INSIDE
THE
NUDGE
UNIT

INSIDE THE NUDGE UNIT

HOW SMALL CHANGES
CAN MAKE A BIG DIFFERENCE

DAVID HALPERN

With Owain Service and the Behavioural Insights Team

Foreword by Richard Thaler

ALLEN

1 3 5 7 9 10 8 6 4 2

WH Allen, an imprint of Ebury Publishing,

20 Vauxhall Bridge Road,
London SW1V 2SA

WH Allen is part of the Penguin Random House group of companies
whose addresses can be found at global.penguinrandomhouse.com

Penguin
Random House
UK

First published in the United Kingdom by WH Allen in 2015

www.eburypublishing.co.uk

A CIP catalogue record for this book is available from the British Library

Hardback ISBN: 9780753556535
Trade Paperback ISBN: 9780753556542

Printed and bound in Great Britain by Clays Ltd, St Ives PLC

Mixed Sources
Product group from well-managed
forests and other controlled sources
www.fsc.org Cert no. TT-COC-2139
© 1996 Forest Stewardship Council

Penguin Random House is committed to a sustainable future for our
business, our readers and our planet. This book is made from Forest
Stewardship Council® certified paper.

To the elected

CONTENTS

FOREWORD

One of the most powerful and pernicious of the many cognitive biases that have been uncovered by behavioural scientists is 'hindsight bias', first investigated by Baruch Fischhoff when he was a graduate student studying at the Hebrew University with Daniel Kahneman and Amos Tversky. Simply put, hindsight bias is the phenomenon that after the fact, we think we knew it all along. Would America elect an African-American as President before a woman? Sure, we all thought that could happen. Did we think in 2000 that fifteen years later most of us would be carrying powerful computers in our pockets that could keep us up-to-date with email, answer nearly any factual question just by speaking to it, and get us anywhere without getting lost? Hardly. But we take our smart phones for granted now.

By a similar process, it is easy to become blasé about the story David Halpern tells in this remarkable book. For example, in 2004, just eleven years ago, I organised a session at the American Economics Association annual meeting that had the cheeky title: 'Memos to the Council of Behavioral Economic Advisers'. None of the participants, including me, ever thought we would see the day that any government institution vaguely resembling such an entity would exist.

Nothing about this forecast changed when Cass Sunstein and I published our book *Nudge*, in 2008. The idea of the book was that it might be possible to use the findings of the behavioural and social sciences to help people achieve their goals, and to improve the effectiveness and efficiency of government policies, without requiring anyone to do anything. We called our philosophy libertarian (or liberal in the UK) paternalism. Perhaps because of the presence of that phrase, commercial publishers shunned the book so we went with an academic press and hoped that a few of our colleagues might read it and continue to push the intellectual agenda. Never in our wildest dreams did we consider the possibility that just seven years later, countries all over the world would be creating new government departments to incorporate behavioural science principles into the design of policies. How did this happen?

The behavioural policy agenda got a jumpstart when one of Cass's former colleagues at the University of Chicago Law School got himself elected president of the United States, and appointed Cass to be the Administrator of the White House Office of Information and Regulatory Affairs. This position was created by President Ronald Reagan and its primary function is to assure that government regulations do more good than harm. During his tenure, Cass was able to use his knowledge of social science, and of nudging, to require many agencies issuing new regulations to incorporate the tools of behavioural science into the design of their policies. In fact, the Obama administration used those tools in a wide range of areas, from health care and financial reform, to healthy eating and energy efficiency. In some cases, binding documents issued by both President Obama and the Office of Information and Regulatory Affairs made sure that behavioural insights were hardwired into the work of numerous government agencies.

The next big breakthrough came when the coalition government of the United Kingdom led by David Cameron announced their intention to create a small team tasked with the job of improving the workings of government using behavioural and social science research.

Having met some of Cameron's team a year earlier, I was asked to come to London for a few days and help get things started. It was on this trip that I first met David Halpern who was then being wooed to take on the job of leading the new team. David and I joined two of Cameron's 'senior advisers' – Steve Hilton and Rohan Silva – (I use the scare quotes because Rohan was not yet thirty) on a one-day trip to Paris to compare notes with some folks in the Sarkozy government who were contemplating a similar endeavour. Nothing came of the French effort aside from an excellent lunch, but we made good use of our time together on the Eurostar to think about what the team might do and other important matters, including deciding what it should be called. We eventually settled on the Behavioural Insights Team, though Rohan prophetically predicted that the formal name of the team would be irrelevant since everyone would just call it the 'Nudge Unit'.

Now, five years later, it is hard to imagine what would have become of the effort had Rohan not convinced David Halpern to come back from the comfortable, good life working at the UK's Institute for Government and as an academic at Cambridge, to resume a full-time role in government. David had a unique background that made him the ideal person to lead this new effort. Not only was he a first-rate academic psychologist with a thorough understanding of modern behavioural science research, but crucially he had also worked in the Strategy Unit at 10 Downing Street in Tony Blair's administration, so knew the workings of Whitehall intimately. He had even written a report urging the application of behavioural science to public policy. I am quite sure there was no one else in the UK better suited to take on this job that was still to be defined.

David quickly formed a small team with a mix of complimentary skills. No member of that team was more important than Owain Service, who quickly emerged as the de facto chief operating officer. (Hint: if you put an academic in charge of something, make sure there is someone on the team who is in charge of making sure things run smoothly.) Through some combination of creating a healthy work environment, good judgment in selecting candidates, and a bit of luck, many other early members of the team are still in place and are now serving in leadership roles.

But even once David was convinced to lead it, and his initial team was formed, few people expected the BIT to be a success. Indeed, on both sides of the Atlantic, the media were pretty sure the nudge agenda was destined to fail. In America the harshest criticism came from the political right, who viewed 'nudging' as some kind of pernicious form of meddling. One particularly nutty talk show host kept referring to Cass as the 'most dangerous man in America'. In Britain the press were of two minds. One was that the idea was just plain silly. References to the famous Monty Python routine using the phrase 'nudge nudge, wink wink' were a common source of put downs. Another came from the most famous example from our book – an image of a housefly etched near the drain in the urinals at Amsterdam's Schipol airport which reportedly reduced 'spillage' by 80 percent – this was considered to be as good as it would get when it came to nudging. The other main criticism came from the political left, who worried that the Tories would use nudging as an excuse for avoiding tougher, presumably more effective policies. Fortunately, neither of these criticisms turned out to be well-founded.

A good example of the potential power of a gentle nudge is the pension reforms that in 2010 were being prepared for a roll-out in Britain under a plan devised by Lord Adair Turner. Under the plan, employers were required to automatically enrol workers into the plan, but employees were free to opt out if they wished to do so. Left-leaning sceptics thought that participation should be mandatory, and that the mere nudge provided by automatic enrolment would not suffice. These fears turned out to be misplaced. At this point, three years into the roll-out, the opt-out rate has been less than one in ten. But these results were not known in 2010, and I think it was fair to say that most observers did not give either the Nudge Unit or its general approach much chance of succeeding.

Of course, some scepticism was warranted. No one had ever tried before to create a special unit of government devoted to implementing behaviourally informed policies, and even those of us involved knew enough about cognitive biases to be wary of overconfidence. Thus one of the team's first decisions was to plan its own demise if things did not work out. Well aware that many new government initiatives fail but yet linger indefinitely, the team built in a sunset clause. After two years, the BIT would be evaluated by the Cabinet Office and unless it could present solid evidence that it could produce results and save the British taxpayers money, it would be dissolved. Practice what you preach is a good philosophy, but the pressure was on!

The initial team had only seven members, a modest budget, and a bit of office space tucked away in the Admiralty Arch. David had no readymade roadmap or obvious role models, but had to show results in two years. Excited, intrigued, and eager to see the process unfold up close, I started including an annual week of teaching in London in the executive MBA programme that the Chicago Booth School of Business offers so I could regularly spend some time hanging out with the team when I wasn't in the classroom, helping when I could. It has been an exciting experience for me, and I am thrilled that David has written this book to let others learn from this experiment.

Now for the spoiler alert. The BIT has been a big success. There are now over 60 employees and the team has been lifted out of UK government and organized as a social purpose company with a mission to help public service organisations across the world. It is currently working with governments across five continents. Furthermore, similar efforts are being undertaken by governments globally, including my home town of Chicago! This book is the story of how that happened.

Of course the team has had its share of good and bad luck, plus plenty of frustration. The insistence that every new idea be tested, whenever possible using randomised control trials, meant that results would come in slowly, and the fine details of every initiative would inevitably be handled by whichever government department held jurisdiction. Needless to say, these sorts of experiments are more difficult to conduct than those run in a laboratory. Still, in spite of these difficulties, much has been learned about specific policy ideas and, just as importantly, how to create an organisation that can investigate the use of behavioural insights to solve real world problems. This first-hand account should be of interest to anyone curious about finding new ways to solve problems in any domain, from the public sector to the private sector to our own lives.

As you read the pages that follow, my only request is the one that I write every time someone asks me to sign a copy of *Nudge*. 'Nudge for good.' Please.

Richard Thaler, July 2015

PREFACE

It is twenty months into the new government, elected in 2010. The Cabinet Secretary, Britain's most senior civil servant, has gathered together the heads of the government departments. Between them, they are responsible for the collection and spending of more than half a trillion pounds and employ more than five million public sector workers.

There are too many to fit comfortably around the table of the Cabinet Secretary's wood-panelled room. Such larger meetings tend to happen in the adjacent room in the old Cabinet Office building of 70 Whitehall, with its roped-off gilded chair in case the reigning monarch dropped by and wanted to look on (not that this had happened in living memory). But on this occasion, they sat around a light and bright room in the recently refurbished 22 Whitehall. It's a minute away on foot, but 400 years away in its history and architecture: a new space for new thoughts. As they gather, the mandarins quietly compare notes, discuss the issues of the day, gossip about who's up and who's down, and deals are quietly done.

The new Cabinet Secretary, Sir Jeremy Heywood, calls the meeting to order. He is, in every sense the Prime Minister's right-hand man: not just the Country's top mandarin, but literally the one to sit beside the Prime Minister in Cabinet to document its decisions and to make sure they happen. The Heads of Departments, or Permanent Secretaries as they are officially called, are curious to see how Sir Jeremy operates and what he cares about. Most know him from his previous roles, but it is still early days for him in the top seat. He is known to be close to, and trusted by, the new Prime Minister David Cameron, but his reputation goes way back. He was Tony Blair's highly regarded Principal Private Secretary, and later returned to No. 10 to be Gordon Brown's Head of Government Policy, a specially created Permanent Secretary role for him. Heywood is the ultimate 'policy wonk', with mastery of detail and strategy across departments; a man whom successive Prime Ministers found indispensable.

On the agenda today is a ten-minute presentation and discussion of government's Behavioural Insights Team, or, as the press and most of Whitehall jokingly call it, the Nudge Unit. For most of those gathered around the table it is the first time they have seen any results from the team. It will, at least, be a fun item to lighten their week. They are old hands. They know the ways of newly elected governments, with their bright new advisers in No. 10. New governments like to talk about new approaches, but many of these approaches are quietly forgotten after a year of two, and with them the advisers that made them fashionable. Ultimately, the challenges and tools of governments don't change much over time.

The Perm Secs, as they are often called, chat, laugh and quietly trade as they settle down. Heywood gets straight down to business, outlining some of the issues that he sees the Government wrestling with in ongoing Parliament. After a brief discussion, he moves the meeting on. 'Today we are going to hear some early results from the Behavioural Insights Team, or Nudge Unit. As you know, the Prime Minister is quite interested in this new approach.' He looks to his left, to the end of the table where I'm sitting with my deputy, Owain Service. 'Most of you will know David already,' he adds, and nods for me to begin.

I have little time so I immediately outline the nature of the approach: it is about introducing a more realistic model of human behaviour into policymaking. The idea is to use this approach to identify low-cost and unobtrusive ways of 'nudging' behaviour. A recently appointed Perm Sec, with whom we have already been working, nods sagely. Several of the Perm Secs are looking at their papers for the day, and one or two surreptitiously check their government-issue BlackBerries under the table. I move to four early results: a slide for each. The Perm Secs have the slides in front of them.

The first is a result from the tax department. The relevant Perm Sec catches my eye as he looks over slightly warily. I explain how we worked with the department to send out different versions of letters to people who owed tax to test systematically if changing the wording based on the behavioural literature would make a difference. We tested whether adding a single sentence such as 'most people pay their tax on time' would boost repayment rates. It did – and by several percentage points, enough to bring forward tens of millions of pounds. The Perm Sec smiles and nods. Though we had spoken to him along the way, it was difficult to be sure if he was fully aware of this trial conducted in his vast department, but he seemed pleased.

The second result is from a trial we had run to encourage people to insulate their lofts or attics. The numbers were small, but the results elegant. The environment department had been asking for money for larger subsidies on insulation, but we had concluded that for many people the biggest issue was hassle rather than cost. With this in mind, we used a leaflet study to compare the effectiveness of offering extra discounts with an alternative one offering an 'attic-clearance service' but that homeowners had to pay for. The attic clearance scheme, despite its extra cost to householders, was more than three times more popular. The Perm Secs chuckle. They see the point. Removing hassle could be more effective than bigger discounts.

The third result is about motoring fines. It shows that adding an image of the owner's car, captured by roadside camera, made the owner significantly more likely to pay unpaid car tax. I mention that the French had tried a similar approach for speeding offences, but had stopped it on account of the marital strife caused by spouses being able to see who else was in the car. Now they just sent them a letter, I explain, threatening to send the photograph if the driver doesn't pay. This causes much amusement – rivalry with our continental cousins runs deep.[1]

The fourth result is from a trial with the Courts Service. We had texted the mobiles of people who owed fines informing them that bailiffs were due to collect in the next ten days. The graph showed how the texts more than doubled payment rates, saving the courts' time and the debtors' money and hassle from bailiffs, and boosting revenue in the process.

One after another, the slides show how small changes in processes, or even just the wording of letters, led to significant shifts in outcomes. More tax collected; more homes insulated; and more fines paid. And the cost? Almost nothing. The Perm Secs aren't laughing now. You don't get to be the head of a department with tens thousands of staff, and budgets the size of small countries', without being able to recognise the political and administrative significance of what they had just seen. Britain, like many other countries, was in the grip of austerity. Most departments faced major cuts, ranging from 10 to 30 per cent. At the same time, the new government was pushing them to deregulate, cut red tape and avoid legislation. In effect, the two main tools that most departments had relied on for the past 50 years – spending money and legislation – had been put in a box labelled 'do not touch' by the new Coalition Government. Here in front of them was a tool they could use. And if the numbers were right, it was a tool that might actually work.

One of the Perm Secs raises his hand. His expression inscrutable, he asks if his Minister had been informed about the trial that had been conducted in his department. For a second my heart sinks. In this particular case, I am not at all confident that the Minister does know, and I'm pretty sure we hadn't discussed it with the Perm Sec.

We had gone, guerrilla-style, to the head of one of his regional services to run the trial, worried that otherwise we would be bogged down in paperwork for months. I fear we are about to be ripped apart for failing to get proper permission from his department, and perhaps, more fundamentally, about the principles of conducting trials at all. It will derail the whole meeting. Instead he grins warmly, and asks for more details to be sent over so that he can brief his Minister, who he thinks will be very impressed.

It is a key turning point. Department heads who walked in as sceptics that spring morning in 2012 walked out, if not as converts, then at least open to the possibility that 'nudging' was worth taking seriously. The ten-minute item took almost the whole hour's meeting. It was the day nudging went mainstream.

A different view on people and government

Human beings are extraordinary. We have evolved to cope with the vast complexity of the world in the blink of an eye. Every day you make tens of thousands of judgements. Your senses and brain are perpetually interpreting the world. Virtually everything you see and hear is ambiguous – the table in front of you could be square, or it could be an odd-shaped trapezoid viewed from a particular angle; and the sound in the corner could be a creaking pipe or a lurking attacker.

We make endless decisions, many so quickly that we barely register them as such. When to stop, or go, at a junction. What to eat and what to wear. Which route to take across a crowded room. And, remarkably, nearly all the time we get it right. We correctly figure out what people mean, and what things surround us. We don't crash into others when we cross a room, or smash our car on the commute to work.

Behind the shroud of our consciousness, a myriad processes race to work out what is going on in the world around us, and how we should respond. From the 'simple' act of seeing a line or edge, to sensing that a friend is angry or sad, our brains ceaselessly infer, overlay and interpret new information and memories. It's an incredible performance.

Because so much of what we see and do is based on inference – or 'fast thinking' – we occasionally get our inferences wrong. We jump at a bursting balloon, or brake sharply at a shadow on the road. Psychologists, and artists, have long studied these 'errors' through illusions and experiments. In everyday life we experience them through jokes or story twists where we suddenly realise our hidden assumptions are wrong.

Some experts and commentators have used the term 'irrational' to characterise the mental shortcuts we use to get through the day. It's not a word I much care for: it fails to capture the remarkable performance of people nearly all of the time. It's also an uncomfortable contrast with the 'rational' but unrealistic models of classical economics, with their assumptions of perfect information and single-dimension comparisons.

Your view of people also shapes your view of government, business and society. If you work on the basis that people are the 'rational utility maximisers' of classical economics, you design tax, legal and welfare systems on that basis, and business models, too. You think that if the benefits of cheating on taxes exceed the likely costs, factoring in fines and the probability of being caught, then people will cheat. You'll think that competitive markets will squeeze out bad providers, and the best will expand to the benefit of all. And you will think that, provided there is information available, people will figure out how best to save, what's healthy to eat, whether to smoke, or do drugs.

The limits of human cognitive capacities, and the naivety and failures of classical economic models, create a powerful case for more regulation and a more active state according to some. Such critics argue that our brains, remarkable though they are, were not made for the modern world. The tastes and surplus of modern food mislead us, with rising obesity across the industrialised nations. Our excessive discounting of the future pulls us headlong towards global warming and destruction. Similarly, it is not difficult to conclude that our brains weren't made for the day-to-day financial judgements that are the foundation of modern economies: from mortgages, to pensions, to the best buy in a supermarket.

Yet classic economic and regulatory models are themselves based on mental shortcuts, or naive models of humanity that do not ring true. They're like ill-fitting suits, because the model on which they are based is a simplistic mental mannequin. In their book *Nudge*, Richard Thaler and Cass Sunstein describe these simplified creatures as 'econs'. These econs consider and weigh up all the options, coolly and accurately, like the Vulcan Mr Spock from *Star Trek*, or the legendary Deep Blue that finally defeated the great chess champion Garry Kasparov (or at least how people *think* it 'thought'). In contrast, 'humans' can't consider 200 million options a second, and our thinking and decisions are fused with emotion. As Dr Spock remarks, our conclusions are – at least to him – frequently 'illogical, captain'.

What would a world look like, and the actions of governments, businesses and communities, if based on a more realistic model of people? *Nudge* popularised and gave a glimpse into a world where governments might use subtler approaches to influence behaviour. It set out a theory; an idea. In contrast, this book tells the story of moving from theory to practice.

A practical approach to government, or business, based on a realistic model of people would be messier than that of traditional economics or law. It would need to reflect the complexity of the human mind – what we do well, and what we don't. It would imply thinking of cognitive capacities as wonderful, but precious resources. When we design services and products, we would need to be respectful of this reality, and remember that people have generally got better things to do than wade through bureaucracy or the puzzling 'rationality' of the state or big business. We would have to design everything we do around people, not expect people to have to redesign their lives around us.

We are perpetually bombarded by subtle influences and cues, and nearly all of us – whether we like it or not – are at least 'accidental nudgers' of a sort. The way a shop is laid out; how an offer is presented; how a form is written – all will have some kind of influence on behaviour. In this sense, the world of nudging is all around us. The question is, do we stumble on blindly, or seek to understand these influences and choices?

An experiment in government

At the heart of this book is the story of an experiment: the Behavioural Insights Team, or the 10 Downing Street Nudge Unit as it came to be called. Set up in 2010 by the new British Prime Minister, David Cameron, it was initially the subject of amusement among the British and international media, and deep scepticism by the mandarins of Whitehall.

The team's objectives read like a mission impossible: to transform the approach of at least two major departments; to inject a new and more realistic understanding of human behaviour across UK government; and to deliver at least a tenfold return on its cost. If it failed, it was to be shut down on its second anniversary – leaving enough time for voters to forget the whole embarrassing episode before the next election.

Over its first two years, the Behavioural Insights Team (BIT) conducted dozens of experiments – 'randomised controlled trials' – across such subjects as healthcare, tax, energy conservation, crime reduction, employment and even economic growth. Much to everyone's surprise, it worked.

BIT's experiments showed that seemingly small changes could have big effects. The team found that adding a simple (and true) statement on tax reminders that 'most people pay their tax on time' encouraged far more people to do so. Such changes, based on social norms and other effects, were shown to bring forward hundreds of millions of pounds of revenue in a year and helped change the way that the Revenue Service operated. Getting the unemployed to think about what they could do in the next two weeks, instead of asking them what they had done in the *previous* two weeks, significantly increased the numbers off benefits at three months, getting tens of thousands back to work faster and trimming millions of days off benefits. Getting rid of a form that employees had to sign to join their pension scheme, but still leaving them the choice of opting out, led to more than five million (and still rising) new savers. Other experiments showed how simple 'nudges' could reduce carbon emissions, increase organ donation, increase quit rates of smoking, reduce missed medical appointments, help students finish their courses, reduce discrimination and boost recruitment. And most of the interventions cost virtually nothing.

It was not all easy. Even with the personal backing of the Prime Minister and Deputy Prime Minister, and a Downing Street base, many inside government remained deeply sceptical. Civil servants and administrators often declared that proposed experiments could not be done or were even illegal. Some of the interventions did not work, and others worked in ways that were not expected.

At the end of two years, however, the results were unambiguous. Designing policy, and the nuts and bolts of public services, around behavioural insights and empirical methods led to better outcomes, easier services for the public to use, and saved money. After a century in the wings, behavioural science had finally moved out of the laboratory and into mainstream government policy.

A short road map to the book

This book is about the application of psychology to the challenges we face in the world today. It explores the results of a small team at the heart of British government which was given the task of translating psychological theory and an experimental approach into action and everyday policy. It also documents some of the trials and tribulations along the way, including the struggles to get mainstream policymakers to take a behavioural approach seriously, and the race to get results before time and political capital ran out.

The Behavioural Insights Team, despite its nickname, actually explored a much broader application of psychology to policy than that described in the original American publication *Nudge*. It sought to apply a more sophisticated model of human behaviour across the whole range of what government does. This story is told in four sections.

The first section provides a short history of 'nudging'. It explores the early academic foundations on which the approach was built, and how they continue to influence it today. It looks at how governments, communities and leaders have – alongside laws, fines and force – sometimes used more subtle ways of shaping human behaviour, but also how early forays into more overtly behavioural approaches ran into difficulties. In the second chapter, a short history explains how in the USA nudge approaches began to be used by President Obama's White House, and how the Behavioural Insights Team came to be founded by Prime Minister David Cameron in 2010. Along the way, we will meet some of the characters who helped make it happen.

The second section of the book looks at how behavioural insights are being applied to the 'nuts and bolts' activities of governments, from persuading people to pay their taxes to encouraging the insulation of homes. Each of the four chapters in this section introduces one of the central approaches used by the Nudge Unit captured in a simple mnemonic – EAST: Easy, Attractive, Social and Timely. We will see how, with minimal cost, the application of behavioural insights and experimental methods are leading to dramatically improved results, and get a sense of why these approaches are being adopted by governments and businesses across the world.

The third section of the book explores the more advanced

applications of behavioural science. This steps up from refinements of letters and processes to how behavioural insights can radically reshape the way we think about the world, and with it policy and practice. It opens by exploring how consumer information and behavioural science are combining to transform how markets work. It moves on to examples of how behavioural thinking led to radically different policy decisions, from the regulation of markets, to getting people back to work faster and helping reboot a faltering economy. For some people, behavioural science goes even further, challenging the fundamental objectives of policy by revealing the foundations of well-being itself. The last chapter in this section explores the impact of the experimental methods that behavioural science has brought in its wake, and that may yet prove to be its greatest and most disruptive legacy.

The final section explores the risks and limits of the rapidly spreading embrace of behavioural science across the world. It examines the practical and political limits of the approach, and why all of us as citizens need to know something about how it is being used. For some critics, nudging by governments is sinister; for others, it is seen as an excuse for governments to stand back from tougher action on important problems. Either way, the argument is made that governments and businesses need to up their game in getting public permission for how they use these approaches. The final, concluding chapter looks at what the future holds for 'nudging' and the application of behavioural insights. It considers whether behavioural insights have anything to add to the deepest and most daunting challenges that face us today, including how we get along with our fellow humans – challenges and frontiers that 'nudgers' are starting to explore.

Suffice it to say that when the time came for the two-year sunset review of BIT, far from shutting the team down the Prime Minister decided to expand it. The Nobel Laureate Daniel Kahneman, whose research has led the field, commended the team's work. The press, civil service and political parties turned – for the most part – from sceptics to supporters.

Love it, or hate it, nudging is here to stay. The history and remarkable results of the 10 Downing Street Behavioural Insights Team have led governments across the world to adopt similar approaches, many advised by the Behavioural Insights Team itself. We are all going to see more use of behavioural insights by governments, businesses, and others in the coming years. Chances are you have already been nudged. It has been a remarkable success, but its very success has raised concerns, too. Like all knowledge, the use of behavioural insights can be a force for good or bad. How we use it is something we must all decide.

▲

A SHORT HISTORY OF NUDGING

People have been 'nudging' each other for as long as mankind has existed. We are always busy persuading and encouraging those around us to do one thing or another. Indeed, many biologists think that much of human development, and our unusually large brains, was powered by the complex patterns of influence that characterised early human, and hominoid, social groups.

Yet when it comes to governments and businesses, many have turned their backs on the messy skills of softer persuasion. Instead, they have packed their toolkits with more recent and fashionable tools, shaped by the modern and 'rational' disciplines of economics and law.

In recent years governments and businesses have started rediscovering this wider set of influences on human behaviour. Partly they have done so out of surprise and desperation when conventional policy tools based on economics and law have failed, but also because of an increasingly nuanced understanding of the human behaviour born of the 'soft' sciences, and psychology in particular.

It has been a fascinating rediscovery.

CHAPTER 1

▲

EARLY STEPS

(Part 1 – theory: 1700–2007)

The greatest and noblest pleasure which we have in this world is to discover new truths, and the next is to shake off old prejudices.

FREDERICK THE GREAT

In the 1700s European leaders and administrators were worried. Their populations were growing, but their diet was relatively restricted. Famine was a constant danger, provoking not only mass starvation, but wars and revolutions. An over-reliance on wheat, or any single crop, presented a particular danger. If the crop failed, disaster would follow.

Against this background, the introduction of the humble potato to Europe had a deep political and strategic importance. But there was a major problem. For those not accustomed to the potato, it was a very strange and rather unappealing foodstuff. It had a taste that was unfamiliar and bland.[1] The way it grew was no less unfamiliar – tubers producing a crop underground, not like the graceful and familiar sweep of wheat and corn springing up out of the earth. It was even shunned by the Church on the basis that the Bible made no mention of the potato, while wheat, in the form of bread, came to represent the body of Christ.

European leaders used a variety of ways to encourage reluctant populations to adopt the potato, some even passing laws requiring their cultivation. Frederick the Great of Prussia took a particular interest in the potato, believing it could lower the price of bread and greatly reduce shortages of cereals in times of crisis.[2] In 1744 he introduced the potato into the diet of the army, and through his reign passed no fewer than 15 orders aimed at driving its adoption and cultivation. But even then resistance to the potato ran deep.

During a famine in 1774, Frederick ordered a national cultivation programme. In a response typical of many towns, the people of Kolberg declared: 'The things have neither smell nor taste, not even the dogs will eat them, so what use are they to us?'[3]

Frederick's initial response was more a violent 'shove' than a nudge – he threatened to cut the noses and ears off any peasant who did not plant potatoes. However, he soon changed tack. In modern parlance we'd say that he used a bit of 'psychology'.

Legend has it that instead of issuing further threats, Frederick ordered his soldiers to establish a heavy and visible guard around the local royal potato fields, yet also instructed them to be deliberately lax in protecting them. At the same time, the local peasants noticed their king's conspicuous admiration of potato flowers as well as the tubers themselves, and sneaked in to steal and plant the 'royal crop'. Within a short time, many potatoes were stolen and soon being widely grown and eaten.

Frederick's interventions provide a striking example of the limits of passing laws and sanctions, and of the power of a more subtle approach to behaviour change. And it paid off. In the years of war that followed, unlike many rival nations the Prussians did not starve or see their population fall. While passing armies could readily raid granaries, potatoes in the ground were much less likely to be taken. The adoption of the potato saved the lives of many, and incidentally helped leave Prussia the dominant power in the region.

The art of persuasion

Frederick was not the only leader to turn to the art of persuasion as a subtler alternative to force. Since ancient times, leaders have sought to impress their followers through statues and monuments that convey power, wisdom and other attributes that they wish to project. Henry VIII lined his palace at Hampton Court with exquisite tapestries to convey not only his wealth and power but also, in the depiction of the story of Abraham, to create a parallel to Henry's own sense of destiny and that of his fledgling but 'special' nation. Similarly, the portraits he commissioned, and the image of power and wealth they project, still influence us today. To many people, the image of Henry VIII is the very personification of a king.

Sometimes leaders have deliberately used their power and influence to alter fashion and behaviour, and religious and cultural practices in societies have often picked up heavily on the behaviour of leaders and the fashions of their courts. Leaders have often intuitively understood this, and through making their behaviour more conspicuous have sought deliberately to change the behaviour of their people.

This has extended beyond religious practice or what names are fashionable for your children. For example, a major turning point in the use of anaesthetics occurred when Queen Victoria elected to use chloroform to ease the birth of her eighth child in 1853. In the medical establishment of the time the use of chloroform was extremely controversial, with the *Lancet* writing that same year that 'in no case could it be justifiable to administer chloroform in perfectly ordinary labour'. But the Queen's use of anaesthesia was a more powerful message than even the medical establishment could resist. When she also used it for the birth of her last child in 1857, the use of anaesthesia to ease the pain of childbirth became widespread, at least among those who could afford it. [4]

Governments, too, at both national and local level, have sometimes turned to more subtle forms of persuasion to influence behaviour.

Between 1910 and the early 1920s, the number of cars on the road in Britain, the USA and elsewhere increased almost tenfold. The rising numbers and greater speed brought with them a new problem – the car crash. In Britain in 1921, following a spate of accidents at Maney Corner, in Sutton Coldfield, outside Birmingham, someone had an idea. They noticed that many of the accidents were caused by the rising tide of ever faster cars cutting the corner and hitting cars coming the other way. The idea? To paint a white line in the centre of the road. It proved highly effective, and within a few years white lines were being painted on roads around the country.

The white line is a wonderful everyday example of a 'nudge', as are many of the prompts that guide our driving every day. Rumble strips alongside the edges of motorways alert us that we are drifting off the road or into the central reservation. Catseyes indicate the separation between lanes, with different colours to highlight turn-offs from the main road. More recently, in many countries speed signs and 'slow down' signs flash back warnings to drivers, the numbers turning to flashing red when the speed exceeds the limit.

Though now mostly forgotten, a similar set of nudges evolved during the time of horse-drawn carriages – nudges designed not just

Figure 1. For this particular 'nudge', the USA was especially fast off the mark, with white lines appearing in several states by 1917 ('Dead Man's Corner' in Marquette County, Michigan, with hand-painted lines in 1917. Photo courtesy of the Michigan Department of Transportation).

Figure 2. The Rotherhithe Tunnel, under the Thames, was opened in 1908. Its repeated sharp corners, now considered dangerous, were partly conceived as a 'nudge' to prevent horses bolting for the light in the distance. (Photo courtesy of Barney Moss.)

for humans but for horses, too. Today's drivers cutting through the Rotherhithe Tunnel, the oldest road tunnel under the River Thames, are sometimes struck by the sharp zigzags along the route. Part of the reason for this was to avoid the docks, but there was another reason and it was not structural. The sharp turns, which restricted the view ahead, were also designed to discourage horses from bolting in the narrow tunnels for the light in the distance.[5]

Though we now take cars for granted, for the first few decades of the rise of the motor car there were few requirements on drivers to learn to drive, and it was often far from clear what the rules of the road were anyway. The British Highway Code, which all new drivers are obliged to learn, has, for most of its history, been just that – a code – a sort of suggestion as to how you might like to drive. Even today, while parts of the Highway Code are embodied in law, indicated by the words 'you must', much of it remains advisory, expressed in the words 'you should'. It is an everyday work of genius, allowing millions of people to travel in relative safety, and powering the lifeblood of the economy through the transport of goods and services. Of course, if you do decide not to follow the rules and thereby put yourself and others in danger, the police may catch you and fine you for 'reckless driving'. But mostly the sanction for reckless driving comes not from the law, but from the angry horns and gestures of your fellow drivers.

Traffic authorities could have responded with more conventional methods, such as introducing strict new laws and bigger fines. Some countries indeed have, but for the most part seemingly gentle cues or 'nudges' have been highly effective in reducing accidents. Often such nudges have been found to be more effective than the use of sanctions and fines (and certainly with horses!). For example, signs that flash 'slow down', or show the speed of drivers going too fast in red, while showing the speed of drivers obeying the limit in a soothing yellow, have been found to be highly effective – and often more so than speed cameras and fines (see Chapter 4). The 'rules' and cues of the road have evolved over more than a hundred years, with a range of approaches emerging to keep us safe from ourselves and each other – and nearly all resting on the creation of new 'habits' and the prompting of each other to keep to them.

There is one issue that *has* brought psychologists into government: war. The conflicts of the twentieth century led governments to employ persuasion on an industrial scale. Winning 'hearts and minds', both at home and among allies and opponents, has often been as important to victory as bombs and bullets.[6] The US Office of War Information, created by Franklin D. Roosevelt, was reputed to have produced more than 200,000 different posters during the Second World War. These campaigns pursued a wide range of objectives, from encouraging people to buy war bonds; eating different, and previously unpalatable, foods; planting 'victory gardens'; and bolstering the preparedness to fight and support the Allies. These campaigns were often highly successful. For example, billions of dollars were raised from US war bonds from the civilian population, including more than a billion from children alone. Similarly, vegetable production from the 50 million civilian 'victory gardens' is estimated to have exceeded that of commercial vegetable production.

These persuasive campaigns, and the behaviour they encouraged, had a dual function. They generated useful resources but, perhaps more importantly, they created a sense of common purpose. An everyday assumption is that attitudes shape behaviours. Yet psychological studies have shown that very often it works the other way around: behaviours shape attitudes.[7] It is what psychologists call cognitive dissonance: when there is a discrepancy between a person's attitudes and their behaviour, such as when you find yourself doing a 'boring' task for little reward, your attitude will often move into line with your behaviour (e.g. you conclude that the task is not so dull after all, and that it enables you to relax and clear your mind). Similarly, someone who has invested in a government war bond, or 'dug for victory', may be more likely to come to believe in the value and objectives of the war itself.

From Frederick the Great's ingenious efforts to persuade Europeans to grow and eat potatoes, to the painting of white lines on roads, we can see that policymakers have – albeit sometimes in desperation – periodically turned to non-legislative tools to try to affect public behaviour. In particular, while laws and punishments have often proved reasonably effective at getting people to *stop* doing something, they are often much less effective at getting people to *start* doing something, and certainly to persist with it.

Nonetheless, such approaches have tended to be at the margins of policy. Across the world, parliaments, presidents and prime ministers battle to bring forward new laws, and occasionally remove old ones. They have fought to increase budgets in many areas and – more rarely – cut them in others. Policymakers have been first and foremost crafters of laws and budgets. Occasionally economists and scientists have broken into the ranks of parliaments and the top civil servants. But psychologists and social scientists? Outside of wartime propaganda – very rarely.

What is a 'nudge'?

A 'nudge' is essentially a means of encouraging or guiding behaviour, but without mandating or instructing, and ideally without the need for heavy financial incentives or sanctions. We know what it means in everyday life: it's a gentle hint; a suggestion; a conspicuous glance at a heap of clothes that we're hoping our kids or our partner might clear away. It stands in marked contrast to an obligation; a strict requirement; or the use of force. For Cass Sunstein and Richard Thaler, originators of the term 'nudge', a key element is that it avoids shutting down choices, unlike a law or formal requirement. But, as we shall see, a 'nudge' is a subset of a wider, more empirical and behaviourally focused approach to policymaking.

Consider how a law actually works. A parliament or executive passes a resolution that says that henceforth there will be a new requirement on people or businesses to do something in a particular way (or not to do something). The lawmaker normally attaches a sanction or penalty to those who fail to comply, such as a fine or imprisonment. But the link between the passing of the law and actual behaviour is very distant. It is premised on an arguably naive model of human behaviour. It assumes that somehow people will have heard about the new law, and realised that it applies to them. It assumes that they will weigh up the costs of breaking the new law, with the risk of being caught, and conclude that they should comply. And it assumes that in the moment and context of temptation, all of this will come to mind, and that these considerations will outweigh other pressures and temptations.

It's a heroic series of assumptions. Unsurprisingly, the passing of new laws is often a far from perfect way of affecting behaviour. Citizens are 'required' to fill in their tax returns on time, but every year millions fail to do so. We're not supposed to drop litter, but parks and public places are often strewn with it. Even the very existence and scale of the courts and judicial system can be argued to be testament to the frequent failure of the law-based approach.

In contrast, sometimes behaviour changes with a surprisingly light touch. For example, over the last decade many countries have introduced bans on smoking in public places. There were grave concerns in many countries that the new laws would be both unpopular and unenforceable. However, in this case, they have proved highly successful. The smoking ban, in the UK at least, has been subject to almost no enforcement. In essence, smoking bans have been self-policed, built around a new social norm – or tacit public support – for smoke-free environments.

Subsidies and incentives have a similarly mixed success rate. Sometimes seemingly small subsidies or taxes have had rapid and dramatic impacts on behaviour. For example, the introduction of a small difference in price between leaded and unleaded fuels in the UK and elsewhere led to a rapid switch to unleaded fuels, and to a much faster transition to unleaded fuels than had been expected. Similarly, requiring retailers to charge consumers a tiny amount of 5p for a plastic bag has been shown to dramatically reduce their use. On the other hand, many much larger subsidies and taxes, such as those intended to drive savings or increase energy efficiency, have often proven to have limited impact.

When things don't work quite as you expect, and it keeps happening, it's time to reappraise the way you think about the world. Nearly all government (and corporate) policies, and the challenges that lie behind them, have a behavioural component. Behavioural analyses start to unpack what makes some policies work and others flop. In so doing, they open the door to alternative and potentially much more effective approaches.

From lab to policy: three strands of research

There is a long and rich history of social and cognitive psychology. For more than a century, scientists have been systematically examining how we see, hear and make judgements and contrasts; and how our behaviour is influenced by the things and people around us. The contemporary application of behavioural science, and psychology in particular, to policy has many routes, but three stand out.

First, the study of perception has gradually laid bare how humans literally 'see' and interpret the world. It is a foundation stone of what is known as 'experimental psychology'. A century of research has shown how our senses are tuned to detect changes, contrasts and personal relevance. We see edges, and the tiniest of differences, but blank out things that do not change. For example, our eyes are 'wired' such that cells that are under a constant level of light gradually habituate and reduce their rate of firing. But if you look at someone's eye very closely, you'll see that it is constantly moving. The net effect is that when a line – and edge of dark and light – falls on your retina, the tiny movements in your eye mean that those cells are being switched on and off, while those in constant light or darkness habituate, leaving your brain to concentrate on the edge of the line.

Similarly, we become accustomed to constant background noises. In a famous example from New York, when the trains in a part of the city stopped working one night the police were flooded with calls from anxious residents reporting the strange noises they were hearing. In contrast, we are very likely to notice if someone mentions our name even in a crowded and busy room.[8]

Figure 3. Mach bands. Each band is a perfectly even grey – cover the adjacent bands to check – but when seen side by side they look as if they are shaded. This illusion is rooted in how our eyes and brain work, serving to highlight edges in the world around us.[9]

This psychology of perception has profound implications for design, pricing, and even what we like and dislike. For example, as consumers we often aren't very good at knowing how much a new product or service should cost in an absolute sense. How much should a good pair of speakers cost? How much should I pay for a Picasso? How much should I pay for a mobile phone that is more secure? We're much better at working out the relative costs of things. Hence, faced with several pairs of speakers, or a selection of Picassos, we'll often be able to give a view on which one is better, and if we're given the price of one of them we'll have a pretty good stab at the price of the others. This gives marketers a powerful tool. If most of the speakers a store sells cost £100 to £750, a price tag of £700 looks pretty steep, and we'll probably go for a cheaper option. But if the speakers are in the range £500 to £2,000, that £700 price tag will suddenly look very reasonable.

The second strand is what is known as 'social psychology' – how our behaviour is influenced by the people and things around us. Its roots also go back at least a century, to early studies that showed that people would cycle faster, or turn handles in laboratories more rapidly, when others were doing the same alongside them. But empirical social psychology really took off in the laboratories of post-war America. This body of work has deeply changed how we think about our fellow humans – and even ourselves.

Most people – and certainly not just psychology students – have heard of the famous 'compliance experiments' of Stanley Milgram, in which subjects seemed prepared to electrocute a fellow subject to death just because they were asked to do so. Milgram showed that ordinary Americans, invited to take part in a 'learning experiment' in a respectable university, would keep administering a steadily increasing shock to the subject that they had just met but who was now screaming and pounding on the wall in the next room for them to stop. All it seemed to take was a man in a white coat telling them that 'the experiment required them to continue'. More than two-thirds of subjects did continue (in Milgram's typical experiment) even though, as far as they could tell, the now silent subject had either passed out or died. [10]

Milgram's work itself built on earlier studies by Solomon Asch showing that most subjects would choose an obviously wrong answer if those before them also chose it. These early results were followed by scores more studies, all showing the power of the situation to shape human behaviour. These ranged from Zimbardo's famous Stanford Prison Cell experiment where college kids seemed to turn into sadists or compliant prisoners depending on the role they were (randomly) assigned, to Latané and Darley's studies showing that groups of subjects would sit unmoving in rooms filling with smoke, or fail to help a fallen assistant in the next room, while subjects sitting by themselves would intervene. [11]

These experiments, in the wake of the atrocities of the Second World War, shocked the world (and America in particular). They suggested that extreme human behaviour was not an aberration, but something that most people would exhibit if the context prompted them. It was a body of work that showed the enormous power of the 'situation' or context on human behaviour, including the influence of those around us. The rise of empirical social psychology marked a decisive shift in approach to the study of human behaviour, from the armchair musings of philosophers into an empirical project. In so doing, it has had profound ramifications for how we think of everything from war and wickedness, to kindness and love.

Third, cognitive psychology has looked into our internal thought processes. To most contemporary psychologists, the ground-breaking work of Amos Tversky and Daniel Kahneman from the 1970s onwards stands out, highlighting the mental shortcuts that people use in everyday decision-making. For example, people generally don't estimate the safety of air versus car travel by dividing the number of crashes over the last year by the number of planes versus cars travelling in the world over that time. Rather, most people use a mental shortcut along the lines of how easily they can recall examples of planes versus cars crashing – what Tversky and Kahneman called an 'availability' heuristic. The more easily the person can call to mind an example, the more likely or common they infer it to be. It's generally not a bad heuristic. It gives you a pretty good idea of how many tigers versus pigeons you might meet walking around the streets of London or New York. But when it comes to aeroplane versus car safety, using the availability heuristic can lead us badly astray. Rare but devastating air crashes make the news and stick in our minds, but the daily death toll on our roads passes largely without comment or lasting attention. As such, most people 'feel' that flying is much more dangerous than travelling by car, despite the statistics – and certainly expressed by mile travelled – suggesting the reverse.[12]

These erroneous estimates can have enormous consequences. For example, in the aftermath of 9/11, people's estimate of the dangers

Figure 4. What our brains are good and bad at.

You can illustrate what our brains are good and bad at with a piece of paper. First, try crumpling it into a ball and throwing it to a colleague. Chances are, they will catch it easily. This is despite the fact that it's an incredibly complex calculation. The thrower has to calibrate the motion perfectly for the weight and the distance, while the catcher has to manage the even more complex task of judging the speed, size, weight and distance of the object, and then calibrate raising their hand to exactly the right point in space and grasping the paper at exactly the right moment. But if you ask them how they did it, they'll probably just shrug their shoulders and say 'I just caught it'. It's an everyday illustration of what our 'fast' or automatic brain can do, and though there's not a machine on the planet that can yet replicate that casual throw and catch, we think nothing of it.

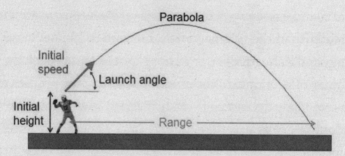

In contrast, now ask your colleague a simple question. Imagine taking that same piece of paper and folding it in half. Then fold it in half again, and again, for a hundred times. Of course, you couldn't actually fold a piece of paper like that more than six or seven times before it got too unwieldy, but imagine that you could. How thick would it be?

I used to ask my students this sometimes. They'd scratch their heads. 'Really thick' one might say, raising their hand, 'like this high, maybe more.' Another would say, 'no – it would be like as high as this building!'

Occasionally one would start to cotton on, 'it's going to be huge, right? Like as far as to the moon?' In fact the answer is way, way past the moon, the sun and the entire solar system. That humble piece of ordinary paper, folded a hundred times, would stretch across billions of light years, well beyond our entire galaxy.

This trivial calculation – even for a pocket calculator – defeats us. Our first instincts are wrong, unadapted to exponential calculations, and we have to engage our 'slow' and conscious thought processes to resolve it. Our brains invisibly ace the complex calculations in catching the paper (thinking 'fast'), but 'simple' calculation of folded paper defeats us (thinking 'slow').[13]

of flying increased dramatically in the USA. As a result, more people decided to drive instead of flying in the year following, leading to a substantial increase in road deaths. This increase is estimated to have been greater than the original death toll from 9/11 itself.

Tversky and Kahneman's work, though rooted in psychology, struck at the heart of economists' assumptions about how people weighed choices and made decisions. It made it crystal clear that people were often prone to errors in remembering, predicting and deciding which experience or option was most painful, risky or likely. Importantly, it showed that these errors were not random, but predictable. This opened the door to canny economists, political scientists and even lawyers not just to abandon their models, but to revamp them using the emerging new insights into how people really made decisions.

Daniel Kahneman was subsequently awarded the Nobel Prize, not for psychology, but for the immense impact of his work on economics. Many others have built on and around this work, for example showing how emotional reactions greatly affect our judgements and thinking, or documenting the variety of mental shortcuts and how they affect performance in a variety of settings.[14] For those who follow the literature, it has felt at times like that period when Victorian explorers were discovering the uncharted regions of the world, bringing back tales of unexplored regions or tracing the sources of great rivers – except this time the discoveries have been in our own minds. And, just as with previous explorers, there have been rival claims, failed missions and the occasional charge of rediscovery – but fascinating all the same.

These three stands have partly come together in recent years, not least through popularisations of psychology by figures such as Cialdini; Thaler and Sunstein; Ariely; and Kahneman himself. These works have played an important role of spreading behavioural insights and psychology into new fields, business and even government.

Behavioural insights and government: early stumbles

Despite a century of research, until recently psychology has had a very weak relationship with policy. Apart from the occasional controversial use of psychological operations (PsyOps) in warfare, or the odd government advertising campaign, psychology has remained the sickly sibling to economics in the policymaking community.

Psychology was sometimes used to help on specific, technical decisions. For example, experimental research from the study of memory was used to help design the UK's postcodes (in the USA zip codes), deliberately mixing letters and numbers to make the sequence more memorable than numbers or letters alone. Similarly, detailed studies of people's capacity to process information from auditory (sound) or visual channels, and then respond to them, was used in the design of control panels in military jets to maximise the amount of information that pilots could absorb and respond to without interference – and to simplify cockpits to reduce fatal errors.

However, psychology remained marginal in mainstream policy-making. This is particularly remarkable given just how large the role of behaviour is in most policy outcomes. For example, the World Health Organisation and others have estimated that more than half of healthy years lost in industrialised nations are due to behavioural factors such as smoking, diet, drinking, unsafe sex, motor accidents and so on (see Chapter 8 for further discussion). Yet this is not what we spend our health budgets, or even our research budgets, on.[15]

Within the UK an attempt was made to introduce more psychology and behavioural thinking into policy in the early 2000s. At that time, I was still a respectable young academic at the Faculty of Social and Political Sciences at Cambridge. I had been involved in some policy thinking in the run-up to the 1997 election and immediately afterwards, but then had settled back to life in Cambridge, albeit with what some of my colleagues regarded as an unhealthy interest in the world outside. Indeed, one of the courses I taught was called Psychology and Policy.[16] It explored how psychology could bring a deeper understanding of the causes behind policy challenges; suggest alternative policy solutions; and perhaps even suggest alternative aims (see Chapter 9 on well-being for further discussion of the last mentioned).

In the wake of Tony Blair's second landslide election victory in 2001, I joined his newly created Prime Minister's Forward Strategy Unit, later to become the Prime Minister's Strategy Unit (PMSU). The unit had been formed to strengthen the capability of Downing Street to think more deeply and long-term about policy problems. Though initially on secondment from Cambridge for 18 months, I ended up staying for six years – a warning, or perhaps encouragement, to other young academics.[17]

Alongside PMSU's major policy reviews, we wrote a series of policy discussion papers – or 'think pieces', as they were called internally. Policy problems don't really respect disciplinary boundaries, but sometimes one of those disciplines or viewpoints is largely lacking and merits an extra push. With this in mind, one of these discussion papers was explicitly designed to explore the implications of psychology and the behavioural literature for policy. We even had Daniel Kahneman drop by for a chat in Admiralty Arch, where we were based at that time (shortly before he was awarded the Nobel Prize).

There was always a bit of wariness about these 'think pieces'. The whole point of them was to push the boundaries of our thinking, and that of Whitehall. On the other hand, that also created the potential risk that a journalist or member of the Opposition might make mischief with the ideas. To address this issue, we took to printing at the foot of every page the words 'This is an issue paper for discussion purposes and does <u>not</u> represent Government policy'. You can still see the statement on the online version of the paper, filed away in the electronic national archives (see Chapter 11, Note 5).

To cut a long story short, the launch of the paper on 'behaviour change' was not a happy one (see Chapter 11 for more gruesome details). After a leak, the paper was subject to heavy press attack, leading the Downing Street Press Office to distance itself from it. Shortly afterwards, a line was added to a major speech by the Prime Minister making it clear that this was not an approach that his government would pursue.

For a government that was already prone to be seen as a nanny state – it was in general expanding the role of the state – the idea that we might start 'messing with people's heads' was seen as a step too far. Our work in the PMSU would have many successes, but this was not one of them.

Still, we did not abandon the approach completely. Within particular domains, such as encouraging giving up smoking, the role of behaviour was palpably obvious and clearly made the case for some behavioural and psychological thinking. The thinking in the PMSU paper also had another specific impact, which was on pensions policy. One of the papers quoted – and highlighted by Kahneman when he came in – was an early piece on 'libertarian paternalism' documenting the powerful impacts of defaults. At that time we had a big review running on pensions, led by an outsider named Adair Turner. I thought the paper on the impacts of defaults so important to the review that I printed off a copy and sent it to Adair and the review team, with a scribbled note along the lines of 'I think this is probably the most important and interesting paper that you are going to read on pensions'.

When the Turner review reported, it recommended that we change the default for workplace pensions from an opt-in to an opt-out. Though the change was set for a number of years in the future – and long after the next election – the policy was ultimately adopted and, as we shall see in Chapter 3, highly effective. It may be that Adair and the team would have found the paper eventually, or reached the conclusion independently. But the changes to pensions saving – not only in the UK, but in New Zealand, the United States and elsewhere – was to prove one of the earliest big wins for behavioural insights in policy.

Other areas in which behavioural insights showed its hand were around issues such as a big push on early years interventions; the introduction of parenting support to reduce crime and improve other outcomes; and some of the ideas around 'respect' and reducing social exclusion.

One more push

Towards the end of the Blair administration the chance arose for one last attempt to get more sophisticated and overt behavioural approaches embedded in policy. In the run-up to the handover of power to Gordon Brown we ran an extensive 'Policy Review' process intended to provide an opportunity to reflect on what had been learnt during Blair's decade in power: what worked; what to drop; and what new ideas might be worth looking into. It was an unusual opportunity – a transition of power and leadership within the Labour government offering an opportunity to revitalise thinking, combining the best of previous reforms with fresh approaches. The Review consisted of a series of papers; seminars with up and coming Ministers and the PM; and even a Cabinet 'away-day'.

A small steering group was established to shape Review process, with political steers from the junior Cabinet Office Ministers Pat MacFadden (previously a long-standing aid to Blair at No. 10) and Ed Miliband (previously an aid to Gordon Brown, and later to be Labour party leader), with me leading on the civil service side, answering to the Cabinet Office Minister Hilary Armstrong and the PM.

As part of the Review seminars in late 2006 to early 2007, we asked Robert Cialdini, the author of *Influence: The Psychology of Persuasion*, if he would come and give a seminar. It proved to be one of the more popular sessions, and we held it in the No. 10 State Dining Room. The State Dining Room was never the most practical for seminars; its long thin table and heavy candlesticks made it difficult to see people alongside you, and its acoustics were better suited to private conversations than a presentation. Nonetheless, the location, wood panelling, historic silverware and paintings always impressed.

Robert was great. I'd first picked up his book years before in the Harvard Coop bookstore, curious to see what my Harvard colleagues were using as texts in their psychology courses, and loved it. Back then it was in its second edition but already a classic: an engaging marriage of famous psychology experiments and the everyday techniques that marketers – and even fraudsters – used to influence people. In person, Cialdini was just as engaging. Drawing heavily on his own work on the curiously fascinating topic of littering, he gave an overview of six broad effects that policymakers should think about. He particularly dwelled on what he called the 'big mistake': emphasising what people *shouldn't do*, instead of what they *should*. He illustrated the 'mistake' with reference to one of his great stories: the problem of people taking the beautiful fossilised wood from the National Park close to his university in Arizona. He explained how one of his PhD students, when visiting the National Park with his otherwise angelic girlfriend, found himself being prodded in the ribs when she saw the signs asking people not to remove the petrified wood. 'Come on,' she urged, 'let's get a piece while there's still some left!'

Cialdini and his students went on to conduct a series of experiments testing the impacts of different signs on the probability that tourists would pick up and take the bits of petrified wood that the researchers would leave dotted along the path past the sign. Sure enough, they found that signs that said 'Many past visitors have removed petrified wood...' made visitors more than four times more likely to pick up the fossils. They were inadvertently communicating that what many people were doing was taking the fossils (a 'social norm' effect – see more in Chapter 5).[18]

Robert similarly showed an old and quite famous anti-littering TV commercial that made you feel bad about littering, but actually *increased* littering by signalling that it was what most people did. In contrast, with a cheesy but effective recycling advert that signalled that most people recycled, and it was only the rare exception who did not, was able to boost recycling by up to 30 per cent.

The junior Ministers present were very taken by the presentation. They could recognise the effects and mistakes Cialdini described in their own policy battles and departments. However, some were also troubled by the acceptability of the approach to the public: 'Isn't it manipulation?' or, as another senior figure put it, 'It's not quite cricket, is it?' Robert's response was simple. 'You are trying to communicate to the public,' he explained, 'but your message is getting mangled and confused. This is about effective communication. You are not doing anyone any favours by failing to get your message across.'

It was a good and practised answer. But it did have a significant downside to a policy audience at that time: it made them think that this was about communication only. In other words, this was interesting material for department press offices, and perhaps for political teams around elections, but not really relevant for core, serious policy work.

Of course, there was a more fundamental problem that hung over the Policy Review as a whole. Blair was nearing the end of his time in office, and the new Prime Minister to be, Gordon Brown, and his allies were in no mood after their long years in waiting to take last-minute advice on policy from a Blair-inspired process. Similarly, as one Minister put it to me, 'as junior Ministers you learn to toe the line – it's very hard, after ten years, to suddenly open your mind to new thoughts and come up with new ideas'.

I left PMSU and No. 10 a couple of weeks before Blair finally stood down in 2007, and Brown took over. I was pretty tired after six years. To the Brownites at that time I would have been seen as too close to Blair – and it's good for government to get fresh blood anyway.

With the near-collapse of the international financial system in 2008, Gordon Brown had plenty on his plate. The Downing Street seminar on preventing littering and stopping fossilised wood being stolen was soon forgotten. Curiously, one of Prime Minister Brown's smartest new political aids, Greg Beales, had worked on the original PMSU paper on behaviour change. In the new No. 10, Greg held responsibility for health. It's no coincidence, then, that one early move of the Brown administration was to float the idea of changing the defaults on organ donation to 'presumed consent' – where people would opt out of being donors, rather than opt in. But even this was not quite the right fight for that time or issue. There was a public and professional backlash against the idea, and the last whisper of the old PMSU paper was silenced for now, in Britain at least.[19]

On the other side of the Atlantic, behavioural approaches to policy were about to get a major boost.

CHAPTER 2

▲

NUDGING GOES MAINSTREAM

... we cannot meet 21st-century challenges with a 20th-century bureaucracy ... Yes, government must lead on energy independence, but each of us must do our part to make our homes and businesses more efficient. Yes, we must provide more ladders to success for young men who fall into lives of crime and despair. But we must also admit that programs alone can't replace parents, that government can't turn off the television and make a child do her homework, that fathers must take more responsibility to provide love and guidance to their children.

PRESIDENT OBAMA, ACCEPTANCE SPEECH, 2008

There has been the assumption that central government can only change people's behaviour through rules and regulations. Our government will be a much smarter one, shunning the bureaucratic levers of the past and finding intelligent ways to encourage support and enable people to make better choices for themselves.

PRIME MINISTER CAMERON AND DEPUTY PRIME MINISTER CLEGG,
THE COALITION AGREEMENT, 2010

Five years after the ill-fated PMSU review, and on the other side of the Atlantic, there was a major breakthrough in the application of behavioural science to policy.

When Richard Thaler, a Chicago economist, and Cass Sunstein, a Harvard academic lawyer, first wrote their book, it was intended to be called *Libertarian Paternalism*, just like the paper on which it drew heavily. Fortunately for them, and for the rest of us, a prospective publisher suggested an alternative title, *Nudge*, under which it was published in 2008*. It makes you wonder how many other great ideas are buried under the weight of an academic title.

As we saw in the previous chapter, many of the ideas and literature that the book drew on were already well known in the psychological literature, and some like Robert Cialdini had helped to spread the ideas more widely. But Thaler and Sunstein gave the ideas a major extra push in at least three ways.

First, as non-psychologists they helped to break the ideas out of psychology, and applied them in an accessible form to problems that faced economists and lawmakers. Second, they blended into these existing literatures new ideas from 'behavioural economics', including a more formal recognition of the widespread power of defaults and 'choice architecture' – or the way in which choices are presented to people.[1] Third, they engaged directly in policy, not least through an old Chicago friend and colleague, Barak Obama.

Obama and Sunstein: 'nudge' comes to Washington

In a move that attracted widespread attention, the new President Obama appointed the co-author of *Nudge*, Cass Sunstein, to be his 'regulatory tsar' in his government in 2008. They had known each other in Chicago, but Cass had long stood out to many as a conceptual

---

* The suggestion to call the book *Nudge* actually came from a publisher they didn't proceed with. Richard Thaler

thinker and academic lawyer, with the ability to look at the world and the law in a refreshing new way.

Cass was also unusually open to statistical and psychological thinking. Long before *Nudge*, he had noticed how courts, and the public at large, seemed to be prepared to pay far more for saving a life in one particular context than in another. It was a line of thinking that was to bring him into the weird and wonderful world of how real people made real decisions.

Though I had read some of Sunstein's work over the years, by the time I met him in person he was already in Washington, as part of the Obama administration. I was still recovering from my six-year haul in government in the UK, a visiting policy wonk from a small, recently created think-tank in Britain called the Institute for Government.

Sunstein's office was in the Eisenhower Executive Office Building, just west of the White House, known as the wedding cake for its elaborate stonework and the grand sweep of steps leading to its frontage. His office was impressive: large and high-ceilinged, with furniture struggling to fill the space and with a beautiful, long-angle photograph of him talking earnestly to the President outside the White House. Cass himself is a quietly spoken and self-evidently reflective, even humble man, albeit with an exquisite mental precision and sharpness of mind. To me, the room did not really fit him, as if it were more space than he was used to or needed.

As head of the Office of Information and Regulatory Affairs (OIRA), within the Office of Management and Budget (OMB), Cass Sunstein was well placed to bring a more sophisticated and behaviourally informed approach into the heart of government. OIRA was originally set up in 1980, and had always been linked to reducing paperwork and the burden on citizens and businesses as a result of government regulation. During periods of Republican administration, it was criticised as acting as an executive-controlled brake to block new regulation. But now, in Cass's hands, the focus shifted on to how regulations could be reshaped to have both bigger impacts and lower burdens. A key tool for achieving this improvement in the cost-effectiveness of regulation was to use the lessons of behavioural economics and insight.

An everyday example that Cass cited was the food pyramid. This was a US Department of Agriculture graphic, first issued in 1992, intended to guide the eating habits of children, parents and schools, and drive underlying production and consumption of a healthy balanced diet. However, many people found it a pretty puzzling graphic. Cass's argument was that this was an illustration (literally) of government trying to be helpful, but actually causing more confusion than good. The issue to him was not that the guidance was wrong, but that it was incomprehensible. He was therefore strongly supportive of a redesigned graphic that people could immediately understand – or would take much less mental effort to interpret – and that might therefore actually affect people's behaviour. This in turn led to the replacing of the 'pyramid' with a simple 'food plate' (see Figure 5) in June 2011. For Cass, this was not a minor detail, but about a fundamental principle: for government regulations and advice to be effective, they had to be intuitively easy to understand. It is a refrain that he continues to use to this day: 'plate not pyramid' he insists.

Figure 5. The USDA food pyramid (2005 version) versus the simplified plate (2011).

OIRA annual reports document a dramatic rise in the cost-benefit ratio of regulations issued, or revised, under the Obama administration. The reports indicate that the improved regulatory quality led to billions of dollars in benefits for the USA. Cass argued that providing information in ways that ordinary people and consumers could more easily understand – such as presenting fuel economy as gallons or dollars per mile rather than miles per gallon – enabled them to make better choices, and improved the functioning of markets. Similarly, the careful refashioning of defaults, or the effective use of transparency, could lead to regulation that was more effective yet also less burdensome on people and businesses.

But Washington is a tough place. Its sharp partisan divisions leave little room for nuanced accounts of how information can be better presented, or the finer points of cost-benefit analysis. Cass himself was described by a leading Republican commentator as 'the most dangerous man in America' for his work to introduce more subtle, behaviourally sophisticated thinking into the world of regulation. The thing is, if you fundamentally don't trust government and want to see its role reduced, the last thing you want is a more effective administrator.

Under Cass's leadership, OIRA had some real successes. Behavioural thinking was embedded in the affordable care act, financial law reform, climate change policy, and consumer protection policy. There were administartive and political limits to what Cass could acheive, but but one thing he certainly did was to open up thinking across the world about more nuanced and behaviourally informed approaches to policy. And if there was one place that was ready to hear this message at that time, it was Britain.

The run-up to 2010: a changing political context

While those in political opposition might not choose it, one thing that a stint in Opposition gives people is time and space to think. They are on the look-out for new and interesting ideas, and in particular ones that resonate with their political objectives and that might also appeal to the electorate.

David Cameron appointed a very unusual sort of Conservative to help him reshape his policies, image and party in the years running up to the 2010 election. Steve Hilton was quick and open-minded, media- and image-savvy, and had a deep scepticism about 'big government'. The Conservatives had been out of power since 1997, and Tony Blair in particular had successfully crushed a succession of Conservative leaders. Cameron and the party were ready for modernisation. While parts of the Conservative party had their doubts, their hunger for electoral victory made them accommodate the more radical ideas of Hilton.

Steve eschewed suits for T-shirts and casual shorts. He was short(ish) and, at that time, slightly round. Never mind suits – Steve eschewed shoes. It was a habit he later brought with him into Downing Street, where he would be spotted padding out of his office next to the Cabinet Room past Cabinet Ministers in suits and ties – in his socks. At the time his shaved head made him look more like a nightclub bouncer than a Conservative adviser to the leader of the Opposition, and later PM. He was generally charming, warm and tactile; and sparky, creative and very imaginative. But he could also be temperamental, had a flaming temper and was partial to expletives. In short, he was the very antithesis of a traditional British Conservative.

Nonetheless, Steve was a Conservative in the sense of combining a deep-seated scepticism about government with a strong belief in letting individuals, businesses and communities make decisions for themselves. His catchphrase and argument, as he would put it, was 'Big Society, not Big Government'.

In the run-up to the 2010 election, Steve, along with a bright young aid to the Shadow Chancellor and previously junior Treasury aid, Rohan Silva, set off on a trip across the USA in search of the most interesting new ideas and minds of the generation. Much of what they learnt was fascinating, but was left on the cutting-room floor. One of the ideas that did stand out was that of 'Nudge'. It suggested that governments might have a viable alternative to legislating, mandating and throwing money at problems – an argument very much in tune with Hilton and Cameron's emerging philosophy. The fact that the new and charismatic US President had brought Cass Sunstein into the administration helped to add glamour and interest, but it was conversations with Cass's dry-humoured co-author, Chicago economist Richard Thaler, that really sold the idea to Steve and Rohan.

Rohan had also picked up on my own work, including a summary in *The Hidden Wealth of Nations*. Published in late 2009, the conclusion of *Hidden Wealth* listed ten top policy ideas that an incoming Prime Minister or President and his team should look at. The list was based partly on the conclusions of the lost Blair-to-Brown Policy Review, but also on a string of other related reviews and academic work.[2] Some of these ideas, and the title of the book, concerned ways in which governments could better facilitate the capacity of citizens to help each other and themselves. Other proposals in the book made the case for dramatically upping government's game on citizen-consumer information; democratic innovations; focusing on well-being; and evidence-based policy. But of particular relevance here, echoing the 2003 PMSU review, Kahneman and others' work, and the Downing Street Cialdini session, was one particular recommendation:

Embrace behavioural economics

Behavioural economics provides a powerful new set
of tools for policymakers and citizens to address the
challenges of today and improve the quality of our lives.
But even though many of the key insights are twenty to
thirty years old, policymakers have been slow to apply
them ... The application of behavioural economics could
offer substantial gains in relation to the environment,

crime, pro-social behaviour, education, welfare and health.
(*The Hidden Wealth of Nations*, 2009, p. 260.)

Drawing heavily on Thaler and Sunstein, Rohan penned an opinion piece in the name of the Shadow Chancellor, George Osborne. The piece made the argument that nudge-type approaches could achieve better outcomes, often at lower costs and with greater respect for personal choice than conventional regulation. For example, the piece highlighted how home energy conservation might be encouraged by giving households feedback on their use relative to their more efficient neighbours, or even by glowing orbs on people's roofs that would signal levels of energy use to their owners and others (see Chapter 5 on social influence for further detail).

The piece attracted considerable attention. It hit the spot perfectly between being slightly crazy – enough to break through into commentator and public attention – but intriguing and plausible enough to stand up to sceptical scrutiny.

Meanwhile, the profound aftershocks of the 2008 financial and banking crises were continuing to highlight deep cracks in conventional economic and policy thinking. The crisis showed that even so-called financial experts, in both academia and the markets, were prone to make serious errors of thought and judgement, with catastrophic consequences. The crisis had shown equally catastrophic failures of regulators and central banks, and of the models of human behaviour that their policies were based on. In this wider context, the Osborne–Hilton–Silva critique of conventional regulation and the prospect of new, nudge-thinking was not so easily dismissed.

Within the administration thinking also begins to change

In parallel to Steve and Rohan's exploration of 'nudge' ideas, a shift was also occurring deep inside the administration of British government itself. The then Head of the civil service, Sir Gus O'Donnell, himself an economist by training and a former Head of the Treasury, had become very interested in the development of new and better models of human behaviour, not least to explain the catastrophic failures of widely used economic models in 2008.

Gus O'Donnell had served as Cabinet Secretary to both Prime Ministers Blair and Brown. In his late fifties, Gus was tall and athletic. He had come to the civil service from a relatively academic – but not private school – background, steeped in econometrics from Warwick and Oxford. One of his first roles in government had been to work on the Treasury's famous Green Book which sets out how rational policymakers should go about doing cost-benefit analysis according to the then latest thinking in economics. His unusual combination of economic expertise with a personable, easy manner soon attracted attention and he became Press Secretary to the then Conservative Chancellor John Major. When Major became Prime Minister in the early nineties, he took Gus with him. Gus later moved back to Head the Treasury (as Permanent Secretary), before finally becoming Britain's top civil servant to Prime Minister Blair in 2005.

Gus's background made him particularly well suited to reflect on the deeper lessons to government of the near-collapse of the banking and financial system in 2008–9, which he had seen up close as Head of the British civil service and Cabinet Secretary. It was palpably obvious to him how badly the Treasury's, and everyone else's, models had performed in the crisis. He could see that the issues reached right into the core assumptions that the models were based on, and in particular the economic or 'rational man' assumptions that he had taught and built into Treasury models himself. Furthermore, if these models were so badly wrong about human behaviour in relation to financial markets, what did this say for policy more widely?

By that time I was at the Institute for Government, which I'd worked with Lord Sainsbury to set up after I had left government when Blair stood down. David Sainsbury had been a long-standing Science Minister in the Blair administration, but was also a philanthropist who had developed a strong interest in addressing the many weaknesses of government. Thinking about this kind of deep, and somewhat technocratic, failure of government was just the sort of thing that the Institute was set up to do. We therefore set about dusting off the old PMSU report on human behaviour and its policy implications. The basic idea was to update the report, bringing in some external academics and producing a summary that could be easily read and understood by policymakers, including Ministers or an incoming government.

The Institute had the resources to do the report by itself. But the point of the exercise was to produce something that policymakers would find useful – and actually use. As it happens, there's a basic behavioural phenomena that applies to both people and organisations around 'commitment': people and organisations are much more likely to do something if they were previously engaged in even a small commitment or helped build it themselves (the IKEA effect). Cialdini gives a neat example, in his early popularisation of the psychology of influence, of a restaurant that was struggling with large numbers of customers failing to turn up for bookings. Staff taking phone bookings were instructed to make a seemingly tiny change: to pause after asking customers 'Would you let us know if you can't make it?' The pause – imagine it in your own head – leads to customers to fill it with a response, such as 'sure', or just 'uh-huh'. And the effect? The number of customers failing to turn up without calling more than halved.

With this in mind, we spent some time agreeing with the Cabinet Office that the report would be jointly commissioned. Gus O'Donnell was delighted and supportive, but there was also support from the then Labour Cabinet Office Minister Liam Byrne, who was quick to recognise the potential of the approach.

To strengthen the team, and broaden its disciplinary base, we joined forces with Paul Dolan, an economist from Imperial College London (and later the London School of Economics), together with a couple of young researchers, Ivo Vlaev and Dom King. I had come across Paul a few times over the years, and was always struck by the sharp practicality and empiricism of his thinking, including his work on behavioural biases and well-being.[3] He had also spent time working with Daniel Kahneman at Princeton, where he had developed a particular interest in 'framing' and 'priming' effects. More particularly, Paul and Ivo had been working on a simple typology of the most robust effects found in the behavioural economic literature, which was exactly what we wanted to form the core of this review. From the Institute, I also added to the team one of our best researchers, Michael Hallsworth, to form a team of five.

The primary challenge was to boil down the large number of laboratory and real-world mental shortcuts, 'errors' and influences into a shortlist that was comprehensive and robust enough to fairly represent the literature – and how humans really thought – but that was still short enough to be a useful tool and guide to policymakers. Paul and Ivo's nascent framework involved four main effects – what they had boiled down to 'SNAP': Salience, Norms, Affect (emotion) and Priming.

I felt the SNAP framework was too narrow. In particular, it felt too thin on the large variety of what those working on social cognition call 'self-serving attributional biases' (e.g. when things go well it's down to us, but when they go badly its always someone else's fault) and on important linked effects such as optimism bias. SNAP was also rather thin on some of the powerful influences documented by social psychology, such as the power of authority (cf. Milgram experiments) or reciprocity (e.g. our strong tendency to help someone who has helped us, in even the most minor way). Michael and Ivo spent several months trawling through the literature, identifying effects that had been vigorously and repeatedly demonstrated; filtering out those that there had been few replications of; and clustering those that seemed to be close relatives of each other. We used these reviews to create groups of related effects, trying to get them down to a robust but more limited and memorable summary of the burgeoning literature.

We also faced another dilemma. Some of the effects referred to *processes* in people's heads, such as 'salience' – for example, how we notice our name in a crowded room, or how a red apple stands out in a bowl of green ones. Other effects referred more to how the *environment* around us was configured, such as 'defaults' or the way in which an option or pathway was set up. From a purist, academic perspective, it felt slightly untidy mixing up these different effects. But from a policy, or practitioner, perspective this distinction was much less important. Given our audience, we decided to err towards the latter.

The final framework – 'MINDSPACE' – was published in early 2010 (see Figure 6). It was designed to provide a simple framework and mnemonic, or memory aid, to help busy policymakers think about what might influence people's behaviour in a given context. As such, it was intended to broaden the policy tools and approaches that could be utilised to achieve public policy goals, from better population health, to recycling, to paying taxes on time. MINDSPACE went on to become the Institute's most downloaded report.[4]

Messenger	we are heavily influenced by who communicates information
Incentives	our responses to incentives are shaped by predictable mental shortcuts such as strongly avoiding losses
Norms	we are strongly influenced by what others do
Defaults	we 'go with the flow' of pre-set options
Salience	our attention is drawn to what is novel and seems relevant to us
Priming	our acts are often influenced by sub-conscious cues
Affect	our emotional associations can powerfully shape our actions
Commitments	we seek to be consistent with our public promises, and reciprocate acts
Ego	we act in ways that make us feel better about ourselves

Figure 6. The MINDSPACE framework (Institute for Government, 2010).

The 2010 government launches the Nudge Unit

Squeezed between Steve Hilton and Rohan Silva, the new Prime Minister's political advisers, in the back of a Paris taxi was not somewhere I thought I'd find myself in the early summer of 2010. It was still the very early days of the new Coalition Government, and we had come to Paris to see if the centre-right administration of Nicolas Sarkozy shared the interest in approaches to government of the new Cameron–Clegg government in the UK, including nudging, Big Society and well-being. It turned out that they didn't.

Richard Thaler was with us, over from Chicago for a few days while we sought to put into action the plan to create the world's first nudge unit. We didn't even know what we would call it at that point. At that time, my role was supposed to be to advise the new unit for a day or so a week, drawing on my knowledge of government and my specific knowledge of behaviour and policy. The politicos didn't mind that I had worked closely with Blair, since the Cameron team quite admired him – and the three elections he won.

It also helped that the Liberal Democrats, the junior partner in the Coalition, were also rather taken with the nudge approach. The two key advisers to the Lib Dem Deputy Prime Minister Nick Clegg – Richard Reeves and Polly Mackenzie – both liked the liberal aspects of 'libertarian paternalism', and also the empiricism associated with the approach.

The wheels of the civil service had already started to turn, seeking to interpret what it was that the new government wanted – or at least a compromise between what the new government wanted and what the civil service thought would be a good idea. The higher rungs of the Cabinet Office had even started to identify people and a nascent team. In the British system, unlike the US, such appointments are almost always made by the civil service, not the politicians – whether rightly or wrongly.[5]

Several ideas were being put together. Rohan was clear that it should be a 'skunk-work'- style unit, based on the famous group of outsiders set up by Lockheed-Martin and charged with coming up with radical new designs for aircraft that its normal teams would not have considered. For others, including parts of the Department of Business, its primary focus should be on deregulation, or at least on slimmer and lighter touch regulation somewhat along the lines being pursued by Cass Sunstein in the USA. For others, including to some extent Steve Hilton and Richard Thaler, it was about bringing in new ways of thinking that could roll back the state while extending choice and freedom for citizens in subtle and empowering ways.

We had spent the day prior to the Paris visit in Downing Street and the Cabinet Office, meeting with the Cabinet Secretary Gus O'Donnell, and also some of the civil servants who were starting to be assigned to the new unit.

Though the trip to Paris was a bit of a dud in policy terms, it did give us a chance to spend a few hours on the train and in taxis hammering out the details of what the new unit might look like and do. The Coalition Agreement between the two parties that formed the new government had a clear statement at the front that the new 'government will be a much smarter one, shunning the bureaucratic levers of the past and finding intelligent ways to encourage support and enable people to make better choices for themselves', and this helped to frame what the unit was about. We all agreed that an early objective would be to try out some of the most prominent and best-evidenced ideas from the wider literature, and from the US in particular. These could provide some early quick wins, and help to establish the approach. For example, we suspected that a version of a successful 'promoted choice' approach to organ donation in Illinois could work well in the UK without needing to go for the 'presumed consent' method that had been proposed by the previous Brown government and abandoned in the face of public opposition. If it worked, it would be a nice illustration of the Coalition's different approach, and of course would hopefully save a few lives.

Other criteria for early priorities were that: the issue was a PM or DPM priority; the intervention was likely to be revenue-producing or saving (given the pressures on budgets); and the intervention was amenable to systematic testing and trialling, with good management data in place that we could use for measurement. For all these reasons, interventions around tax and fine collection were identified as an early target, if at all possible.

A surprising amount of time was spent discussing what the new unit should be called. First, the decision was taken not to call it a 'unit'. The new administration was generally keen to make government smaller, not larger, and particularly at the centre.[6] Meanwhile, some senior civil servants were happy to go along with the idea that this was something that could be tucked under the wing of someone or something else. The idea of a 'team' seemed a nice, soft alternative to a 'unit', implying the idea of more permeability and openness to the inclusion of experts from outside government.

More difficult was what the main part of the title should be. An early front-runner was the Behaviour Change Team, but this made Richard Thaler's inner Chicago economist and US instincts feel very uncomfortable: was it really the primary role of government to 'change' people's behaviour? Behavioural Economics Team was also mooted, but was a little too narrow in its disciplinary base (and would have made Daniel Kahneman, a psychologist, despair). Behavioural Science Team was another possibility (which Steve quite liked), but risked offending all those at the softer ends of the government community who felt that policy was more of an art. The word science also felt a bit harsh to other parts of No. 10. There were also serious concerns about its acronym – it risked ridicule as it was without its staff introducing themselves as being from the BS team.

By late July 2010, the Behavioural Insights Team was ready to be launched. It was to be minute – just seven or eight people with an annual budget totalling less than £0.5 million. It was to form a tiny sister unit to the much bigger PM's Strategy Unit (a relic of the Blair years), and would be based alongside it in Admiralty Arch. It was to be staffed by civil servants from a mixture of the PMSU and the business department's Better Regulation Executive (BRE). Finally, it was to be given special access to No. 10 and the Deputy Prime Minister's Office through a special steering board, which was to be chaired by the Cabinet Secretary personally.

However, there was to be one extra change that was to affect me in particular. By the end of the trip to Paris, Rohan and Steve had become very concerned about who would lead the new team, a concern shared by Richard Thaler. The deputy director who had been chosen by the civil service to lead the team didn't really know much about behavioural economics or psychology. This is not unusual for the British civil service, which has a long tradition of putting people in charge of things that they don't know much about. It's generally considered that smart generalists can get the hang of most things, though it's not clear why you would want to move them on after 18 months once they *had* got the hang of it ... The person concerned was a competent and ambitious deputy director who had been drafted across from the BRE, but she had neither a background in the behavioural literature, nor a good relationship with Steve and Rohan, a particular problem given Steve's short temper. Her background also rooted the team rather firmly in the deregulatory space, a prime interest of the business department, but less so the broader ambitions of No. 10.[7]

As we headed out from St Pancras, Rohan started working on me in earnest to get me to lead the new team. He had clearly already discussed it with Steve. My agreement had been to advise the new team a day a week, perhaps two at a push, while continuing my role at the Institute for Government. To come back to Downing Street to lead the team, even four days a week, would mean effectively standing down from my role at the Institute, and I had already spent a long time in No. 10 in the Blair years. But I knew he was right. It was double or quits. It was a high-risk programme: a small team; a new idea; a crazy challenge; a sceptical civil service; and complex coalition politics. The chances of success did not look good to start with, and, without someone at its head with a strong relationship with the key players in No. 10 and the rest of the centre, it was almost bound to fail. So I agreed, albeit on loan from the Institute. For the summer, I held to the idea that I would continue to work at the Institute a day a week. But I should have known better: by October I gave up on the fiction and came in full-time.

Together we set the objectives of the team. It read like a mission impossible. With our team of seven we were to:

▲ Transform at least two major areas of policy.
▲ Spread understanding of behavioural approaches across Whitehall.
▲ Achieve at least a tenfold return on the cost of the unit.

If we failed to achieve these objectives, it was explicitly stated that BIT would be shut on its second anniversary. The decision to set up BIT with a default that it be shut after two years was based on my own experience of government, plus the desire to create a sense of urgency and momentum. I had seen too many units set up by previous governments that had failed to deliver, but limped on because no one got around to shutting them down. This way we would have a clear, time-limited target. It also enabled us to live by our own principles: we had effectively switched around the normal default of government teams so that the Prime Minister and Cabinet Secretary would have to make an active choice to keep the team going (see Chapter 3 for more details on defaults). If it hadn't worked, I would go back to the Institute for Government and BIT would have disappeared long enough before the election for voters and commentators to have forgotten about it.

With the sunset clause in place, recruitment of the team really did feel like a scene out of the movie *The Dirty Dozen*: pulling together a group of grizzled fighters with an unusual set of talents and a 'nothing left to lose' mentality. They were being asked to sign up to a mission that most considered very likely to fail, and though they weren't actually going to be dropped behind enemy lines and shot at, it was going to feel like it at times. Fortunately, the British civil service has many talented young people, especially in the old Prime Minister's Strategy Unit, and a high enough turnover rate that a two-year project linked closely to No. 10 was something quite a few were interested in. Remarkably, and testament to the team, many of the original recruits were still with the team five years later, among them Rory Gallagher, a brilliant and energetic policy analyst from the PMSU with a PhD from Cambridge, now leading our work in Australia and Singapore, and Sam Nguyen, our second ever recruit, a young and talented economist drawn from the Home Office, now leading our work on employment and growth. The successes that followed would be down to the efforts of those early recruits.[8]

Some of the team members would change as the early focus and methods evolved. By November 2010, the original deputy director moved to another role and was replaced by a returning PMSU deputy director, Owain Service, with a background in strategic policy and a social science degree from Cambridge. This set in train an important early lesson for BIT, and for similar teams that may follow it: it was critical to get the mix of skills and personnel right. With Owain on board, we set about refining the team that would enable us to put in place a new kind of approach to policy. We needed a team who knew the behavioural literature, were capable deploying robust methods for discerning 'what works', and who knew their way around the political and administrative complexities of government. For example, we recruited Laura Haynes, a Cambridge PhD on loan

Figure 7. The Behavioural Insights Team in the Treasury courtyard in early 2014. By this time, the team had grown to around 18 people, or around 14.5 full-time equivalents. The baby in the foreground belonged to Felicity Algate, team lead on consumer markets, and was not involved in any behavioural experiments, to my knowledge. Team member Rory Gallagher was absent, having been seconded to help Singapore and New South Wales, Australia.

from the NAO, and later the excellent Michael Sanders from Bristol, and then Harvard, to lead our own research, evaluation and analysis work. Another team member, Maren Ashford, would go on to expand BIT's innovative approach to working with business through a sister unit we created, the Cabinet Office Partnerships Team, still operating today.

We were also helped by the setting up of a parallel Red Tape Challenge team with an explicit focus on deregulation more generally. With the Red Tape Challenge team set up to trawl through 20,000 or more historic rules and regulations, BIT was able to focus on areas where we could add most value. The Red Tape Challenge could call us in when needed, and I sat on the deregulatory Star Chamber to look out for areas where a behavioural solution might help.

In July 2010, much of this was still ahead. The BIT, or Nudge Unit as everyone soon called it, was the first of its kind in the world, applying behavioural science in a systematic way to a range of policies at the very heart of government. BIT had the support of the key political advisers around the Prime Minister and Deputy Prime Minister, Britain's top civil servant, Gus O'Donnell and the wise counsel of Richard Thaler; as well as the good wishes of a small clutch of other academics. But against the team – or at least indifferent, unaware or sceptical – was Parliament: 70,000 civil servants around Whitehall; 450,000 civil servants across the UK; five million public servants; and of course the media and public. Back in the USA, behaviourally informed policies were quietly being adapted on an increasingly large scale, through Cass's skillful hands. But even there, the idea of applying behavioural economics to policy continued to encounter some abrasive politics in public. Applying a better model of human behaviour to policy was a nice idea, but the history books are littered with nice ideas that didn't work out.

We are often asked by other governments and organisations, many of whom we now advise, what the key ingredients are for setting up an impactful Nudge Unit or similar. We've summarised them in a mnemonic – 'apples':

Administrative support – ensure you have senior level buy-in 'inside the system'. For us, it was key that we had the support of the Cabinet Secretary, the UK's most senior civil servant, and that he personally agreed to chair BIT's steering board. This was a very powerful signal to the rest of government, and gave us key leverage when we needed it.

Political support – governments are also political projects. The take-off of BIT was greatly facilitated in 2010 by the interest and support of the Prime Minister and Deputy Prime Minister, and their close aids. At the very least, you need to think about how the approach fits with the political narrative and instincts of the government – and public.

People – getting the right mix of skills and expertise is critical. You need subject expertise (see below) but at least as important is having people with battle-hardened experience of government and large organisations, and personal relationships with those who you will need as allies.

Location – so much of government, as of life, is about being in the right place at the right time. Don't rely on luck. There are certain places where people regularly bump into each other and much impromptu business is done. In the UK this includes the lobby of No. 10, Parliament and on the streets around Whitehall. Choose a close location over a fancy office 20 minutes away.

Experimentation – embrace empirical methods. You'll need to demonstrate to sceptics that your new approach works, and to quantify the impact. But, more fundamentally, you should follow a logic of test, learn, adapt – behavioural science is well suited to experimental approaches, and human responses are complicated and hard to perfectly predict.

Scholarship – know the behavioural literature and details of the challenges you are engaging with. Everybody has some knowledge of psychology. You need a team who really know what they are talking about, and are plugged into the latest thinking and results. Identify your local and relevant academic experts, and form an expert advisory group.

Figure 8. Key ingredients for the creation of an impactful Nudge Unit – 'apples'.

▲

CHANGING THE WORLD A NUDGE AT A TIME

In government, as in life, you must walk before you can run. BIT was set up to make a difference, and – if it worked – ultimately to transform policy and practice in a range of areas. It sounds good to say that you are going to transform the way something works, or transform how a business or department runs, but it's not necessarily a good strategy to persuade those who actually run it.

Large government departments and businesses have many moving parts. Telling the head of a large government department or organisation that you want to make a few changes in the way they run their operations is no small matter. For example, the head of a tax office in a medium-sized country will have 50–100,000 staff, and be responsible for collecting hundreds of billions of pounds in revenue that every other department will rely on. To those who have spent years oiling and tuning it, what to you look like a 'few' ingenious changes will to them look like a dangerous risk of throwing grit into the cogs of their great machine. They know perfectly well that if the changes you make lead to things going wrong, tax collection not happening, or mistakes being made, support from your political masters will evaporate. And chances are they'll have to pick up the pieces.

With this in mind, BIT deliberately started its work with small, relatively modest changes. We sought to make such changes in letters and communications, testing if behaviourally informed alternatives would work any better, or worked on internal change processes, such as the Prime Minister's commitment to reduce the energy use of government departments.

In the early days, BIT leant heavily on the MINDSPACE framework to help guide its work, and to inform the many seminars and workshops that the team conducted across the major government departments to spread understanding and capability in the approach. This capability building was important to develop support for the approach, to identify specific opportunities and ideas for interventions within the departments, and to build their capacity to use the approaches for themselves. But after the first year or so of battle-hardened application, and many workshops and conversations, we developed a slightly simplified framework for day-to-day use. It is this framework that will be used to organise this section of the book, and will hopefully help you, the reader, remember and use what you have learnt more easily.

The first public appearance of this simplified framework was at a series of seminars in Harvard and the East Coast of the USA in 2011, and partly as light-hearted tribute to that location it became known as the EAST framework. Just like MINDSPACE, EAST is a mnemonic. If you want to encourage a behaviour, you should think about making it:

- ▲ Easy.
- ▲ Attract.
- ▲ Social.
- ▲ Timely.

The EAST framework does not cover every nuance of the behavioural literature, but it does offer a good starting point. Members of BIT spend a lot of time reading the latest academic papers and studying the literature and find that frameworks like EAST enable a rapid engagement of a new problem – a sort of mental checklist that can be run through quickly to enable the identification of some simple ideas for early testing.

The study of human behaviour reveals that many of our abilities as human beings rest on mental shortcuts or heuristics. It also leads you to respect these heuristics. EAST is a mental heuristic of mental heuristics. Like all heuristics, it will miss a few angles, but it should get you quite a long way.

CHAPTER 3

▲

EASY

John was in his late twenties. He had decent grades at school and a job he enjoyed. He was already an assistant manager, and rising fast. His employer, a large retailer, offered good benefits, including a great pension. He remembered the details from when he first joined, and from a seminar they did for staff the previous year. For every pound he put in, his employer would put in the same again, and the government added more on top. It was a no-brainer, and he knew it. The only problem was, John hadn't actually signed up.

Like many people, John knew that he should start saving for his pension, and it was something he actually wanted to do. He'd seen his grandparents struggle with money, and though one or two of his friends joked that you should 'spend it while you're young', he knew that a few pounds put away now would be worth a lot more in the future. But it also involved paperwork, a bit of hassle, and it didn't feel like something that had to be done today. Retirement was years away. It was something he could do tomorrow; a consideration in the back of his mind. 'Yes', he thought, 'I'll do it tomorrow, or maybe next week.' This week was, after all, a bit busy.

In 2012, something happened. His employer wrote to him to say that, as a result of a small change in the law, they would now automatically enrol him in the company-sponsored pension scheme unless he indicated that he would rather not. If he didn't want to enrol in the scheme for now, it was simple. He just had to ask to leave the scheme within a month, and he would get another prompt in a couple of years' time. The 'default' had been flipped: from one in which John would have to actively choose to join a pension scheme ('opt in'), to one in which he would be automatically enrolled on to the company pension plan unless he said otherwise ('opt out'). John read the letter, and went to a short talk on the new arrangements. It was a bit of a relief. He didn't have to do anything. His pension was sorted.

John was not alone. Within six months of the change, initially for large UK firms only, more than a million new savers started pensions. In short, more than 90 per cent of eligible workers chose *not* to opt out. The proportion of the employees of large firms saving for pensions rose from just over 60 per cent, where it had hovered for decades, to over 80 per cent (the overall percentage is pulled down by those who were not immediately eligible for a pension, such as those on extended leave). By early 2015, this simple change in the default had led to more than five million extra UK workers saving for their pensions.[1]

The power of a simple nudge – changing the default

This stunning result illustrates the power of a simple 'nudge' to change behaviour, and to turn around a policy problem that had defeated generations of policymakers. For more than half a century, policymakers on both sides of the Atlantic had wrestled with the issue of how to get more people to save for pensions. Despite subsidies running into many billions – more than £20 billion ($30 billion) per annum in the UK and $100 billion in the USA – millions of people apparently preferred not to save. It was enough to make many experts conclude that there was something deep in Anglo-Saxon culture against saving – we just preferred to live and spend for today.[2]

The primary tool, employed on both sides of the Atlantic for decades, had been the use of generous tax breaks and subsidies to encourage people to save. And yet, as one leading economist put it, many people continued to 'leave the money on the table'.[3] Recent analysis by Raj Chetty, a brilliant Harvard economist, has shown just how cost ineffective such tax subsidies are. His analysis, using European data, shows that every $1 of taxpayers' subsidy to encourage people to save more for their pensions led to a miserly 1 cent of extra saving by workers.[3] The main effect of these huge subsidies was simply to encourage a small minority of savvy savers – perhaps 15 per cent – to move their investments into the most tax efficient schemes. In contrast, changing the default to one in which savers were asked to 'opt out' was shown to lead to substantial increases in saving literally overnight – and very little reduction in saving elsewhere.

Changing the default also beats 'financial education' hands down. A wide variety of studies, by David Laibson, Shlomo Benartzi and other behavioural economists, showed that financial education – though often called for by industry and some politicians – had very modest effects. These studies showed that financial education, such as seminars on saving, left participants feeling more knowledgeable and intending to save more. However, participants' enhanced intention to save more generally failed to translate into actual increases in savings. In contrast, changing the defaults – allowing people to opt out of future saving, rather than opting in – had much bigger impacts on medium- to long-term savings behaviour.

Still, just because changing the default works, is it what people really want? Policymakers on both sides of the Atlantic worried greatly that many people would object to the idea that they had been automatically enrolled in a pension. 'Not so,' explains David Laibson, professor of Economics at Harvard. He is one of those rare breed of academic economists: patently brilliant, but also comprehensible to the rest of us. 'It is hugely popular. US survey data suggests that 9 out of 10 workers who have experienced the pension opt-out support the changes in 401k defaults. And even among the small minority who do opt out, more than 7 out of 10 of *them* still think the opt-out is preferable to an opt-in arrangement.'[4]

As well as being extremely effective, changing the default so that savers are automatically enrolled illustrates how we can often achieve better outcomes by making it easy for people to do things that they would quite like to do, if only it were more straightforward.

If you want to encourage something, make it easy

It has become one of Richard Thaler's favourite sayings. As we saw one Minister after another, one policy challenge after another, sooner or later – normally sooner – the mantra would appear. If you want someone to do something – pay their taxes, recycle, or take on an extra employee – a pretty good start is to 'make it easy'.

It is so simple, so obvious, it should hardly need saying at all. And yet, across the world, governments and scholars have been slow to learn the importance of this most basic behavioural principle.

In economics there's a phrase that captures this simple concept: 'friction costs'. As in physics, from where the phrase is borrowed, it helps explain why otherwise 'perfect' models might sometimes throw out predictions at odds with messy real-world observations. For those who studied physics at school, the words 'calculate, ignoring frictional effects ...' will be familiar. Economists have deployed similar simplifications to make the world more amenable to elegant mathematical models.

But in the real world of things, of people and of bureaucracy, friction matters a great deal. Just as a real weight pushed across a real table will soon grind to a halt as a result of friction, a human impulse to do something soon grinds to a halt when it becomes a hassle. Hence John, the character at the start of this chapter, really did mean to start saving, and to get that 'money on the table'. He just didn't get around to it because it was an effort, involved tedious paperwork and was less attractive and urgent than all the other things he could be doing in the next hour or day. Frictional costs are not a peripheral issue. Rather, they often make all the difference between something happening or not, be it a stone rolling down a slope, or a policy succeeding or failing.

From stealing motorbikes to suicide – the power of 'friction'

In 1980, the Federal Republic of Germany (West Germany) introduced spot fines on motorcyclists not wearing helmets. The primary motivation was to reduce head injuries, but it had an unexpected and dramatic impact in a totally different area: thefts. In the wake of the change, motorcycle thefts fell by 60 per cent, and stayed down.[5]

You might think that if a person intended to steal a bike, this change in the law would not make that much difference: they just had to remember to bring a helmet with them, or to steal one, too. But, it would seem, most offenders did not do this. It was extra hassle, and required forethought. Riders often carried their helmets with them, rather than leaving them on the bike. In short, the requirement to wear a helmet introduced 'friction' to the act of stealing a motorbike, with dramatic consequences.

Criminologists Pat Mayhew and colleagues, who studied the effect, tested whether thieves had simply switched to other forms of crime. They did find evidence for slight increases in car and bicycle thefts, but nothing close to the 100,000 reduction in motorbike thefts. Nor was it a peculiarly German phenomenon: they documented similar reductions elsewhere. Texas saw a reduction of 44 per cent in motorcycle thefts from 1988 to 1990 following the requirement to wear helmets, and Britain and the Netherlands saw comparable reductions in thefts of a third or more when laws were changed to require the wearing of helmets in the 1970s.[6]

The big impact of friction, or hassle, is not limited to would-be thieves or, as we saw at the start of the chapter, would-be savers for pensions. Humans have a deep-rooted tendency to take the line of least resistance, be it cutting the corners across a park, to deciding what to watch on TV, to what to eat. Try putting out a selection of fruit in the office, or even at home, and see what's left at the end of the day. Chances are it'll be the oranges. They are just that little bit more hassle to eat compared with an apple, or that master of convenience the banana.

Even the most serious decisions in life are affected by friction. You can intuitively see why an orange might get left in the fruit bowl, and even why workers might never get around to starting a good-value pension because of the hassle of filling out a form. But what about the ultimate decision of all: whether to end your own life?

In the early 1960s the suicide rate in England and Wales began to fall. It was not unusual for the rate to fluctuate from year to year, so at first it went largely unnoticed. But from 1963 the suicide rate for both men and women fell for seven consecutive years. In less than a decade the suicide rate fell by around 30 per cent. Was this some wonderful result of free love? But if so, why was this trend not being seen in other countries over the same period? What was going on?

The answer came when researchers broke the trends down by type of suicide.[7] It turned out that the falls in suicide concerned one particular method: carbon monoxide poisoning. Until the early 1960s in Britain, one of the most common ways of committing suicide was to 'stick your head in the oven' – you turned on the gas, put your head in the oven and the carbon monoxide in the gas would quietly kill you. But in the early sixties the source of the gas in people's ovens began to change following the discovery of North Sea gas off the coast of Britain. Unlike the previous gas that had been derived from coal, the new North Sea 'natural gas' had much lower levels of carbon monoxide. Putting your head in the oven with the new, seemingly identical North Sea gas (carbon monoxide has no odour) might give you a headache – and could put you at risk of blowing up your kitchen – but it was unlikely to kill you.

You might think that the decision to end your own life, given the gravity and the number of ways of doing so, would not be defeated by discovering that putting your head in the oven no longer did the trick. It is clear from the trends in Figure 9 that at least a few poor souls – mainly women – did find other ways to kill themselves. But the overwhelming result of this method of suicide becoming ineffective was to reduce the overall suicide rate: most of those who would have

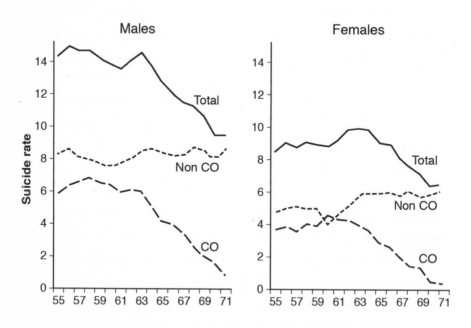

Figure 9. Trends in suicide rates per 100,000 in England and Wales, 1955–71, involving carbon monoxide and not involving carbon monoxide.

killed themselves with the oven did not go on to kill themselves by another means.

Friction – even small amounts of extra effort or hassle – matters greatly, and often much more than policymakers and citizens ever thought.

Simplify, reduce hassle and take out friction

As we have seen, hassle and friction have big impacts on behaviour. This simple insight opens the door to many policy interventions – as well as its use and abuse by companies. Businesses work hard to make it as easy as possible for you sign on to a new deal: to get a mobile; to try out a new product for ten-day period for free; or to walk out of the showroom with a new car. However, most will not make it as easy to return the product or end the deal. They'll go to great trouble to make sure that when it comes to paying the instalments or renewing the subscription, it happens automatically. They'll want to make sure that it's an effort to opt out and end the subscription, but as easy as possible to leave it to renew. If it's a product you are happy with, there's no problem. But if you aren't sure about it and genuinely want to try it out, thinking you'll cancel it in the offer period is generally a mistake; the frictions are now working strongly against you – and probably much more strongly than you anticipated.

As a modern consumer, you almost certainly recognise these types of offers, but they still work just the same. For example, my deputy Owain Service particularly hates the kinds of special offers that require you to claim the money back after you've got the product. Being a determined and frugal sort of person, he's tried out a few. Suffice it to say, there's plenty of friction involved in getting the 'saving' back. As the literature shows us, even a small amount of friction will defeat most of us. Hence the retailer, or manufacturer, can afford to offer dramatic discounts on the ticket price provided there's a bit of effort involved in claiming the money back. The fact is, most of us will never get around to it, even though that's what helped to persuade us to make the purchase in the first place.

Businesses can also take out friction in ways that consumers can find very helpful. For example, pharmacies can make life much easier for patients on repeat prescriptions by automatically sending by post a new batch of the medication just before the old prescription runs out. This can save both patient and doctor quite a lot of hassle in getting and collecting a new prescription, and saving everyone tens of millions of pounds in the process.

We'll return to the issue of how governments and regulators should respond to such practices – good and bad – on behalf of consumers in a later chapter, but for now let's note the basic rule. If you want to encourage a particular behaviour, make it easier. If you want to discourage it, make it harder.

Curiously, many policy and business interventions stumble at the first, most basic step: communication. There's little point in passing a law, introducing a benefit, or running a public information campaign intended to influence behaviour if no one knows about it. Similarly, don't expect much impact if the information is so dense and complex that it is not clear what is being asked of the person it is directed at. As such, the most fundamental application of 'make it easy' is to make sure that information, messages or requests are clear and simple to understand.

When you last received a letter or message from government, or big business, was it clear what it said and what it was asking you to do? Or did you have to read it three times – after which it was still not clear? If you were asked to pay a bill, was it obvious how to pay, or were there three different addresses, several phone numbers and the 'how to pay' details buried somewhere on the back?

Many people assume that these are trivial details. They are certainly not the things that senior government officials or the heads of business worry about. But they should, because the effects are substantial. Laboratory studies show that an easy-to-read message is not only more likely to be understood, it is also more likely to be believed. By way of a simple illustration, subjects are more likely to believe a statement as true when it is written in bold rather than standard text.

In BIT – just like many citizens and businesses on the receiving end – we came across many official letters and communications that looked as if they had been written by a committee of lawyers or technical administrators (and often were). For example, correspondence about fines often uses the language of the court, with words like 'distraint' that even my spell-check doesn't recognise, let alone most people.

We tested the effects of simplifying such letters, texts and websites experimentally. We found that tax letters written in plain English, with a clear, simple request at the beginning, could often be 200–300 per cent more effective than the originals we compared them with. And, generally speaking, we found that 'less is more'. For example, we found that click-throughs by businesses to get further information in response to emails from a major government agency could be increased by 40 to 60 per cent by reducing the volume of text in the email. Similarly, we found that sign-ups – from stopping smoking to youth skills and employment programmes – were significantly increased when the website landing pages were simplified and de-cluttered.

Even armed with this evidence we couldn't always convince the relevant department to simplify and de-clutter. In one case, it took us three years to get a single letter changed (we are a persistent bunch), albeit one sent to 8 to 12 million people a year. Sometimes the stated reason would be quasi-legal – that the wording of the form was actually specified in legislation. More commonly, the problem was blamed on old IT systems that were difficult and expensive to change, sometimes because the contract with the IT provider was

People often joke about how bad doctors' writing is, but in clinical settings this is no joke. In the UK alone thousands of clinical errors a year arise from misreading doctors' scrawls on patient charts. For example, there is a thousandfold difference between 'microgram' and 'milligram', but in a hurried or abbreviated scrawl it is easy to get the two mixed up. Furthermore, previous studies have shown that other medical staff will often follow what they think are instructions from a doctor, even if these may put the patient's life at grave risk (a good example of the 'Messenger' effect described in the MINDSPACE report).

Dom King, a co-author of MINDSPACE, and now a surgeon at Imperial College London, had noticed how routinely these kinds of errors were being made. He felt he could probably help save many more lives by doing something about these frequent errors than he could in a lifetime of operations. With a small amount of funding and support from BIT, Dom ran a trial of a redesigned hospital patient chart to reduce errors and make it easier to read what doctors had written, and especially their medical prescriptions. These changes made the new form look much more like the kind you will probably have filled in when coming into a country at border control – boxes that encourage you to write one letter or number at a time, and standard questions answered by ringing your answer (see below). The form was also designed so that you could always see the patient's name, even if you were on the third or fourth page, so you wouldn't accidently write the information in the wrong chart.

Figure 10. Reducing medical errors – by making it easier to read doctors' handwriting.

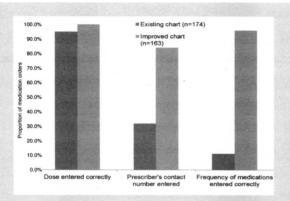

In a trial in two hospitals, new versus old patient charts were checked for errors (such as misread drug or dosage) as well as missing or unreadable information (such as the name of the doctor in case someone needed to check or clarify something). The improvement in accuracy was dramatic.

poorly written, which made any change prohibitively expensive. And sometimes, of course, the blockage was political – with either a big or small 'p': the department was at war with the centre that month and in no mood to comply with a request from an arm of No. 10.

The next step up from simplifying messages and communications is to simplify processes. The changing of defaults to make things easier, as in the pension opt-out, is an example of much wider class of interventions that revolve around taking out bureaucracy and the hassle of paperwork. In the USA the reduction of paperwork was a centrepiece of Cass Sunstein's later work in the White House, with an underlying ambition to save billions of hours of Americans' time every year.[8] As BIT and others have been able to show, the benefits of reducing such hassle extend to far more than just time and irritation.

A powerful everyday example is provided in an intervention involving pre-filling college application forms in the USA.[9] Low-income families, with children approaching college age, were offered a free service to pre-fill the college application forms using their tax and income information. The researchers found that pre-filling the forms, which took no more than a few minutes and cost just a few dollars, increased university enrolment from these lower income families by around a quarter (34 to 42 per cent), and increased the proportion receiving a scholarship by around a third.[9] The researchers also found that giving information, the standard government response, made no difference at all. Clearly the intervention was extremely cost-effective: a great many forms can be pre-filled for the equivalent cost of an expensive new scholarship or outreach programme.

Our work in BIT soon taught us to be almost obsessive about taking out such frictions. Even the tiniest extra hassle can make a significant difference. For example, in one series of letters from our tax department, the HMRC, taxpayers were given a web address where they could find the online tax forms to complete. If the recipient typed in the address, it took them to the HMRC's webpage with the tax form clearly on it. All the person had to do then was click on the form and, of course, fill it in. It turned out that just under one in five people who received these letters did indeed go on to fill in the form and pay their tax as a result. We ran a trial testing a tiny change. The trial compared the effect of the original letter to one almost identical except that the web-link took people directly to the form, instead of to the page with the form on it. In other words, it saved people a single click, albeit at the cost of a couple of extra characters of text. The result? A 22 per cent increase in the proportion of people completing their tax forms in response to the letter.[10]

Of course, it would have been great to have been able to pre-fill these forms, too. You can imagine the effect of doing this – filling as much of a person's information from other sources as possible – if simply removing a single click can increase rates of completion by more than 20 per cent. Indeed, this is a lesson that many tax authorities are learning, and that technology can increasingly help with. We need to redesign our tax systems so that they do more of the work for taxpayers. In our view, much of what tax authorities consider fraud and evasion are really much more about people having better things to do than wade through the complexity of tax forms.

There are other kinds of hassle and friction apart from paperwork. A no-brainer to help save the planet, or at least reduce emissions and save citizens money, concerns energy conservation. The stand-out example of this in colder countries is to encourage people to insulate their lofts, or attics. An uninsulated roof typically accounts for around 25 per cent of heat loss from a house, and 30–45 per cent through uninsulated walls. Insulating a loft, or adding cavity wall insulation, costs a few hundred pounds/dollars, but immediately reduces bills. As such, it looks as if it should be a no-brainer for homeowners, too: the payback period for loft insulation is typically one to two years, and for cavity insulation one to four, depending on building type. In other words, the consumer is getting between 25 and 100 per cent interest on their investment per year, an outstanding deal by any account.

On top of this, many governments have spent billions subsidising and promoting such insulation. Given this, it was puzzling that there were still people who had not installed such insulation – and that our energy department was asking for even more money to increase subsidies on insulation. How much more of a return might be necessary? After looking at the issue, and talking to industry and householders, we concluded that the problem was less about money and more about hassle. Specifically, people couldn't bear the thought of having to clear out the contents of their lofts.

To see if this was the case, as mentioned briefly in the Preface, we ran a leaflet trial with a commercial provider offering households in different areas of London one of three offers:

- ▲ A home insulation service at a low, but standard cost.
- ▲ A home insulation service with a substantial extra discount if any of your neighbours also booked the same service

(the idea being that it was cheaper for the installer to do a couple of houses in one go, and that you were more likely to insulate your home if a neighbour went in with you).

▲ A home insulation service combined with a loft clearance service, albeit at a significant extra cost to insulation alone.

This was not a perfect trial in methodological terms. The different leaflets were tried in similar but separate local areas, and not therefore perfectly randomised and total numbers were small. Nonetheless, the effects were still striking. Compared with the basic offer, the extra discount made almost no difference. People certainly liked the idea, but the increase in uptake was very small and not statistically significant. In contrast, the loft clearance offer, despite costing several hundred pounds extra, had a three-times higher level of take-up.

It wasn't that cost did not matter. In a later variation, which involved offering the loft clearance scheme at cost in order to lower the price, uptake was even higher (at around five times the standard offer). But the trial powerfully illustrated that, at least for the minority of households that had yet to insulate their lofts, it wasn't the price of the insulation that was the barrier, but the fact that they couldn't face the hassle of clearing their lofts. It is certainly an important reminder to look carefully at what the real behavioural blockages are to a policy before presuming that the answer is an ever bigger tax subsidy.

Putting a bump in the road

Sometimes the answer may be *more* friction – at least when we are trying to encourage people *not* to do something, or to pause for thought before doing something that they might later regret. Many of the decisions we make in life are really done with our 'system 1', or autopilot parts of brain, as Daniel Kahneman has laid bare. In some situations, the role of the 'nudger' may be simply to put a bump in the road to jolt the person's 'system 2', or active reflection, back on.

Indeed, adding a bump in the road is not just a metaphor. Speed bumps, or sleeping policemen as they are called in Britain, and textured road surfaces on the approach to junctions are intended to jolt the inattentive driver into slowing down or paying more attention as they approach a residential area or busy junction.

Other examples of such bumps include introducing mandatory cooling-off periods for financial products; having a required delay between a store offering cheap up-front credit and the person's ability to use the card (even if just 30 minutes); measures to check the behaviour of gamblers, such as requiring a break in machines after they have been used for a certain period; and requiring that certain products, such as cigarettes, can only be sold over the counter.

Even suicide, as we saw earlier, is influenced by how easy or difficult the act is. The extraordinary reductions in suicide resulting from changes in levels of carbon monoxide may have happened by accident, but the insight can be used to make deliberate changes that have reduced suicides. For example, a number of countries have introduced legal restrictions on the number of paracetamol tablets and similar everyday medications that can be bought in one go. There is not much to stop the determined buyer from going into several stores in a row and buying many more pills, but it has been shown that in the UK alone such measures were associated with around 70 fewer suicides a year as a result of paracetamol ingestion (a 42 per cent reduction), and an even bigger reduction of 61 per cent of patients needing a liver transplant as a result of damage from paracetamol.[11] Similarly, there is evidence that where such pills are required to be sold in pop-out packs, rather than loose in a bottle, this also reduces suicide rates since the pills have to be taken out one at a time. A little friction, it turns out, is not always a bad thing.

Conclusion: make it easy – the '101' of nudging

It is curious that many of the early expert explorations of behaviour, and the popularisations of psychology, weren't very interested in the power of everyday hassle and friction.[12] Perhaps it just seemed too obvious. But sometimes we overlook the importance of the so-called obvious, as has itself been documented by some of the leading figures in the field.[13]

At the very least, it is worth noting how the world around us, and our own behaviour in it, is perpetually being shaped by the 'make it easy' principle. It is really easy to join a gym, or subscribe to a magazine. Conversely, it can take a Herculean effort to end your membership or the subscription, even though 'in principle' it looks simple enough (at least it did when you joined). Similarly, walk into a store to set up a new phone contract and you will have it in minutes. Seek to end the contract, and transfer your number, and you will be stuck on the phone for an hour …

Businesses, governments and householders can use adding friction to good purpose, notably in the form of 'target-hardening' to reduce crime. It might seem silly that closing a window or strengthening a lock would make much difference: if a thief wants to get in, surely they can just break the glass or use a crowbar? That's both true and 'rational' but the evidence shows it makes a big difference. The headphones on the aeroplane will have a different jack from the ones back home – I am sure you did not intend to take them anyway, but if it did cross your mind you would have looked at the jack and thought 'hassle'.

Partly by evolution and partly by design, the commercial world is full of examples of frictions removed, and frictions added, to shape our behaviour, but we can also use these same approaches on ourselves. You like to have chocolate in the house, but you are afraid you will eat too much? Why not put it in a tin on a shelf you have to stretch to reach and open the container before you get what you want? In other words, have the chocolate around, but make sure you deliberately add a few extra frictions. Want to save for something? Consider a regular auto-transfer to another account. Add more friction by transferring it to an account for which you do not have a bank card.

So, too, for policy. Policymakers should never forget to ask the question 'could we make it easier?' It might be a bit harder for the administrators, behind the scenes, to design a tax or health system that makes it easier to fill in a form, but it will generally pay out in spades. Better still, try to get rid of the form completely. Make it easy. Take out the friction. And certainly give 'making it easier' your best shot before spending an extra billion or two on tax subsidies.

CHAPTER 4

▲

ATTRACT!

You are about to walk into the supermarket. It's not your favourite thing to do in the world, but you get a certain pleasure from it. When you think about it, you find yourself there quite often, probably more often than you need to be. But though you might not appreciate it, a modern supermarket is a masterpiece of behavioural engineering, and, in particular, of the behavioural principle of 'attraction'.

Even before you enter the supermarket, thoughts and impressions start to edge into your mind. Fresh. A little hungry. Though you can't make them out individually, the splash of green from the fresh veg and fruit is clearly visible from ten paces away before you walked through the door. As you pick up your trolley (easy) and move towards that swath of green, the stack of beer catches your eye. You half look at the price, but have already concluded it's a good deal. The heavy box fits so nicely on the flat base of the trolley; no risk of crushing that fresh fruit you are about to buy. You pick up some veg and salad, glistening green and even pre-washed (not a fleck of the soil it came from); the carrots, cucumber and broccoli together like an echo of how they are grouped in your own mind from pre-school onwards. Now the fruit, similarly clustered, the greens, reds, and yellows almost glowing against each other. As you add them to your trolley, some part of your brain glows a little, too, the virtue of this healthy freshness you have collected.

Onward through the aisles and finally to the checkout. You look at your overflowing trolley. The queue is not too long anyway – just one person ahead. Would you look at that? A magazine catches your eye. Britney Spears looks terrible. And a royal baby, eh? Just drop it in. Oh, and some gum. Need some of that. Hate breathing fire on people after lunch. And you only came in for a couple of things...

Sportacus comes to Downing Street

I had not met Sportacus before we had him in for a seminar in Downing Street. My kids were a little too old to have seen his show on TV. He looked a little different in a smart grey suit than in his

Figure 11. 'Sportacus', played by Magnús Scheving (Photograph courtesy of Daniel C. Griliopus.)

TV persona, but even in the suit you could tell he was muscular and his movements sharp – he had been a European champion gymnast more than once, and you could tell.

One of the team, Maren Ashford, who had a strong marketing background, thought we could learn something from Sportacus that we weren't going to get from the public health literature. Sportacus – real name Magnús Scheving – was the central character on a TV show he created and starred in called *Lazy Town*. The basic idea was simple: to create an entertaining show aimed at young kids that made a healthy lifestyle fun and 'automatic'.

In the show, kids were constantly on the move, doing things to get their counterparts at home off the sofa and active, keeping them flexible and fit. The kids in the show would recharge and get their energy from 'sport candy' (fruit and vegetables). You can picture the scene: children running around, stretching and wheeling their arms, brandishing carrots and munching on apples. Sportacus's mission in life was to beat the marketers at their own game – to make a healthy lifestyle fun, attractive, and at least vaguely natural. I am not sure Downing Street – in the dining room appropriately enough – had ever seen anything quite like it.

Magnús knew he was up against formidable opposition. One of the video clips he showed was of a playful demonstration with adults in a supermarket. In one clip, adults were given two minutes to fill a trolley with as much healthy food as they could, which they could have for free. They hurtled off around the aisles, filling their trolleys, but before long they were stopping themselves, putting back items they realised weren't healthy at all. After two minutes the trolleys would be checked. Few were full, and many still contained items that clearly were not very healthy.

Then the adults were asked to do the task again, this time with a twist. Now they would be blindfolded. This time the objective would be to fill their trolleys with unhealthy foods. Strikingly, the adults were very good at this, and most of the trolleys were overflowing even before the time was up.

Magnús's point was that we lived in a world where marketing and supply made an unhealthy lifestyle both easy (see Chapter 3) and attractive. In the academic literature, it has been called an 'obesogenic environment', a term widely attributed to the public health expert Boyd Swinburn. We will see more of these wider forces in the next chapter, but for now let us unpick the simple idea of making something more, or less, attractive.

The two sides to attraction

There are two basic elements to 'attraction', both of which you will see in every aisle of every supermarket as products battle it out.

First something must attract your attention. Your brain is receiving thousands of signals every second: which do you attend to? What matters, and what is just noise? Which products, letters and emails make it to the top of the pile marked 'response needed'? Cognitive psychologists refer to an 'attentional spotlight' to capture the idea that the mind can consciously only focus on, or attend to, a narrow amount of the large field of stimuli that are presented to it. In this small field of our attentional spotlight, we use our brain to integrate a more complex array of information, such as you are now turning these shapes on the page into words, sentences, and extracting the meaning. As you do so, your eyes can still see the whole page, and indeed much of the room beyond. But this wider visual field is on 'monitor only' – you'd notice if a light started flashing or something moved, but it's outside your conscious attention. By way of illustration, scan the page ahead and see if you can see a triangle. Found it? See how fast it caught your eye? That's because your brain can effectively scan the whole page at once when looking for a simple attribute. But try and find a specific word, like 'goods', and you'll have to use your attentional spotlight, scanning the lines to see which symbols and lines together make up the word.

Supermarkets have learnt to arrange fruit and vegetables as contrasting blocks of opposing colours – such as reds against greens – to make them stand out more dramatically. Indeed, you might note the hand of evolution here, too: the bright colours of ripe fruits attract our attention against a sea of green, a beautiful deal between a plant wanting its seed spread and our primate ancestors wanting a ripe meal. Similarly, most supermarkets have learnt to make sure that the fresh fruit and brightly coloured 'best buys' catch your eye long before you even walk into the store, a call to your unconscious brain to help attract you inside, and to prime you for the fine goods you will find there. If you want to influence behaviour, you will often have to do something similar: to attract attention or some basic form of engagement before you have a chance to persuade or encourage.

Second, if a signal, product or choice does manage to break through, how will it be assessed? What will it be filed under – yes, no or maybe? Is it good value? Will I like it? Our brains very rapidly, and largely unconsciously, assess things and people according to a few key dimensions. Susan Fiske, perhaps the world's leading expert on social cognition, has documented how people almost instantly categorise things and other people on two key dimensions: positive or negative emotional reaction (warm or cold), and competence. These reactions are thought to lie deep in our evolutionary development, enabling us to sift out threats and opportunities. For example, you might see an older person and 'feel' or react to them as 'warm' (positive) but perhaps not very competent. They are not a threat, and you might even help them. A homeless man with a bottle in his hand might also suggest a sense of low competence, but perhaps elicit a cooler emotional reaction. Catching sight of a work colleague, you might 'feel' towards them as warm and competent – someone who can help you. On the other hand, you may react very differently to another colleague following behind; the competence remains but the affect turns to cold – here is a threat, a rival, your brain warns. Susan Fiske has shown the same very fast reactions occur in response to groups, ethnicities and even nationalities.

These same reactions kick in when you see an object or a product. For example, seeing a little old Fiat car – perhaps you feel 'warm' towards it – it's cute – but don't 'feel' it's very 'competent'. On the other hand, your feelings towards a Mercedes might be 'cold' but very competent. These fast reactions offer a glimpse into how our brain navigates the world. The skilful advertiser knows these effects well, and seeks to tweak the attributes and associations around products to make us feel more favourable towards them. For example, they

Figure 12. As part of a programme to get more people to move, VicHealth in the city of Melbourne funded a spectacular painting of the staircase of the Southern Cross station, where around 800,000 commuters pass through each day. The artwork led to around 25 per cent more people taking the stairs during rush hour, and 140 per cent more during the rest of the day. Sadly, the artwork was only there for one month (August 2014). It was followed by a giant image of a popular drink. (Photograph courtesy of the City of Melbourne.)

will seek to create an association in your mind between something you feel positive about, such as a movie star or beautiful face, and the object they want you to be interested in or buy.

You can even use this same approach on yourself. Want to get yourself to exercise more? Don't just do it as chore, or something that you know you 'ought' to do. Instead try to incorporate into it something that you would enjoy. This might mean walking with a friend, or choosing routes to jog or cycle that take you past an attractive view. Studies have shown that kids are much more likely to engage in exercise, and persist with it, if it is presented as a chance to see the outside world or nature, than if it is presented as being healthy. Chances are you'll find it works for you, too.

Supermarkets and retailers get our attention in many ways. Some are obvious, like bright signs and labels. Others are more subtle, such as how the juxtaposition of red and green, or blue and yellow, make the objects appear brighter and more eye-catching. Smells, lighting, and location all affect what we notice. For example, items placed on the ends of aisles, which our eyes naturally scan as we turn corners, attract our attention. Putting a non-alcoholic drink in a supermarket end-of-aisle sale increases sales by 52–114 per cent and alcoholic drinks by 23–46 per cent.[1] This is an equivalent effect to a decrease in price of 22–62 per cent per volume for non-alcohol categories – no wonder producers will pay handsomely for those key end-of-aisle spots. Not only are effects like this large, they also persist over time. Temporary sales promotions can actually lead to an increase in consumption that lasts for six months after they have stopped.[2]

Another simple approach to catching someone's attention is to personalise. As demonstrated as early as the 1950s, people tend to hear their name being mentioned even in a noisy room (the so-called 'cocktail party effect'). It is pretty clear, therefore, why marketers have learnt to put your name on the letters and emails they send you.

Attention, salience and personalisation: paying taxes and fines

These same lessons of 'attract!' or 'attractive' apply to governments. You can see them at work in propaganda and recruitment posters from the two world wars, such as 'Britons [Lord Kitchener] wants you!' with Kitchener staring and pointing a figure right at you in 1914. Across the Atlantic, an almost identical image of Uncle Sam pointing and declaring 'I want you for US army!' They may not have been grammatically correct, but they are images that stick in our minds even a century on. To be effective, such a 'nudge' (both posters were looking for volunteers), or call to action, needs first to attract our attention: both posters have the word 'YOU' in extra large capital letters, together with a direct gaze and pointed finger, all likely to seize our attention. It is not clear, however, how effective these posters were in the second aspect of 'attract!' – that the underlying offer be an appealing one. Contemporary advertisements for the military on both sides of the Atlantic dwell much more on the opportunity for adventure and excitement, than a cold demand or call to duty, and are likely to be much more effective as a result (at least to a modern audience).

A simple example resting heavily on 'attract!' is shown in one of a series of trials conducted jointly between BIT and the UK tax and revenue services (HMRC). In the British system, as in those of many other countries, doctors and other public service professions have two sources of revenue. In the case of doctors, they receive a main salary from their hospital or practice, but many often receive extra cash for working privately. The tax on their salary is deducted at source (*easy!*), but the extra earnings, as in any occupation, are supposed to be declared for tax purposes. Unsurprisingly, this doesn't always happen.

In this trial we compared the effectiveness, in terms of responses and subsequent payment of tax, of various letters to a sample of doctors. As can be seen in Figure 13, sending a generic letter from the HMRC reminding them to declare extra earnings was not very effective, with only around 4 per cent responding. In contrast, a letter that made reference to doctors and medics specifically, noting that they often had extra earnings, led to a fivefold increase in responses to 21 per cent. We also tested a further letter, designed to catch the reader's attention and jolt them into specific action. Again the letter made specific mention of medics ('we know that many doctors receive extra income'), but also politely noted that the HMRC took the previous lack of response as an 'oversight', and ignoring this letter would now be taken as an active choice. As can be seen, this letter led to around a ninefold increase in response. We also tested similar approaches on other professional groups that HMRC suspected of being 'economical with the truth' about their earnings. It was not just doctors that responded to the adapted messages – we found similar uplifts in payments in relation to other professional groups too (such as everyone's favourite, plumbers).

We found that even quite simple cues can have a significant impact. In another trial, led by Rory Gallagher in Sydney with the

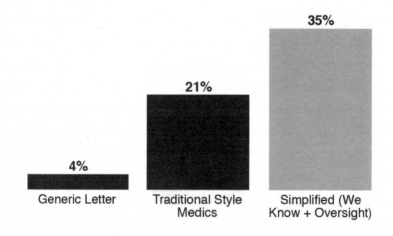

Figure 13. Three different versions of letters asking doctors to declare private earnings for tax purposes.

state of New South Wales, we adapted a letter reminding people to pay overdue traffic fines, the main addition being to add a stamp at the top of the letter reading 'pay now' in red letters. This led to repayments without further action rising from around 14 to 17 per cent, worth around $10 million a year and, equally importantly, saving residents around $4 million a year in extra penalties and preventing more than 8,000 drivers a year from having their driving licences cancelled or suspended. The saving on printing costs alone, for the extra correspondence avoided, was estimated at $80,000 a year. In a substantive sense, the message of the letter was unchanged, but pulling out the key words in red letters helped both to attract people's attention and to prompt them into action, saving them and the state time and money.

A key challenge for tax authorities is getting people to open a letter in the first place. It turns out that an official-looking brown envelope does not always make it to the top of our in-tray – literally or metaphorically. Drawing on the wider literature, including an Irish trial sticking Post-its on to the front of notes to get more attention, we thought we would test the hypothesis more systematically.

We sent out 5,000 HMRC letters in a white rather than a brown envelope, and had someone scribble on the front a personalised message: 'David' – or the relevant name – 'you really need to open this'. The new envelope raised the response and completion rate in previous non-responders from 21.8 to 26.0 per cent – a 4.2 percentage point increase. It did cost a little bit to get the 5,000 envelopes done this way – indeed, HMRC were sceptical because of this extra cost – but when they calculated the rate of return on the investment they found it was more than 200:1. It might not be that we should scribble on every envelope sent, but it is a powerful illustration of how every detail matters.

However beautiful your envelope is, it will not be very effective if it is stuck at the bottom of a pile of other papers. In work for the UK

Courts Service (officially Her Majesty's Courts and Tribunals Service), we followed how they collected unpaid fines, right up to the point at which the bailiffs were called in. It was a sad business. But one of the observations made by Rory and the team when they returned from their visit with the bailiffs was the reaction of the person who owed the fine: one of surprise. In all likelihood they received many letters saying they owed money, most of which they habitually ignored. Indeed, inside their front doors there were often piles of unopened mail. No wonder they were surprised. We wondered if there was some other way we could get these people's attention before the bailiff turned up – a pretty dire outcome for everyone concerned.

As is often the case with our approach to changing the world one nudge at a time, we noticed that there were a few maverick officials who were doing things a little differently. In the Courts Service there was a Fines Support Officer who had observed that simply drawing people's attention to the fact that a bailiff was about to come round was a good way of prompting payments. He did so by texting people. But he did not have any real evidence for the impact beyond his gut instinct, and he was just one individual operating from one Courts Service facility. So we worked with the Courts Service to test this hypothesis. Ten days before bailiffs were due, a random sample of debtors received a short warning text message that if the fine was not paid the bailiffs would be sent in. We compared the amount paid by the group of people who received the text with another group who were only sent the final warning letter (those getting the text also received the same letter). The text proved highly effective. It doubled the amount paid, thereby also sparing quite a few people a visit from the bailiffs, and saving quite a bit of money given that the bailiffs rarely got a good deal on the items that were confiscated and sold.

We also tested some other slight variations on the text. Adding in a reminder of the amount due was marginally more effective, but not reliably so (we ran the trial twice to check the results). But adding the person's name at the beginning of the text was significantly more effective, trebling the amount paid relative to receiving the letter alone.[3]

Finally, we also tested the use of an image in catching people's attention. Previous trials in the commercial world have found that adding a photograph can have a significant impact: a picture of a smiling woman on an invitation for a loan leads people to be significantly more likely to take up the offer. It worked particularly well on men, among whom it proved to be more effective than cutting the loan rate by more than a percentage point a month.[4] Similarly, images have been shown to be far more effective in attracting attention and subsequent donations to disaster relief funds than bald facts and statistics. With the image of a single child, typically donations doubled.[5]

A specific challenge concerned people who persistently failed to pay their car tax. In the UK, non-payers are identified by certain traffic cameras that automatically check number plates against car tax records. Most people pay when prompted, but a minority fail to pay even after they have been picked up and written to more than once. We were asked to help with these persistent non-payers. Could a nudge, or bit of behavioural insight, really help in a case of such persistent non-payment?

We tried two approaches. First, we did our standard approach of rewriting the subject line of the letter in plain English: 'pay your tax or lose your car'. This is what the standard letter said, but just in a more roundabout way. It did lead to a small improvement – around 2 percentage points (or a 5 per cent increase) – in payments. Our second arm included the image of the car, taken from the original traffic camera shot. This was much more effective, increasing the payment rate by 9 percentage points (more than a 20 per cent increase). The licensing authority was very pleased with this: even a couple of percentage points increase translates into significant sums of money.

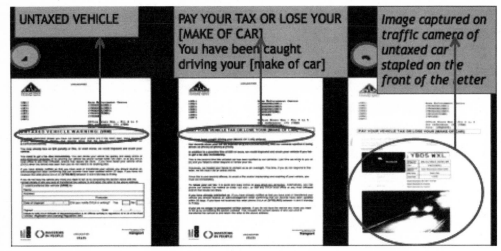

Figure 14. Three versions of a letter to persistent non-payers of car tax.

There's more to life – and catching attention – than fines and threats

Governments have a wide array of fines and sanctions to use in cajoling their more reluctant, or forgetful, citizens into changing their behaviour. We might think of these interventions as more 'prods' or shoves than nudges. As we have seen, these can be significantly improved with a few nudges and behavioural insights in the mix. But the very availability of such sanctions means that governments are arguably rather neglectful of other, frankly nicer, ways of attracting people's attention and influencing their behaviour.

A classic illustration of using 'attract!' as an alternative to fines or sanctions is in reducing speeding by drivers. In the USA alone, more than 10,000 people a year die in speed-related car accidents, with an associated economic cost of around $40 billion, leaving aside the human tragedy and human costs involved. For many years, the police focused on using speed cameras, or tailing police cars, to catch and fine speeding motorists.[6] Until well into the late 1980s, the primary tactic was to use hidden police cars and cameras to catch motorists unaware. This may have been good for collecting fines, but studies showed that such a surreptitious approach wasn't very good at reducing speeding or unsafe driving.

One early study compared the effectiveness of extra police patrols with putting up a sign giving drivers feedback about the percentage of drivers who were staying inside the speed limit, manually updated once a week. (see also next chapter on social influence). It was found that the extra police patrols were around ten times less effective than the sign.[7] This was replicated in other countries, with generally similar results, leading, in many cases, to a change of strategy. In the UK, for example, the police moved from concealed speed cameras to ones that were obvious to motorists, employing bright yellow reflective material to catch drivers' attention at night, with frequent roadside warning signs on their approach. Though not uncontroversial – many people are attracted to the idea of punishment – the strategy moved from capture and sanctions, to catching attention and warning, and particularly around junctions and roads known to be dangerous.

In more recent decades, technology has allowed the spread of signs that give immediate feedback to drivers about their driving speed. Studies have shown these signs to be effective, typically reducing average speeds by around four to eight miles an hour, or 10 to 15 per cent, though once drivers have passed the signs their speed gradually creeps up again. They seem particularly effective when combined with additional cues to make the reason for not speeding more salient, such as reminding drivers that they are close to a school, entering an urban area, or approaching a complex junction.

Extensive studies have been undertaken on whether the effectiveness of such feedback signs drops off over time, a key concern of many critics. Studies show that though they lose some effectiveness over time, they still remain effective. For example, installing speed feedback signs in school districts in parts of the USA was found to reduce average speeds by 5.1mph in the initial few weeks, and a year later the signs were still reducing average speeds by 3.6mph. Another study, looking at the effectiveness of speed feedback signs at the key transition from highway (55mph) to urban (35mph) zones across a range of areas found average speeds reduced by 6 to 8mph, and that the effect was maintained over a year later.[8]

A different way of making an offer more attractive, often employed in the commercial world but rarely by governments, is the use of lotteries. It is a curious thing that governments very readily fine their citizens for late payment or non-compliance, but they almost never reward them for paying on time, or complying. Part of the answer, interestingly reflected in focus groups, is that many people feel that

Figure 15. In Copenhagen, Pelle Hanson and his students used a simple but effective method of 'attract!' to reduce littering. With the permission of the city, they painted the bins brighter colours (previously they had blended in), and painted footsteps leading to them in similarly bright colours. Using his students to do observational studies, they found that the changes led to an increase in litter going into the bins by around 45 per cent. The use of painted footsteps is now being trialled in the UK in a similar way, and, as part of a joint trial between BIT and the state of Victoria, Australia, to increase walking through the use of steps instead of escalators.

their fellow citizens shouldn't need to be paid for doing the 'right thing'. On the other hand, if the reward is not automatic, but more in the spirit of a friendly thank-you, then people start to feel much more positive about it.

An elegant application of this approach was trialled in Sweden, once again building on the example of reducing speeding. Rather than just using speed cameras to catch and fine speeding drivers, those who drove within the speed limit were recorded and entered into a lottery. The idea was that the lottery would be funded out of a portion of the fines on those who were speeding. Over a three-day trial period in a multi-lane road in Stockholm, average speeds were reported to have fallen from 32 to 25kmh.[9]

The use of a lottery in a public service scenario is nonetheless controversial. We had suggested the use of a lottery on a couple of occasions, but did not succeed in getting one in place. With this in mind, we decided to see if we could find an area in which a lottery might help address a public service need. Some rare examples did exist. For example, a number of London councils had combined to enter into a £25,000 prize lottery those people who switched their Council Tax payments (local tax) to direct debit, thereby saving the councils a considerable amount of money and hassle. Indicative estimates were that the savings generated were more than ten times the cost of the prize.[10]

We needed something a bit boring, but nonetheless still important, to test whether a lottery could be an effective and acceptable way of making a certain behaviour more attractive in a public sector context. At that time, local governments were wrestling with a change in the voter registration system, away from 'household' registration (where one person could register everyone in the home) to one where individuals were more responsible. The argument for the change was that it would reduce fraud, but the change also resulted in extra work in getting some local voters to sign up to the register, with the risk that some would never get around to it (such as students or some low-income groups). Working with Peter John of University College London, we used this as an opportunity to test out a lottery. We compared the effectiveness of three approaches: a standard letter from the council reminding people to register to vote; a similar letter but with an offer to be entered into a lottery for £1,000; and the same but with a lottery of £5,000. Sure enough, it made a difference. The £1,000 lottery led to an extra 1.5 percentage points of voters registering (from 44.8 to 46.3 per cent). Interestingly, the £5,000 lottery worked slightly better, but not much, lifting the registration rate by 1.9 percentage points.

With this result in mind, we worked with the British Treasury to see if we could do something similar to the Stockholm and voter registration trials, but on a much larger scale, with tax payment. There was already a system for fining people £100 who were late paying their taxes. The set-up led to a rush on tax returns the day before the deadline, which was sometimes so overwhelming that it crashed the system as well as making staffing very difficult. Our argument was that, by way of a gentle nudge and encouragement, we should enter into a lottery those people who submitted their tax returns early, with the prize money coming from fines accumulated from late payers. We proposed giving people an additional entry for every week they made their returns early (also creating a series of natural early deadlines, an additional part of the nudge). Like the Stockholm trial, the elegance was that the overall effect would be fiscally neutral: if it was an overwhelming success (i.e. if people made their returns on time), the prize money would drop accordingly (though we urged that a baseline prize should be offered to provide some certainty and attraction).

We very nearly got the lottery through, but at the last minute senior Ministers expressed concern that a wealthy person might win it, and it would be seen as unfair. After all, in the British tax system not everyone has to complete a tax return, and those who do tend to be on higher earnings. Ministers are democratically accountable, and it is right they should ultimately call such decisions (see Chapter 11). Still, it remains a good idea, and I am sure a government somewhere will try it soon enough.

Honour, shock, curiosity and fun

Governments should be straight, honest and fair, but that shouldn't preclude a consideration of at least some of the other motivations that make humans, well, *human*.

Non-financial incentives are very powerful drivers of human behaviour and often considerably more so than financial incentives. In a modern society, having children doesn't make much sense from an individual's financial perspective; indeed, the lifetime cost to a parent of having a child will typically run into many hundreds of thousands of pounds. It's clearly not financial incentives that drive the urge to have children for most people.

One approach is to use 'goal substitution' or supplementation. This is a technique used to make something that we know we 'ought' to do more appealing or attractive. It's the equivalent of putting a sprinkle of sugar on medicine. The psychologist Dan Ariely gives a powerful personal example of how he would plan which movies to watch in the evening after difficult, painful and ongoing medical treatment. You would think that the reward of saving your own life would be enough motivation, but often it proves not to be, with low completion rates of the therapy. Dan used the movies as a way of making the treatment more attractive, and he found it worked.

One of my favourite examples of where government did think about a problem in this way was when an arm of the US Air Force was facing public opposition to its flying over or close to residential neighbourhoods. Someone had the bright idea of circulating much more information about the different aircraft being flown. Though that didn't reduce the noise level, it certainly changed reactions to it – and as any cognitive psychologist will tell you, most perception is interpretive. 'Look – it's the new F15!' feels very different from, 'it's another bloody plane flying overhead'.

As an aside, as battles continue over airport expansion in the UK and elsewhere, I'm inclined to think that a similar technique might be used to persuade potentially affected residents as to the benefits of a new runway or airport by offering them generous annual vouchers for flights and holidays around the world from the airport. Rather like the US Air Force's approach, it might dramatically change how you feel about the noise and be more effective than cash alone. 'That's my holiday to Barbados this year!' you'd think as a plane roars over, giving you a personal and positive interest in the outcome of expansion rather than simply seeing it as an irritation.

Most governments still hand out 'honours' in some form – a rare and overt use of a non-financial reward. These may be medals for bravery in combat, or civil awards for great generosity or other contributions to society. If not the reason why people behave in the way they do, the award of such honours does seem to be a powerful and extra motivating force behind it.[11] Soldiers generally don't fight for the money. More likely their motives include a desire for adventure, honour, to do the right thing, to fight for their colleagues, unit, family and country. Despite the power of such motivating forces, and their validation through honours, the average economic textbook has little or nothing to say on them. Even in policy, they are too readily thought of as a dusty relic of the past, rather than an important form of 'attract!'.

Advertising campaigns are one area where governments occasionally let their hair down, at least with the help of NGOs and creative agencies. 'Shock' is certainly a tool that has been used to attract attention, ranging from encouraging people to practise safe sex and avoid drugs, to wearing a seat belt. It is almost certainly the case that some of these campaigns have been highly effective, though unfortunately they are rarely evaluated to a standard that would get past an average junior Treasury official, let alone a tough-minded evaluator (and rightly so).

Some of these campaigns are quite sophisticated. For example, those working on campaigns to encourage people to install and maintain smoke detectors through the eighties and nineties found they had a major problem. If the advert was too softly-softly, it would fail to attract people's attention let alone motivate them to buy, install and maintain a smoke detector. But if the campaigns were too graphic and shocking, people's psychological defences kicked in – 'that's not me or my family'. After extensive testing, they found a way through, which was to retain a shocking and potent message, but to remove any images of people that triggered the easy defence of thinking 'yeah, that guy is not me' or 'that child is not mine'. Instead, in a child's scrawled handwriting, with a burnt toy to the side, the message said, 'Daddy forgot to change the batteries ...' There is no doubt that many lives have been saved, and the overall casualty rate from fires greatly reduced, as a result of the widespread installation of smoke detectors – although it is hard to isolate the effects of any one campaign.

A number of campaigns have used other emotions with a more subtle twist than raw shock. One such campaign encouraging people in the developing world to wash their hands was found to be highly effective by triggering disgust at the *thought* of eating food before washing, though very little of the advertisement actually focused on washing per se. Similarly, graphic anti-smoking campaigns that showed tumours and fat dripping out of cigarettes and on to clothing are believed to have been highly effective. It is interesting to reflect that disgust triggered by the image of dripping fat should be more powerful than the threat of death (which, arguably, our psychological defences shield us from). Similar campaigns have recently been advocated by doctors who argue that alcoholic drinks should contain calorie labelling, rather than information about how many 'units' of alcohol they contain, the idea being that some individuals (unaware of what an unhealthy intake of alcohol actually constitutes) might cut down on their drinking when they realise a glass of wine is equivalent to a slice of cake.

Other campaigns use humour and fun to attract attention, with the best of them carrying a well-judged strapline. Australian public service advertisements have become particularly famous for their humour, as well as their disarming bluntness. For example, anti-speeding adverts in which an attractive woman raises her little finger to infer a speeding driver's sexual inadequacy. Another recent advert, aimed at reducing binge drinking, humorously plays with the idea of not needing to have an excuse not to have another drink.

In the commercial ('snake eyes'), a guy responds to his mate's urging to have another drink by explaining that he can't because he's on antibiotics. When pressed further, he explains that it's the

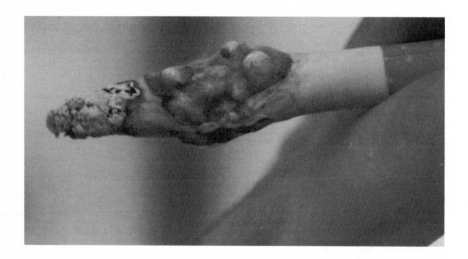

Figure 16. This 'mutation' anti-smoking campaign played heavily on disgust: 92 per cent of smokers noticed the adverts – the highest of any similar campaign. (Courtesy of Public Health England.)

result of having been bitten in the eye by a snake, which has become very attached to him – and the shot jumps back to see him with a patch on his eye and a snake sliding round his neck. It is effectively a form of 'psychological inoculation' – preparing the person for the question and the fact that they don't need to have an answer as to why they shouldn't drink alcohol. The closing message also draws on psychological principles, explaining that 61 per cent of young Australians do not drink to excess (see next chapter on social influence).

Humour, fun and curiosity are neglected forces of social change and nudging. But this is starting to change. One of the components of the First Lady Michelle Obama's anti-obesity campaign in the USA, which appears to be showing quite promising results, is a two-year deal that allows the use of *Sesame Street* characters in the promotion of fruit and vegetables. There is now good evidence that making healthy food more fun can dramatically increase its consumption – just as it can for unhealthy food. Christina Roberto and colleagues at Harvard's Psychology of Eating and Consumer Health (PEACH) have found that associating a *Sesame Street* character with a piece of fruit or vegetable substantially increases the likelihood of a child choosing to eat it – and makes them feel it tastes better. Purists might not like the idea, positing that kids should 'naturally' prefer healthy food, but pragmatists should celebrate the result.[12] It is not just that you've found a way to nudge the behaviour of an individual child, it's that you've found a way of shifting consumption patterns in a way that has the potential to move an entire market (see Chapter 7 for further discussion).

A recent study conducted in schools in the Netherlands found that children's consumption of wholegrain brown bread, which was otherwise just a third of that of white, could be virtually doubled by cutting it into fun shapes. Other studies show that such interventions are especially effective among low-income children, where the need is greatest.[13] It is also likely that much of the recent trend in the US away from the consumption of sugary drinks is being driven, or reinforced, by the promotion of other fun and pleasant drinks that are less unhealthy.

These ideas have started to attract real attention, but their application is still in the early days. For example, there is interesting ongoing work on whether curiosity could be an effective motivator to get people going to the gym more often, or to turn up for medical appointments. Would you be more likely to keep an appointment if it came with a couple of interesting questions to which the answers would be given at the surgery, or if you were told that a previous patient had left a message for you to collect (and that you might leave one for someone else)? Gamification is another area of ongoing interest, with games and video content aimed at: encouraging people to exercise more; teaching kids maths; addressing prejudice and extremism; helping with career choices; and reducing drug and alcohol abuse in the army.

Conclusion – attract!

In the previous chapter we saw how reducing friction is a potent way of clearing the path to 'make it easy' for people to do something that they probably already intended to do, but hadn't got around to. Yet for many behaviours, removing friction may not be enough: that stone will still not roll, that person will not move, without an extra gentle nudge.

In terms of behavioural science, 'attract!' involves two linked elements. First, it involves breaking through and attracting attention. There's nothing desperately complicated about this, but still governments, and sometimes businesses, miss its importance. Passing a law, or applying a sanction, may have little or no impact if the person or entity it is aimed at fails to notice.

To attract attention, something has to stand out: in the language of psychology, it has to be salient. Salience can be increased through personalisation, relevance or contrast – standing out as different from the background. Changing the colour of an envelope, the use of images that can reach out to us on an emotional level; and addressing a person by name can all increase the impact of a communication or intervention. Typically, such approaches increase responses by a few to 10 or 20 per cent. Occasionally, when combined, the impact can be very dramatic, such as increasing the impact of a request to pay unpaid tax nearly tenfold relative to a generic letter. Similarly, signs that give drivers immediate feedback about their speed relative to the limit have been found to be more effective than increased police patrols, and the effects of these 'smart' signs persist over time, especially around key junctions where drivers tend to know that they should slow down but fail to notice how fast they are going.

Second, the suggestion or offer itself has to be attractive, or at least persuasive. Using financial incentives can be effective, but it is just one tool among many. It matters who the message, advice or invitation comes from – a so-called 'messenger effect'.[14] Seeing a politician on the news suggesting your kids should get vaccinated may have little impact, but seeing the Chief Medical Officer or a senior doctor, white coat and stethoscope around their neck, suggesting the same thing is much more likely to be acted on. Non-financial incentives, such as curiosity and fun, can be powerful motivators, too. Air miles, and related schemes, work so well partly because they cannot be easily monetised. We like to engage in a 'game', to collect points and progress, and tend to be attracted to things that are perceived as scarce or associated with others that we like or respect. We are also, of course, motivated to do right by others, such as to help our children strive and succeed, and to develop and actualise ourselves (see Chapter 5 on social influence and Chapter 9 on well-being).

When we do use financial incentives we can still use behavioural insights to give them greater impact. For example, rather than a small incentive thinly spread, people may be more motivated by a chance to win a bigger prize in a lottery. Similarly, since we care much more about the present than we do the future, an incentive (or sanction) that is front-loaded – i.e. weighted to the present – can have far more impact for the same level of cost than one in the future (see Chapter 6 for further discussion).

Of all behavioural insights, 'attract!' is probably the one that has most often been used by businesses and marketers, sometimes in ways that may border on ubiquitous or even annoying. Nonetheless, despite the familiarity of this approach, it remains widely used for good reason.

Despite its use by business, except for very specific campaigns, such as encouraging people to quit smoking or exercise a little more, few governments have really thought about 'attract!' very much, let alone engaged more broadly with the motivations and emotions that guide and influence human behaviour. Even in business, outside of marketing more nuanced thinking about what really motivates people and attracts their attention is surprisingly rare. For example, managers tend to focus too much on extrinsic rewards, notably money, and much less on all the other factors that tend to motivate people to take up a job or to work hard. Itself illustrating a behavioural effect, managers tend to think of themselves as being motivated by a wide range of factors, such as job satisfaction, but when thinking of others they tend to neglect these intrinsic factors and instead focus overly on pay and rewards. Often they would be better off walking the floor and saying thank you than worrying about the annual bonuses.

Like other nudges, 'attract!' will be most effective where you are prompting or reminding someone to do something that they know they should probably do anyway, such as slowing down as they approach a school or paying an overdue fine. Attract! is certainly a useful tool to have in your armoury, not least to help shape your own behaviour when you want to, be it a Post-it on the door or reminder in your diary, or a deal with yourself for when you've finished a piece of work.

CHAPTER 5

▲

SOCIAL

It's a cold winter's day and the wind is whipping off the river as you get off the bus and walk to your office. You head towards the main entrance, where you can cut through the building and on to where you are going, your mind already on the day. You can just make out the sign on the swing door asking you to use the revolving doors instead. You're contemplating pushing the revolving door as you approach it, vaguely wondering if it will be stiff, or if someone will push on it the other way from the other side, catching your foot as they do. But just then, the person ahead of you pushes through the swing door, glancing at the sign as they do. The blast of warm air catches your face and you follow them through.[1]

The behaviour of those around us is a powerful influence on what we do. It is almost impossible not to follow the gaze of a crowd. We laugh twice as often at a comedy show when we watch it with someone else. The more fellow diners we have around the table the more we eat at dinner. And we're more likely to take the stairs, or take the revolving doors, if the person ahead of us does so.

As someone skilled in, or learning, the art of nudging, you need to understand a wide range of influences on behaviour. Like your children, or students, these influences are all interesting and special in their own way. If I had to choose one of these many influences on behaviour as especially interesting I'd say it's social influence. It's probably not surprising, since I used to teach social psychology at Cambridge, but perhaps I can pass on a little of that interest before we go any further.

As discussed in Chapter 1, human beings are deeply social beings. We are constantly influencing each other. In your next few meetings, try watching people's body language more carefully. People really do follow each other. If someone leans back and puts their hands behind their head, the chances are someone else will do the same, especially if the person who initiates the movement is more dominant or in a senior position. Or try touching or gently rubbing your nose or the side of your mouth as if you were wiping something away, particularly if you are glancing at someone else just before, or as, you do it. Chances are, within a minute or so they will do the same. We are genuinely very attuned to each other. These influences, or social habits, spread through entire organisations and even nations. If you want to understand human behaviour, you have to understand this web of influence that perpetually flows between us.

Picking apart social norms

An everyday example of the power of social influence is littering. Imagine you return to your car and find that someone has stuck a flyer under your windscreen wiper. Do you remove it to throw away later or, if there is no rubbish bin in sight, do you chuck it on the ground?

Picture the scene. You probably think, like most people, that you wouldn't throw it on the ground. But then you look around the parking lot and see that there are dozens of such flyers already on the ground. So what do you do? You probably drop it as well.

Experimental studies into just such a situation as this by Robert

Cialdini and others have found that people are around eight times more likely to drop the flyer when other flyers are already littering the ground, than when the car park is flyer-free. We may not like or approve of littering, but when it seems that many others around us are doing it we follow the crowd.

This powerful form of social influence comes from what Cialdini calls a 'descriptive' or 'declarative' social norm': what we see others doing or what the evidence indicates that they are doing. Such descriptive social norms need to be distinguished from 'injunctive' social norms: what we're *supposed* to be doing or what others approve of.[2] It's a key distinction. Lawyers, politicians and managers are generally in the business of constructing and enforcing injunctive social norms: this is what you are supposed to do. Cialdini's work shows that if you run into a situation where an injunctive norm is running against a descriptive one, it's the descriptive norm – what others are actually doing – that tends to win out.

We can see why it makes sense to follow the behaviour of others. If everyone is running away and screaming, it's probably a good idea to do the same, even before you know exactly what's going on. Maybe it's a tiger, or a tsunami, or an attack by an invading army: but whatever, it may be best to examine the detail later. Similarly, when visiting a new place, it is probably a good idea to choose the restaurant that is busy, especially with knowledgeable locals, than the one that's empty.

A key point to note is that often we don't directly see the behaviour of others, but infer it. For example, in the case of litter it is not that we actually see everyone dropping it, but the fact that it is lying on the ground tells us that they must have done it. Similarly, when out walking, worn footpaths and trails tell us that many people have passed a given way, even though we haven't actually seen them. The worn pathway is still a useful clue that we're probably heading in the right direction to the nearby river or town that we are seeking, and that the path we are on is a safe route to take.

In the modern world this pattern of social inference is as powerful as ever, and perhaps even more so. The recommendations on e-shopping sites that show us what other people bought or looked at strongly influence behaviour. It is also generally useful. Buying a camera? Many people also bought this handy tripod. Buying that DVD? Many people also viewed this box set, which costs almost the same but has all three series, not just one. Clearly, other people's behaviour contains lots of useful information, particularly when we're not quite sure what to do.

Systematic studies of consumer choice confirm that these social influences are very powerful and tend to be self-reinforcing. When students choosing music on an online site are given information about what others liked, this leads to dramatic 'tipping effects' compared with choices that are not informed in this way. Even low-level feedback about what others liked amplifies the popularity of some songs and suppresses that of others.Quality does play a role: songs that are independently rated as very good tend to do better, and those that are independently rated as very bad tend to do less well. Nonetheless, in repeat experiments, which songs become popular depends heavily on whichever song first gets recommended. The feedback creates a 'winner takes all' dynamic, at least in these experimental conditions, with that winner strongly depending on whatever got recommended on the first round of feedback. [3]

In the 'real world', other sources of information normally come in to help inform those early judgements, such as expert reviews. But social influence – seeing the choices of others – then amplifies these differences. It is no wonder, then, that Robert Cialdini, an early expert and populariser of social influence, ensures that later additions of his book shout from the front cover that 250,000 copies have been sold.

Such social influence can have a dark side, too. Every social psychologist knows the name Kitty Genovese, the woman brutally attacked and killed in the early hours of the morning in a New York suburb in 1964. Her screams and extended struggle in the street woke many of her neighbours, some of whom watched as she was killed, yet did not offer help or call the police. The murder gave birth to the phrase 'diffusion of responsibility', and led to some of psychology's most famous experiments in order to explain why nobody intervened. In these experiments, Latene and Darley showed how strangers in a group will watch each other to decide what is going on, and how to react.[4] For example, in their famous 'smoked-filled room' experiment, subjects were filling in forms in a waiting room when smoke begins to enter. They found that a person on their own was almost certain to get up to investigate, such as going into the room next door to let someone know that there is a problem. However, when there was a group of eight people they were much less likely to do anything. Instead they would generally look furtively at each other, trying to figure out what was going on, but not actually taking action. Just as in the Genovese murder, the subjects look to each other's responses to decide how they should react. Is this really an emergency? Surely someone else has already called? If no one else is doing anything, I guess it must be fine ...

The Latene and Darley experiments on bystander intervention create artificial, though plausible, situations where people are unsure what is going on, and where there's no obvious leader or immediate cue to tell them the 'right thing' to do. As an aside, if you ever are in such a crowded situation in need of help, a pretty good idea is to point or look at someone in particular and say 'I need help!'

In much of life, situational cues and prior knowledge generally remove much of this ambiguity, giving us a strong sense of what others are doing, and what we are 'supposed' to do. We know we're supposed to be quiet in libraries, and loud at parties; to stand on the right on the escalator in London (and the left in Sydney) and to say thank you to our hosts at dinner. We know that we're not supposed to walk around naked in the office, comment on the body shape of other people or hit other people every time they annoy us. We call these social norms – the software or 'habits' that make societies and economies work.

Social norms in policy

Social norms, and the inferred behaviour of others, are powerful forces on our behaviour. But they are also prone to error, not least in the inference itself.

Suppose you are a first-year student at university. You are a bit like one of Latene and Darley's subjects, in a strange environment and trying to figure out the rules of the game. It's your first time away from home and a host of new behavioural opportunities lie before you, not least 'sex, drugs, and rock'n'roll'. How many drinks should you have? Should you try that drug? Condoms? The list goes on and on.

Your parents have told you to 'be careful' and 'sensible'. Your tutors have warned you not to take drugs, to be respectful of others, practise safe sex, and to be moderate in drinking. But how moderate is moderate? The fact is, a key influence on your behaviour is going to be your sense of what everyone else is doing. But how do you know what that is?

As you sit in your room trying to wade through a textbook in the evening, you hear shouting and laughing in the quad outside. It's a sound you hear every evening and from it you infer that drinking and partying is an integral part of student life. But what you don't hear are all the other students like you trying to read in their rooms. Sure enough, students systematically overestimate how much other students drink, have sex and do drugs.

This matters. These skewed estimates in turn strongly influence behaviour in a self-reinforcing way. For example, if our estimates of crime, or the trustworthiness of our fellow citizens, are being driven by a few highly visible examples of crime or bad behaviour, it will likely change our own behaviour in ways that we would not otherwise have chosen (see also Chapter 9 on well-being). If a few high-profile cases convince us that every other adult is a paedophile, then we won't let our children out of our sight or allow them to explore the world around. Our estimates of risks may spiral badly out of alignment with reality. We'll end up terrified of strangers, but neglect much more serious dangers, such as the swimming pools of our neighbours, carbon monoxide poisoning from an untested heater or the dangers from our own speeding through the neighbourhood.

This insight highlights a key lesson for student advice and behaviourally focused campaigns more generally. Factual information about how excessive drinking damages your liver, or not using a condom puts you and your partner at risk of STDs, has a role, but it can often be overpowered by a false estimate of what other people are doing.

Giving students, and others, more accurate information about what others are doing can in turn moderate unhealthy or dangerous behaviour. This can range from simply providing factual information along the lines of 'the vast majority of students drink in moderation' to more qualitative information, such as that your partner will think it normal to use a condom. For example, one study conducted in US university campuses showed that attempting to encourage stair use by putting up signs next to elevators that explained that stair use is a good way to get some exercise did not work. In contrast, a sign telling people that 'most people use the stairs' was highly effective, increasing stair use by 46 per cent.[5] Furthermore, even when the sign was later removed, a higher level of stair use continued.

The use of social norms lies at the heart of one of the most famous early series of interventions conducted by BIT. The idea was simple: tell late paying taxpayers the truth – that nine out of ten taxpayers paid on time. To give credit where it is due, the idea was based on

Robert Cialdini's work on social norms, not least his presentation at Downing Street in 2006, with a first version of the intervention drafted by a UK-based associate of Bob, Steve Martin. The first trial in the series was actually initiated, not by BIT, but by a civil servant named Nick Down who was responsible for chasing a block of £600 million of unpaid personal income tax to HMRC. Nick sent out thousands of letters to late payers, and chased them to complete their returns and pay whatever was owed. Inspired by Cialdini's work, Nick wondered whether a social norm-based approach could be built into some of the HMRC reminder letters.

The first version showed promising results, but it was not a true randomised control trial, which left it open to criticism that it was hard to isolate the impact of the letter from other changes that had occurred at the same time. BIT therefore worked with Nick's team to see if we could more systematically test the impact of the social norm message, and to explore whether further variations on it could perform even better.

To make sure that HMRC felt comfortable with the work, and that we would be able to set up the trials and analyse the data correctly, we arranged for someone from the team to be seconded directly into HMRC. With the cautious support of the head of the HMRC, we arranged for a talented young researcher, Michael Hallsworth, who had also co-authored the MINDSPACE report at the Institute for Government, to be seconded to the tax department. It made HMRC much more comfortable to have the person running the trials under their own wing, and meant that the data for the analysis could be kept inside the department without running into statutory barriers. This secondment was probably key to the success of the trials, and an important wider lesson to those seeking to spread new approaches into the necessarily secure world of tax collection.

Sure enough, adding the single (truthful) line that 'nine out of ten taxpayers pay on time' raised the payment rate by around 1.5

percentage points, or about 4.5 per cent, even in a letter that had already been stripped and simplified ('make it easy'). This might not sound a lot, but if you are in the business of gathering hundreds of millions of pounds or dollars, and the marginal cost of the intervention is essentially zero, then this is very valuable indeed.

Cialdini et al.'s work also gave clues about messages that might work even better. His work suggests that people are more influenced by the behaviour of those they see as being more like themselves than by people in general. For example, guests are more likely to reuse hotel towels, thereby saving energy, if told that previous guests had done so, rather than people in general. On this basis we tested the line that 'most people in *your local area* pay their tax on time', and found this raised the payment rate by more than 2 per cent over control.

Similarly, a little known exception to the rule that the more litter on the ground, the more likely a person is to discard a leaflet is that you are even less likely to drop litter in an otherwise perfectly clean environment with a single piece of litter than one with no litter at all. The single piece of litter seems to remind us that littering is the exception, and that disposing of it properly is the norm. This finding helped to shape the line that 'most people with a debt like yours' had already paid ('debt norm'). This was even more effective than the local social norm. Combining the two approaches into one, explaining that most people in your area had already paid, and that you were one of the few yet to do so raised the repayment rate by 5.4 percentage points, or an impressive 16 per cent increase in payment rate relative to the control letter. Not bad for a single extra line of text in a letter that was going out anyway.

One concern, regardless of whether the revised letters were effective, was that those receiving the letters would not like them. In fact, the revised BIT letters were actually associated with a dramatic reduction in complaints. One likely interpretation is that people preferred a short and courteous letter that reminded them that their fellow citizens were more virtuous than they thought, to the alternative – threats.

Reciprocity

Social norms are one of a number of pervasive social influences on our behaviour. Another powerful one is reciprocity, and even the simple act of asking from one person to another.

Imagine if a fellow passenger on a train, a stranger, leaves his bag unattended while he goes to the lavatory. While he is gone someone else confidently picks up their bag and walks off with it. Would you intervene?

You might hope that you would, but if you are honest with yourself you know you probably wouldn't. Experimental studies show that most people, at least in North America, do not intervene.

Imagine, however, that your fellow passenger had asked you to keep an eye on the bag while he stepped away. Would you intervene then? Almost certainly. Indeed, if the person hadn't said anything at all, but had simply caught your eye and smiled before stepping away,

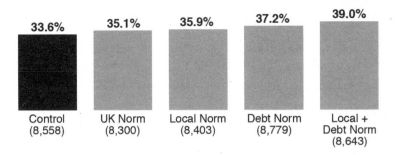

Figure 17. Tax payment rates by late paying individuals, one month (23 days) after receiving five different versions of a reminder letter. The 23-day measure was used because this is the threshold used by HMRC before sending further reminder or enforcement letters, with further costs incurred.

experimental evidence suggests that you would have been much more likely to intervene.

One area in which this type of direct ask, or reciprocity, is used is by charities hoping that you will give them some money. In its most basic form, charities have learnt that it is effective to have volunteers on street corners directly asking people to give. Another approach is the way some charities have learnt that it can be highly effective to 'give' a potential donor something in order to initiate the impulse to reciprocate on a mass scale. This could be by including a small gift, such as a pen or a penny in the envelope along with the request. Many people, myself including, find this approach annoying, but it can be effective.

As it happens, the 2010 Coalition Government, and the Prime Minister in particular, were keen to encourage giving, and we therefore conducted a number of trials to help charities in this area. We were interested to see if we could find effective, but less annoying, ways of encouraging giving. Working with Michael Sanders (who later joined BIT as Head of Research), we conducted a series of trials to help understand how giving might be encouraged beyond the usual approach of ever greater tax breaks. We found that effective approaches to encourage giving often involved social influence.

One trial, inside a large government department, involved trying to increase payroll giving: that is when people decide to make a regular donation directly from their monthly salary to a charity. Charities themselves particularly like this form of giving, because it establishes an ongoing and regular donation, and creates a direct connection with the donor. For donors, it makes the act of giving much less of an effort, and is also more tax efficient, in effect amplifying the impact of any gift. The primary intervention that we wanted to test, alongside just making it easier, was a series of alternative emails sent from people inside the department to their colleagues.

We found that 2.9 per cent of people chose to start payroll giving when sent an email from a colleague asking them to support a charity in this way, whether a charity they already supported or a new one. This in itself was quite impressive, given the 70,000 employees in the department, and testament to the generosity of the staff. However, when the email also included a picture of the asker, the number deciding to support payroll giving more than doubled to 6.4 per cent.

To be really effective and impactful, we needed to show whether similar approaches to encouraging giving would work in private sector contexts. In a trial set inside an investment bank, Michael tested the efficacy of a variety of different approaches intended to encourage the bankers to give the equivalent of one day's salary to a charity supported by the firm. The control group received a general email about the scheme, and some information about it. This led to a respectable 5 per cent pledging a day's salary. Bringing in a (minor) celebrity to the office pushed this up to 7 per cent, but much more effective was to simply give a tiny tub of sweets to staff along with the leaflet about the scheme. A personalised email from the CEO of the bank (see 'Attract!' above) was also pretty effective, while combining the personal email and the tub of sweets led a stunning 17 per cent to give a day's salary. In all, the experiment raised more than £500,000 for charity (see Figure 18).

The sweets, and personal email, were powerful because they created a sense of personal connection and reciprocity. As well as triggering the dynamic of reciprocity, we also chose sweets for an additional reason: a previous study among doctors had shown that giving sweets to someone tends to put them in a good mood, and being in a good mood makes the person more open-minded in their thinking.[6] Both these effects may have helped.

Commitments, eyes and faces

A closely related effect of reciprocity is a social commitment. We'll learn more about these in later chapters, but let us note for now what these are and why they relate to social influence. Part of the power of reciprocity is that it draws us into a commitment with someone else, however weak that may be. For example, if friends invite you to dinner you will generally feel some obligation to invite them back, if not for dinner then at least for drinks. In other words, when someone helps or gives to us, it tends to leave us feeling we owe a commitment to them.

In a modern market economy, where things are bought and sold and contracts drawn up, this older, deeper form of reciprocity and commitment may feel like a relic of our past. But it has a logic and pattern to it that is deeply ingrained in our habits and thinking and, to a much greater extent than most of us realise, continues to form the foundation of much of the modern economy itself. When someone helps us, we 'naturally' feel a sense of obligation to that person or institution.

Public services, and businesses, often help people. Particularly where someone goes the extra mile to help, the desire to reciprocate creates a natural opportunity to invite a commitment in response – to make a small ask. For example, finding out how a service or business might be improved is a very valuable piece of information: a natural

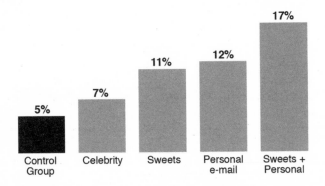

Figure 18. The percentage of bankers encouraged to give a day's salary to charity by different approaches. The personal email combined with the gift of a small tub of sweets led to more than a tripling of giving relative to a control group who received a general email and a leaflet about the scheme.

time to ask someone to give such feedback is after the service has just done something for us. A doctor has just given a person medication: an ideal time to ask the patient to try to quit smoking or exercise a little more. Curiously, public services are very poor at making such asks, or inviting people to make commitments. But when they do, as we shall see in later chapters, these can be very effective ways of 'helping people to help themselves'.

We are such social creatures that even the suggestion that someone is present or watching us has been shown to influence our behaviour. Several studies have indicated that eyes or faces looking at us tend to make us behave more virtuously. Hence, posters with faces looking at us have been shown to increase substantially the likelihood that people will, for instance, clear away their trays in a canteen or use an honesty box in an unsupervised environment, while other images and messages had little effect.

BIT has not conducted a systematic study using this approach, but after a discussion of this wider evidence base with our colleagues at HMRC, they decided it was convincing enough to build it directly into their national campaign to encourage people to declare their incomes in full. We had something more subtle in mind, but you get the point (see Figure 20).

The human, or personal, touch

Given the success of the trial with the investment bank (mentioned above) in raising money for the charities they supported, the bank invited Michael Sanders back for a follow-up study the next year. This offered him an opportunity to test a further variation of using social influence to encourage giving. We had already shown that adding a personal connection to the request was highly effective in a government context and were keen to test this in the commercial context. This time we arranged for people to recieve an email from

We're closing in on undeclared income

Go to gov.uk/sortmytax
If you've declared all your income you have nothing to fear.

HM Revenue & Customs

Figure 19. In the UK, HMRC incorporated eyes into its 2012 campaigns on the basis of behavioural evidence that they tend to increase honesty.

someone within the division or group of the bank highlighting that they had chosen to give. Unlike in the government example, this email came from someone the individual was likely to know, or at least know of. The effect of this intervention was stunning, leading to more than one in three people who received the email giving a day's pay to charity, more than doubling the impact of the previous best intervention from the year before, or around seven times more giving than in the control who just received a leaflet and a standard email.

The effects of a personal touch are not limited to giving. Many aspects of government activity – and business services – involve human exchange, often asking or encouraging a person to do something, though too often the human element is squeezed out. This is a mistake, and, frankly, a bit of a shame. This point is nicely illustrated by one of my favourite BIT studies.

We have done quite a lot of work to try to get unemployed people back into work faster (see Chapter 8 on growth, for more detail). In doing this we noticed that jobcentre advisers, whose role it is to help the unemployed back to work, would sometimes book people into a local job fair or recruitment event. Sometimes the advisers would send a helpful text to the jobseeker to confirm that they had been booked a place. But only around one in ten would actually show up. One member of BIT, Elspeth Kirkman, hypothesised that a more personal touch might make a difference.

As we suspected, adding the recipient's name at the beginning of the text increased the proportion turning up by 5 percentage points, or 15 per cent, just as would be predicted from our work on personalisation elsewhere (see 'Attract!', above). What if the adviser also added their own name? The number turning up rose even further, to 18 per cent. And how about if the adviser instead wrote: 'I've booked you a place ... Good luck!' Now the proportion turning up rose to an impressive 27 per cent, a nearly threefold increase (see Figure 20).

What I like about a trial like this is not just that it worked so well, and at such minimal cost, but its humanity. Behavioural approaches aren't just about invisible nudges that pull in a bit more tax revenue or help deliver on some worthy but distant outcome. At their best, such interventions are about understanding who we are; about connecting and communicating with each other better; and, frankly, about designing services for human beings, instead of 'econs'.[7] Put it this way, imagine if it was you who received that confirmation about the job fair – which text would you rather get? And how do you think that unemployed person would feel getting that text relative to the others? Would they not walk into that interview with their head held a little higher, their confidence a little stronger?[8]

Avoiding the 'big mistake'

In his 2006 Downing Street seminar, Robert Cialdini had one message that struck particularly deeply, and led to quite a bit of nervous laughter around the State Dining Room. He talked about

Figure 20. The proportion of jobseekers turning up at a job fair, depending on the reminder text they received.

how often policymakers, in his opinion, not only missed the power of social norms and influence, they often inadvertently used them in a way that actually backfired (see also Chapter 2).

He argued that too often, in their haste to impress upon colleagues or the public the gravity of a particular issue, policymakers would inadvertently reinforce the very behaviour they were trying to discourage. For example, a campaign concerning knife crime would end up communicating the message that most young people carried knives, or a campaign to reduce tax evasion or benefit fraud would inadvertently communicate that everyone was at it. Such campaigns, or speeches, were the policy equivalent of putting a 'no ball games' sign on a high brick wall – well meaning, but almost bound to prompt the thought, well, now that you mention it, that is a great surface for a ball game.

In the years since that seminar I have lost count of the number of examples of Robert Cialdini's 'big mistake' that I have seen. In most cases the effect has not been evaluated but we know enough about of the power of descriptive social norms to be troubled. Examples include: posters telling immigration officers that some of their colleagues have been caught and punished for selling work visas ('Never thought of that – I wonder how much they made'); signs in doctors' surgeries about the number of people who missed their appointments in the last month ('... so I'm not the only one'); and national campaigns bemoaning the low number of women on top company boards ('well, we've got a woman on our board of twelve, so that's pretty good, then').

Unfortunately, certain institutions in society also inadvertently make, or amplify, the 'big mistake'. The media itself is one of these, albeit echoing our own human interest in stories about crime, threat or deceit. No wonder that the majority of the public, in the UK and elsewhere, continue to feel that crime is rising (at least at a national level), despite every reliable measure documenting its fall over the last 20 years. Similarly, welfare and regulatory systems often inadvertently signal that most people are not to be trusted, since they are routinely built around the assumption, and associated checks, that people are cheating and breaking the law. The evidence on social norms suggests that such signalling is likely to increase levels of cheating.

Yet it is often possible to flip around these campaigns and effects. Take the example of getting more women on company boards, an issue widely championed by campaigners and indeed Prime Ministers, but often embodying a clear example of the 'big mistake'. The normal centrepiece of campaigns to get more women on boards is a statistic along the lines 'isn't it shocking that only 25 per cent of board members are women?' (less in some countries). It is shocking, but it's also likely to be a message that inadvertently normalises the situation. On the other hand, if such campaigns made the equally valid point that '90 per cent of companies have women on their boards', then the signalling is very different. Following discussions with Iris Bohnet, an expert on gender inequality, and Emily Walsh, special adviser to the UK's Business Secretary, parts of the UK's campaign to encourage more women on to boards was indeed reframed in this way.

Cialdini's 'big mistake' provides a clear example of why governments and businesses can benefit from learning even just a little about behavioural insights. Even if you have no interest in actively using nudge approaches you should at least want to know where you have inadvertently stumbled into deploying them against yourself.

Conclusion: the behaviour of others shapes and amplifies what we do

It turns out that one of the most powerful, but underused tools in the policymakers' armoury is simply to provide a more accurate echo chamber of what others are doing. Since, in general, policy is aligned behind what the majority of people are already doing – such as paying tax and not hurting others – it is a tool that can be applied widely.

However, it has obvious limitations, too. Reflecting the social norm isn't going to help much when most people are doing the 'wrong' thing. For example, most industrialised countries are wrestling with the problem of obesity, so reflecting these particular social norms is likely to backfire. Indeed, there is specific evidence that obesity is 'contagious' – when those around you get fat, so do you, and with it your sense of what is healthy shifts, too.[9] This can raise difficult issues, including occasionally the temptation to 'nudge' the presentation of numbers to prevent the situation getting worse. The weight curves given to US parents to plot their child's development, for some years, have not been the actual weight curves of US children. Rather, they are distributions of 'healthy weight', driven by the concern that if parents used the actual weight curves of US children it would exacerbate the problem of obesity even further (see Chapter 11 for further discussion of the ethics of behavioural approaches).

But 'social' is about more than social norms. It is also about nurturing the human and personal touch in the design of services. At its most basic, this is little more than using someone's name, but it can be much more. We are profoundly social beings. Understanding social influence can not only help achieve better outcomes such as paying our taxes or getting people to job interviews; it also has much deeper effects that we shall return to in later chapters, and particularly the effect on well-being.

One might ask if the effects of many nudges, and social norms in particular, are limited to a particular cultural context. It's something we've considered, too. Recently, BIT was asked by the World Bank to look at the very low payment of taxes in a particular Central American country. We weren't sure if our approaches developed in the UK would work in such a different national context. Led by Simon Ruda and Stewart Kettle, we tried a range of alternatives in a letter trial not unlike that presented earlier in this chapter. Some were based on appealing to national pride, others on the threat of audits and so on. Perhaps to everyone's surprise, the version that proved most effective was based on – you guessed it – social norms.

Though cultures and habits across the world may differ, it seems that in essence we are all social beings. We are influenced by what others around us are doing (declarative social norms), and particularly by the behaviour of those we know or feel are like us; by the desire to reciprocate; and even by the idea of other people observing us. At the very least, policymakers need to be aware of these effects; if they do not necessarily actively use them, at least they should avoid creating inadvertent nudges that work against their stated intent.

Finally, we as citizens should not underestimate the power of social influences on our own behaviour. It can be very helpful to get feedback on what others are doing, such as when deciding where to stay or what to buy. But we should also be aware of where our inferences about the behaviour of others might be wrong, or obscuring other factors that we care about. I have two children who will be leaving for university in the next couple of years. I'd hate them to end up drinking too much or driving too fast just because they thought that's what all their peers were doing.

CHAPTER 6

▲

TIMELY

There's a reason why retailers want to know if you are having a baby and will trawl through your purchasing data to figure it out. Having a newborn baby is wonderful, but it also means you buy lots of things you've never had before, and it will inevitably disrupt your life and routine. For a retailer, that's a perfect storm. You need to go shopping, and with your normal routines disrupted you might be persuaded to switch products, brands, and even retailers – for lots of items, not just baby gear. It's a big opportunity for a store that you go to regularly, and an even bigger opportunity for a rival if they can figure out the right moment and product to tempt you with.[1]

Governments might not be interested in getting you to switch where you buy your groceries, but they are quite interested in getting you to change your behaviour, including around the birth of a baby. And with good reason. Public health professionals are aware that smoking and drinking during pregnancy, for example, can significantly affect a child's short- and long-term health. More than that: they also affect subsequent educational attainment, juvenile offending and employment. In addition to wanting the best for mother and child, the entire community ends up bearing the costs of a child suffering foetal alcohol syndrome.

Figure 21. Many countries now add warning labels to alcohol, and other products, intended to create timely prompts to reduce risky behaviour.

When is the best time to intervene? In this case, after the child is born is clearly too late. Should it be at school, long before the young adult becomes a parent? Yet giving advice to teenagers, potentially years before they are even thinking about having a child, seems far from perfect. For most young parents-to-be, initial healthcare seems the obvious place to give advice in the early months of pregnancy. But even here there are limitations. Some young mothers may not come into contact with healthcare professionals until shortly before the birth of their baby.

An alternative approach is to pursue wider health education, and to introduce labels on potentially harmful products, such as cigarettes and alcohol, warning young, pregnant women to avoid them. But even these labels have serious limitations, not least since most people do not read labels; discount risks; and in some cases, may not even realise they are pregnant. There is an additional issue that some of the most at risk, such as heavy smokers, systematically underestimate their own personal risk – they rationally know that smoking is dangerous, but tend to think it will be other smokers who will die from the habit (see also Chapter 4).

When is the right moment?

Timeliness matters in several senses, and it is worth distinguishing these before we continue.

First, timing matters in a simple, causal sense. It is often better to intervene early: 'a stitch in time saves nine' is an old adage but a good one. There is nothing especially behavioural about this but there are psychological processes that have this sort of dynamic, too.

Second, even when a habit or behaviour is established, it turns out that there are certain key moments when an intervention is much more likely to affect changes in behaviour. This is why retailers want to know whether you are going to have a baby, because it identifies a time when you are especially likely to be persuaded to buy new products and potentially to switch your habits in other ways as well.

Third, there are a set of issues around what psychologists, and increasingly economists, call 'time inconsistent preferences'. For example, you really want to get fit, and lose a few pounds – but right now you are a little bit peckish, and there's some cake in the kitchen ... We all know how this story ends. There is also the fascinating issue of the perception of time itself, and how the future and past are broken into psychologically meaningful chunks, not the even segments of a clock. Fortunately, it is possible to design interventions that can help people act in ways that are more consistent with their underlying preferences, and to escape the trap of our present desires.

We shall use this loose framework to organise the sections of this chapter, though, as we shall see, all three aspects of timing can come together to help shape a more effective intervention.

Intervening early, before a habit or pathway is established

One of the most famous illustrations of the importance of timing in psychology comes from the phenomenon of 'imprinting'. It has been documented for more than a century how certain species, most famously birds, latch on to whatever larger moving object they first see in the period after birth. Konrad Lorenz showed how young geese could be imprinted in this way to follow a human being, or even an

Figure 22. Konrad Lorenz documented how many species appeared to have critical periods during which they would learn specific relationships, and that, once this limited period passed, the learning was 'stamped on' or 'imprinted' permanently. He was awarded the Nobel Prize in 1973 for his work. (Getty Images.)

inanimate object, in preference to another goose (see above). This attachment, or preference, could be extremely persistent right into adult life.

It is generally considered that human beings show much more malleability in their learning, but, nonetheless, at least some similar effects appear to exist. For example, longitudinal studies have shown that having a mother with maternal depression in the first six months of a child's life is associated with marked reductions in that infant's IQ at the age of 11, all other factors taken into account. It is thought that the disruption of the rapid mother–child interaction, or 'meshing', in early life stunts the infant's development of the social skills and engagement in their environment in a way that leaves a permanent mark. Similarly, it appears that children exposed to more than one language as young children, despite an initial delay in language acquisition, later acquire fluency in both languages in a way that is distinctive throughout life.

Such 'critical periods' matter in childhood and adult life, too. Most of us have the experience of picking up bad habits somewhere along the line, such as in a sport, driving or the use of language, that we later find it hard to shake off. In this sense, it is important to intervene before habits, or repeated behavioural patterns and associations, become entrenched.

In the policy world, a good example comes from a programme known as the Nurse Family Partnership (NFP), originally developed and tested by David Olds in the USA. The programme involves a nursing practitioner befriending and supporting a young at-risk mother from the pre-natal stage through to the child's second birthday. It is a well-validated programme that has been shown to reduce violence and abuse of the child, improve educational attainment and even reduce the child's rate of offending at the age of 15 compared with children from a similar background who did not participate in the programme (at least in the USA).

A less well-known but fascinating detail of the NFP that Olds noted when we introduced it into the UK was that the programme worked much better with mothers having their first child. Indeed, it wasn't clear that it had any effect at all on mothers giving birth to their second or later child. In essence, the habits had already been established with the first child. This isn't a marginal detail. It is an expensive programme, and so it is incredibly important to make sure that it is focused on the right people, and at the right time, to whom it will make a difference – young, first-time mothers.

In general, we might take as an opening mantra something like 'learn it first, learn it right'. One example of this, relevant to many policymakers (and parents!) is that it is important to give corrective feedback early when a problematic behaviour is developing. If a person breaks a rule, or does something 'wrong', and gets no reaction, that behaviour may soon become firmly established. Later on, when a sanction is introduced, it may have to be very severe to have any effect at all.

To illustrate this, consider someone starting a small business for the first time. Among the many things they will have to learn to do are their accounts and their tax returns for the business (or for themselves if they are self-employed). There will be many things going on but their primary focus will be on the business itself rather than getting their tax return in on time. Many revenue services have found that if a new business pays its taxes on time in the first year, this sets the tone. If they don't get into the habit of keeping good records from the outset, filing tax returns on time tends to be much harder in the future. Tax inspectors and accountants are very familiar with small businesses coming in to see them a few days before, or just after, the end of the tax year with bags of receipts and bits of paper and a soulful look on their face. Many of the smarter tax authorities have therefore learnt that it is worth putting a lot of effort into helping and encouraging small businesses in their first year of life to get their first tax return right and in on time. This pays great dividends over time.

We saw clear evidence of this effect in our trials. In the previous chapter we saw how simple nudges could, in general, be effective in encouraging people to pay their taxes on time. But when the data were analysed carefully we found that the effects of such nudges were uneven across the population. The nudges were generally around two to three times more effective among those who had generally paid their tax on time before than among those who had been late paying their taxes in previous years. The nudges still had some effect on the previous late payers, but the effects were consistently diluted – particularly in the case of the more mildly worded nudges.

The problem, at least for the tax authorities, is that once someone gets into the habit of paying their tax late, or not paying it at all, it's quite hard to get them to change. They've got used to receiving numerous letters, and 'shoves' such as fines rather than being nudged. It is no surprise that one extra phone call or nudge will have less effect, however elegantly and politely it may be put.

A similar logic lay behind our advice to the Home Office to write to people before their visa was due to expire, rather than waiting until it had expired and only then prompting them to take action. When this was run as a randomised control trial it was indeed found to be effective, raising the number of people recorded to have left the country by around 20 per cent.[2] Better to get to people before they have got used to the habit of ignoring the law – and, indeed, before they discover that many of its enforcement mechanisms are far from perfect. It's generally cheaper, too.

Finally, the same lesson often holds at the micro-level of everyday behaviour. We saw in Chapter 5 how people often look to each other to see what the 'right' behaviour is in an unfamiliar setting. This insight has very practical implications in relation to the timing of interventions, especially concerning crowd behaviour. As many police forces, school teachers and parents in charge of parties have learnt, it is important to establish early on the 'right way to go on'. Hence it is generally better and more effective if the police intervene around incidents of violence early in the evening in a town centre crowded with drunken revellers. A wave of the finger, or a shake of the head early on, to stop aggressive behaviour becoming entrenched or spreading through the crowd, will generally be more effective than leaving it until there are running fights or battles. Similarly, many teachers and leaders soon learn that they had better follow a 'tight-loose' rule: enforce the good behaviour you want to see early on and you will generally find that later you can be much more relaxed.

Key moments to prompt or reshape established behaviour

In much of life we have plenty of choices about how to behave or what to do. Sometimes these choices are conscious, but often there is something in the situation that nudges us to follow one 'script' or another.

Let's take a simple example: honesty. In many situations a little bit of forgetfulness, a white lie, or even downright cheating will be in our best interests, at least short-term. It can be both tricky and expensive to build bureaucracies and systems designed to check whether we are telling the truth. The classic response is to crank up the cost of dishonesty, perhaps through larger fines and punishments, but the net effect may be far from perfect. Greater punishments may encourage more honesty, but also create the need for elaborate and expensive judicial mechanisms to make sure that we are not punishing the innocent. Even when such systems have been built, it often feels as if they result in quite a lot of hassle for the honest, while still remaining far from foolproof at catching the cheats. If only we could just 'nudge' people to be honest ...

Consider what happens when a witness is called to give evidence in court. The first thing the witness is asked to do in the box is to raise their hand and swear an oath to tell the truth. They are then questioned as to what they witnessed.

We know from other studies that people like to be consistent, which strongly suggests that making people promise to tell the truth before they give evidence is a good idea. But notice what we don't do. We don't first summon people to give evidence, and then, after they have finished, ask them if they were telling the truth.

It seems almost ludicrous that we'd ask people to tell the truth after they've given evidence, but that's exactly what we do in many parts of government (and business). In particular, we often ask people to fill out forms and then, at the very end, ask them to sign the form to confirm that what they've said is true.

To be fair, there are quite a few different reasons why we ask people to sign forms at the end. One important reason for a signature is to confirm your identity, and that you have consented, read or agreed to what is on the form. But an important second reason is often to declare that what you have written is true. So why put the signature at the end? What if forms asked you to sign an honesty declaration before, rather than after, filling them in?

Dan Ariely, Max Bazerman and colleagues tested this idea in the USA in a series of lab studies and found that people were indeed less likely to cheat if they signed a declaration of honesty before rather than after the opportunity to cheat.[3] They also tested the idea in an elegant real-world study on car insurance, where drivers were required to estimate how many miles they were likely to drive in the coming, or typical, year. The more miles you drive, the higher your insurance is likely to be, so drivers do have an incentive to 'underestimate'. When the signature was brought to the top of the form, drivers declared on average an extra 2,428 miles, or a little over 10 per cent more. This in turn cost the average driver around $97 extra, a significant amount. Signing the honesty declaration before they filled in the number made them significantly more honest.[4]

Quite often policymakers are so focused on the 'what' – the intervention at hand – that they pay little attention to the critical question of 'when' (and 'where'). For example, imagine you want to encourage more people to walk, cycle or take public transport to work. There are lots of ways you might do this, such as putting in cycle lanes (easy), emphasising that many others walk to work (social), or making public transport more comfortable and frequent (attractive). Some governments have even funded one-to-one transport advice for workers, intended to encourage more to leave their cars at home. Unfortunately, many of these strategies are not very effective, although there is one big exception – among people who have just moved house. You can see why. If you've just moved house, your journey to work habits have yet to fully form, and you will be much more open to the suggestion of alternative options than if you have already been driving to work for the last five years.

One everyday application of a timely intervention is providing information to consumers around, or just before, the moment of purchase. Most people would rather buy appliances that use less energy and cost less to run. In most countries, appliances now have some kind of energy rating on them, but it is not immediately obvious how to trade off an A+, A++ or even A+++ rating against the cost of the appliance (see also discussion in Chapter 7 about making these ratings easier to understand). Based on earlier work by Greenudge in Norway, BIT ran a trial, led by our environment lead Marcos Pelenur, with a large retailer in the UK expressing the energy efficiency of appliances in terms of how much they are likely to cost to run over the products' typical lifespan (typically around nine years).[5] Sure enough, when labels had this extra information consumers tended to buy slightly more expensive but more efficient products, at least in a product class with high usage costs, such as washer-dryers. Clearly, the effectiveness of the intervention rests on supplying that information while the consumer is still deciding what to buy.

Another important example comes from the welfare state: does the timing of when people receive payments matter? For everyday forms of expenditure, this might not seem a very important question, but a lot of expenditure is not every day – rather, it is 'lumpy'. Rent has to be paid at the end of the month, but the temptation to drink or have a meal out might be every day. Some forms of expenditure are even more irregular, such as paying for car servicing or paying your tax. An increasingly popular innovation in welfare systems is to use benefits to encourage certain types of behaviour, through what are known as 'conditional cash transfers' (CCTs). For example, several countries have implemented systems that 'reward' children and parents for school attendance: if you miss too much school, you lose some of your benefits.

One such scheme, in the city of Bogotá in Colombia, gave families extra money every two months provided their children had been attending secondary school at least 80 per cent of the time. Analysis showed that this scheme was effective at boosting attendance, but

Subconscious priming: a nudge too far?

In the 1970s and 1980s, psychologists found that it was possible to subconsciously 'prime' people's responses to words or ideas. Subjects would 'see' a word flashed on a screen in front of them, followed almost instantly by a 'masking' stimulus such as a random pattern. Psychologists such as Anthony Marcel at Cambridge found that they could adjust the timing to the point that the person could no longer tell you what the word was, or even be sure if they saw one, but nonetheless the word could still be shown to influence their behaviour. For example, if the unseen word was 'bread', the subject would later react faster to the word 'butter' than to an unrelated word such as 'nurse'.[6]

These results attracted much attention and controversy because they suggested how people's behaviour might be influenced without their conscious awareness, such as frames being added into movies to prompt us to buy a particular product. Similarly, more recent experiments have suggested that people can be prompted to be more or less helpful to others, such as picking up things that someone has dropped, according to whether there are images of money (e.g. dollar signs) or a neutral image (e.g. fish) on the screensavers in the room.[7] The dollar signs seem to make people less likely to help others, priming a sense of self-reliance, 'time is money', or, more controversially, of 'selfishness'.

Such priming effects influence our behaviour in many ways that we are not fully aware of. Hearing a word in a conversation may bring an idea to mind, or smelling bread as we walk down a street might prompt us to feel hungry and to stop and buy some food where otherwise we would have skipped a meal. But primes don't have to be subconscious to be effective, such as the honesty prompts described earlier, or the use of 'anchors', such as introducing a high number before negotiating your next pay deal. It's an important question as to whether or not governments should be in the business of using subconscious primes (see Chapter 11).

one disappointment was that many children still dropped out of school at the end of the year, failing to complete their education or matriculate from high school. One explanation for this seemed to be that, despite the extra payments, many families failed to re-enrol when they needed to in December. The programme was therefore restructured so that a third of the extra payments for attendance were held in a bank account and instead released as a lump sum in December when enrolment was due. This led to a dramatic increase in enrolment and matriculation rates.[8]

One recent, and remarkable, result illustrating the power of a timely intervention comes from some work we were assigned on recruitment. We were asked to look at what might be done to narrow the gap between white and ethnic minority recruits into a major public service: the police. To set the context, for a number of years British police forces have been keen to increase the number of ethnic minority recruits to levels closer to those in the wider community. However, despite numerous changes, including introducing an online, centrally conducted exam (which can therefore be marked ethnically blind), considerable differences remained in the recruitment rates across groups. Particularly strikingly was that the pass rate for this online exam was around a third lower for ethnic minorities than for white applicants, despite the intention being that it would help narrow the gap.

Simon Ruda, who leads the BIT work on crime, together with Elizabeth Linos, who was working on organisational psychology in the team, investigated the issue in more detail. Theories abounded as to why this gap was occurring. Some thought it must be to do with mastery with English, which sounded plausible. Others controversially argued it was cognitive ability, and that the test standard would need to be lowered to boost numbers from certain groups. Simon and Elizabeth thought that motivation and expectancies might be part of the story, so we tested adding an extra line to the email instructions

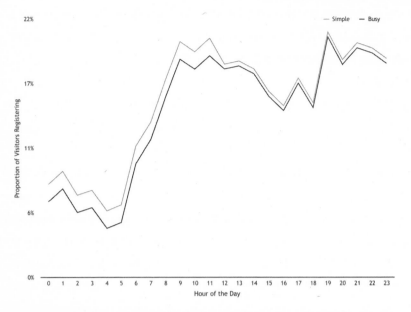

Figure 23. The proportions of people visiting a quit-smoking webpage registering for a 'quit pack' by time of day and complexity of the site. People were much more likely to register for the pack in mid-morning and in the evening. A simplified webpage was also more effective, but especially in the morning. [BIT data]

to applicants with the help of one of the regional police forces. Just before the link to click-through to take the test, we added a line asking applicants to reflect for a moment about why they wanted to join the police and why it mattered to their community. We made no other changes.

This timely prompt made no difference to white applicants. However, for the ethnic minority applicants it boosted their performance dramatically. The ethnic minority pass rate rose from around 40 to 60 per cent, entirely eliminating the difference with whites.

We did not test sending police applicants' messages at other times, but we very much doubt that the same spectacular result would have occurred had we sent them a similar motivational message in a different email or letter a week before. We can certainly be sure that it would have made no difference if we'd sent it to them with their test results. Timely prompts can clearly make a big difference.

Choosing for our future selves – 'time-inconsistent preferences'

A series of studies has shown that what we choose for our future selves often differs greatly from what we choose for our present selves. Around three-quarters of (Danish) workers chose fruit over chocolate when the prize was due to be delivered the following week, yet the majority instead chose chocolate when offered the choice at the point of delivery.[9] Similarly, most people choose a healthy snack option over an unhealthy one for later in the day – especially if they have just eaten – but the reverse is true when asked immediately before the snack is available. The same appears to be true for other forms of consumption: most people choose a 'highbrow' movie (such as *Schindler's List*) over a 'lowbrow' one (such as *Four Weddings and a Funeral*) when deciding what to watch next week, but the reverse when thinking about that evening.[10]

We are, in the words of Danny Gilbert, prone to be trapped in our present. When we've just finished a huge Christmas lunch, we push the plate away and say – in all seriousness – 'I'm never going to eat again.' Yet chances are we'll be snacking before the end of the day. Behavioural economists link this to 'hyperbolic discounting': the further into the future a cost or benefit, the disproportionately smaller it becomes relative to immediate costs and benefits. We also know that this discounting curve is not smooth, but drops away more sharply with the boundaries that our minds use to divide up the future. Viewed from Monday, three or four days away is pretty close, but viewed from a Friday, three or four days away is another world away – it's next week.[11]

The inconsistency in our preferences also applies to the past. When people are asked how much they would pay for an object, such as a souvenir mug or pen, they give a much lower figure than the one they come up with after they have been given the item. Known as the 'endowment effect', this doesn't seem just to be a negotiating strategy. Rather, it seems to be that once we've mentally labelled something as ours, we value it much more highly than we did before. That's one of the reasons so many of us find our homes full of bits and pieces that we really should have thrown out long ago, and if we saw the same type of thing in other people's homes we'd surely think they should throw them out.

Time inconsistency is also aggravated by the fact that self-control is like a precious good that we use up. Lab studies show that people are much more likely to choose chocolate cake rather than a healthy snack after taking part in a task that requires self-control.[12] Similar effects appear to impact on professional judgements, too. In a now famous study, Danziger *et al.* found that judges moved from around 65 per cent favourable parole judgements at the beginning of the day to close to zero by late morning. After lunch, positive judgements surged back up to 65 per cent again, before dropping away by the end of the day.[13] Recent studies have shown similar results with other professional groups. The incidence of hand-washing has been found to fall across care workers' 12-hour shifts, with the drop accelerating the more stressful the shift was. Furthermore, the shorter the break before the shift started, the faster the rate of decline.[14] Similarly, doctors have been found to prescribe more antibiotics as the day wears on. The rate is partly reset after lunch before it drifts up further through the afternoon, ending at around 20 per cent higher than when the day began.[15] It's an effort to say no to patients who you feel probably don't need antibiotics, and an effort to keep washing your hands. We've seen similar effects in BIT analysis, too, such as the changing probability that social workers will bring a child into care through the week. Decision fatigue, as psychologists call it, has very wide effects and is often far more powerful and pervasive than we realise.

Yet we're not powerless in the face of our immediate desires, or the slow drip of decision fatigue. Studies have shown that most people are aware of their own 'time inconsistency', and will, when offered the opportunity, often deliberately bind themselves in to 'do the right thing'. For example, experiments have shown that savers often choose financial products that restrict their access to high savings accounts rather than ones that allow withdrawals at any time. Similarly, smokers seeking to quit, and people hoping to lose weight, will often seek to avoid environments that are associated with, or tempt them into, their habits. Rather like Odysseus listening to the song of the Sirens in Greek mythology, we choose to lash ourselves to a metaphorical mast.

Policymakers, and indeed companies, can greatly help by offering products and services that allow people to shape choices for their future selves, and help them resist moments of temptation that they may later regret giving in to. For example, in the USA many states and casinos now offer the option to gamblers to self-exclude themselves from gambling (though without hard constraints other casinos and firms may find the temptation to reach out to such gamblers irresistible). The principal tool is normally to offer a 'commitment device' to the individual. This is essentially a form of contract, or more usually a 'compact' (because it is not legally binding), whereby the individual can constrain their own future choices.

An everyday example of a commitment device is marriage: two people committing to be faithful to and care for each other for the rest of their lives, or at least for a while. Another less onerous form of commitment device is to make a promise, or place a bet, such as 'If you catch me smoking in the next year, I'll give you that signed football shirt that I know you want.' This type of promise forms the basis of the web platform stickk.com, on which more than a quarter of a million commitments have been made. People use it to help themselves quit smoking, drugs or watching porn, as well as to commit to positive self-betterment such as getting fit, losing weight, or learning a new language. At the time of writing, the site claims that it has helped people complete more than 300,000 workouts, and has prevented more than 2,500,000 cigarettes being smoked.

Speaking at a seminar in Downing Street, the co-founder of stickk Ian Ayres offered thoughts about what made for an effective commitment device. He felt it was important that the objective be clear, and that the self-inflected punishment be something that would genuinely 'hurt', such as making a donation to a political party you deeply disliked. He also highlighted the importance of choosing a partner to enforce the commitment who was close enough to know whether you were succeeding, but not so close that they would let you off the hook. Hence, for example, he had concluded that entering a commitment contract with your wife or husband not to smoke, or to exercise more, was not particularly effective because they tend to let you off the hook when you fail to get to the gym or sneak out for a smoke after a stressful day. Instead, it was better to get a workmate or a friend (but not someone too close) who would probably catch you if you broke your promise, but would also seek to enforce the deal or punishment.

Helping people to address this time inconsistency offers a rich variety of possible policy interventions. One example, of relevance to David Cameron's interest in strengthening the 'Big Society', is how we might encourage more giving and mutual support, and charitable giving in particular.

Michael Sanders, the BIT member who heads our research team and leads on charitable giving, conducted a series of experiments that showed that people were much more likely to give some of their earnings or winnings to charity if they were asked before, rather than after, they received the cash. In a variation on this approach, we wondered if we could help achieve the Prime Minister's soft ambition that people might leave 10 per cent of their wealth to charity in their wills.

You could sense the wheels of the Treasury nervously turning around how large a tax subsidy might be necessary to achieve this 'legacy-10' commitment. If our estimates on the scale of conventional tax subsidies required to get people to save for pensions were anything to go by, then the Treasury were right to be nervous. So while the Treasury sweated, we set about organising a trial to see if a timely intervention could achieve the PM's ambition without a tax subsidy at all.

The first question is, when was the right time to ask? Our conclusion, unsurprisingly, was when people were writing their wills. With this in mind, Michael organised a trial with one of Britain's largest groups of lawyers that helped people write wills. We asked the group if they would be prepared to add a couple of specific questions into their script for the writing of wills about charitable giving, and they agreed.

The control groups simply received the standard script. Under these conditions, around 5 per cent chose to make a bequest to charity. In a second, randomly assigned group, clients were specifically asked if there were any charities they wished to make a bequest to. Asking the question led to a doubling of the numbers of people who chose to make a bequest to charity (see Figure 24). Under a third condition, clients were asked a more empathetic question, that also drew on social norms (see Chapter 5). It was worded: 'Many of our customers like to leave money to charity in their will. Are there any causes you're passionate about?' When asked this question, the proportion giving in their wills rose to 15 per cent, or treble the control group. Even more strikingly, the level of the average bequest also doubled (from £3,300 to £6,700), so that the average level of the bequest to charity increased sixfold over the baseline condition.

Of course, many people still chose not to give, as is their right. In later chapters we shall return to the question of the ethics of such asks, as well as the well-being impacts of giving and a more detailed breakdown of these results. But for now let us note that simply adding this question at the time people were making the decision took just a few seconds, was not considered intrusive, and led to a significant voluntary uplift in giving, but without the enormous cost of a further tax subsidy. Indeed, it strongly suggests that if everyone was asked a similar question when drafting their wills, the ambition to get 10 per cent of people to give to charities in their wills would be easily achieved, and the charitable sector greatly boosted as a result.

Another approach to reducing time inconsistency is to prompt people to think about the details of *how* they will do something in advance. For example, when writing to let people know when they can get a flu jab, it has been found that adding a box at the top of the letter to encourage them to write down the date when they will get the jab makes them significantly more likely to get the vaccination. Adding an extra box to encourage them to write in the time as well makes them even more likely to get the jab.

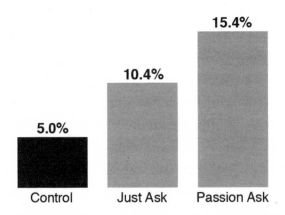

Figure 24. The proportion of clients giving money to charity in their will, across three conditions. When clients were specifically asked if they would like to give to charity in their will, the numbers giving doubled, and trebled when asked in a more empathetic way (see text for wording).

This approach is known in the behavioural literature as encouraging 'implementation intention': encouraging people to think not just about what they want to do, but when and how, makes them much more likely to see through their own intentions. Such approaches have been used to encourage a range of behaviour, from voting to getting a job (see Chapter 8).

Bringing the elements of timely together

Effective interventions often bring together all three elements of timeliness. The intervention is targeted before the behaviour has become entrenched; the intervention is aligned to a moment when it is likely to be most salient or when the existing behaviour is disrupted; and its design will help the person overcome their own time inconsistency – helping them to do what their future self would have wished.

The restructuring of conditional cash transfers, as in the example concerning Bogotá outlined earlier, illustrates all these elements. Though a central point in that example is to ensure the release of the money at the key moment just before the decision about schooling is to be made, the intervention is also clearly designed to help parents and children address their own time inconsistency.

Similarly, interventions that offered farmers the opportunity to purchase fertiliser with free delivery just after the harvest – when they have cash in hand – have been found to be a highly effective way of boosting production. This very simple and cheap intervention led to an increase in farmers' use of fertiliser from 26 to 42.5 per cent – a two-thirds increase. A plausible alternative was also tested, which was to offer purchase with free delivery of fertiliser just before it was due to be used. This also boosted use, but to a more modest 35.6 per cent: still impactful, but not as effective as making the offer when the farmers had the most cash in hand.[16] Again one can see that the more impactful intervention brings together an understanding of time inconsistency with a timely offer. The researchers also compared the effectiveness of these timely interventions with a much more expensive subsidy. They found that offering the fertiliser with free delivery after harvest was as, or slightly more, effective as a 50 per cent discount on the cost of the intervention – a much more expensive approach.

The beauty of timely interventions that combine these elements is that they can be very simple, effective and popular – either as interventions in themselves, or as ways of enhancing existing interventions. Let me conclude with a couple of final recent examples from the Behavioural Insights Team around education.

Working with Todd Rogers of Harvard, BIT's Raj Chande, Elspeth Kirkham and Michael Sanders wanted to see if timely prompts to students or their parents might increase attainment. In the first series of studies, the team simply texted parents a few days before their child was due to do a maths test to warn them it was imminent. That's it – very simple. They found that the texts increased performance by the equivalent of a month of extra teaching on average, and two months of extra teaching for the bottom quarter of students. In essence, it encouraged parents to talk to their child more about the subject, and encouraged the child to study more.

As an aside, the team also asked the parents and children afterwards if they would like to receive more such texts in the future. Perhaps unsurprisingly, the vast majority of parents said they did want to receive such texts in the future, but the kids? More than 80 per cent said they would like their parents to get such texts in the future. They might have got a little extra hassle, but like Odysseus, they wanted to be lashed to the mast to be prompted and encouraged to study harder.

In a second series of studies, we wanted to see if we could reduce the drop-out rate of young adults in further education courses.

The team analysed the pattern and timing of drop-outs and then designed a series of short text messages to students to encourage them at high-risk times. For example, a student might receive a text saying that many found the course tough going at this point, but within a week or two would find themselves back on top. Note how the message itself drew on work about how we find it difficult to escape our current moment and difficulties, and see past into the near future. The result? The drop-out rate fell by 36 per cent. And the cost? About £2 ($3) per student.[17]

Conclusion: timing matters

Much policy, in business and certainly in government, pays scant attention to timing. Laws and incentives are presumed to apply evenly across time: it is just as wrong to steal in the morning as in the afternoon. But human behaviour is not like this. We are much more likely to change our behaviour at some times than others. We are more likely to give to charity before Christmas than after it, but much more likely to want to save for our pensions after Christmas than before it.

There are some examples where governments do vary punishments or encouragements by timing. Australia varies the penalties for speeding, so that at on certain days an offence will attract 'double points' – and make this clear on road-side messaging. Similarly, most governments are shrewd enough to realise that it is wise to gently remind citizens when it is coming up to the time to fill in their tax returns, and courts offer discounts for fines paid by a given date.

But, in general, the commercial world is far more attuned to the importance of timing, prompting us with linked offers when we are most likely to be interested; varying prices through the year, and even through the day on some websites. At their most sophisticated, businesses actively identify key periods when our normal habits have been disrupted and we are most likely to be amenable to buying or switching products and services, including in ways that may push the boundaries of acceptability (see Chaper 11).

Ironically, public services are often present at key moments in life when people are amenable to advice and change, and may actively welcome help to change their behaviour. For example, someone who has suffered a heart attack may genuinely want advice about how they, and others in their family, might change to a healthier lifestyle. Adults with poor skills may become interested in learning when their children start going to school. People who have escaped unemployment and benefits might be happy to encourage someone else into employment, if only we thought to ask. Finally, policies, products and outcomes can sometimes be greatly improved by helping people to plan and anticipate in advance (encouraging our 'implementation intentions').

When set alongside the other elements of EAST – make it easy, *attractive*, and social – timely interventions can be highly effective. Just like swinging for a ball with a bat, or catching a ball in our hands, the timing of interventions can make all the difference between a flop and a roaring success. Intervene before the behaviour has been established if you can; look for when the intervention is most salient or disrupted for other reasons; and try to help people overcome their own time inconsistency. Bring these elements together, and you'll probably hit the ball for six.

Figure 25 (opposite). Summary of EAST, and Section 2.

	Headline	Things to think about	Examples
Easy	Make it easy. People are much more likely to do something if it's easy and low-hassle	▲ Simplify ▲ Friction: remove, or add it to inhibit ▲ Defaults: set the easy path as the healthiest, safest option	▲ Pensions: millions more saving as a result of auto-enrolment ▲ Suicide: reduced when easy routes blocked ▲ University entry: 25 per cent more poor students go when forms pre-filled
Attract	People are drawn to that which catches their attention, and that which is attractive to them	▲ Personalise: use recipient's name; make relevant ▲ Salience: make key point stand out ▲ Messenger: experts and named individuals beat anonymous or distrusted sources ▲ Lotteries: make incentives more attractive ▲ Emotion: as important as reason	▲ Tax: 10 times more doctors declared income with salient letter ▲ Giving: 2 times more donations to emergency appeals with story of one child versus statistics of millions affected ▲ Courts: 3 times more likely to pay fines with a personalised text
Social	People are strongly influenced by what others are doing or have done	▲ Norms: what are others actually doing ▲ Networks: a friend or colleague recommends ▲ Reciprocity and active commitments: promises ▲ Reminders of others: eyes and faces	▲ Litter: 8 times more likely to drop flyer if others already on the ground ▲ Tax: 16 per cent more likely to pay if informed that most people 'pay on time' ▲ Giving: 7 times more likely to give when learning that a colleague already gave
Timely	Interventions are more effective before habits have formed, or behaviour has been disrupted for other reasons	▲ Habits: intervene before they become established ▲ Key moments: when behaviour is disrupted ▲ Priming and anchoring: the power of what just came before ▲ Time inconsistency: discounting of the future	▲ Development: two-thirds more farmers take up fertiliser offer after harvest when cash-rich ▲ Health: 3 times more workers choose healthy option a week ahead than on day ▲ Tax: 2 times more less likely to respond to nudge if late paying previous year

SECTION 3

▲

BEHAVIOURAL INSIGHTS AS A POLICY TOOL

It is sometimes said that the work of BIT, and 'nudging' more generally, is about little tweaks. 'Isn't what you do really just about better communications?' I'm often asked. As we have seen in the previous section, a lot of the work of BIT and behavioural scientists has focused on communications. BIT refined and tested more effective letters to elicit more unpaid tax. We tested and adapted websites to increase the numbers quitting smoking or joining the organ donor register. And BIT advised on media campaigns to make them more effective.

Yet much of the work of BIT from the outset was to advise and adapt government policy. Governments, and Prime Ministers, are confronted with an endless array of challenges and choices. Many of these are externally driven. Sometimes crises blow up that require rapid action, such as the protests and blockages that nearly derailed Tony Blair's early administration, and at one point threatened to do the same for David Cameron. Such situations demand rapid action, with the best guess of those gathered around the Cabinet table as to how such actions will play out. Other policy challenges have deep roots and long shadows, such as obesity, unemployment, productivity or climate change. These are the subject of recurrent discussions and argument, both public and private. Most old hands will have concluded that 'there is no magic bullet', and will be sceptical of new solutions and ideas when so many options have been tried before and failed.

Policy decisions are the lifeblood of government, and of many businesses, too. What to invest in and what to cut? Which rules and regulations to expand or create, and which to scrap? Where to push harder and where to back off? If behavioural science − or any other new approach − is to prove itself, it is in this battleground of policy and strategy advice that its proponents must make a difference, or else be content to be a footnote in history. Furthermore, to make a real mark, and not just a smudge on the wall, the advice given has to prove 'right': it has to have been adopted, impactful and effective. It is this wider battleground that this section explores.

CHAPTER 7

▲

DATA AND TRANSPARENCY

In many countries people can save money by switching their electricity or gas supplier. By 2010 in the UK most people could save around £200 per annum or more by switching. But in a given year, only 1 in 10 did so.

This apparent reluctance to switch would have surprised the economists and lawyers who designed the new, privatised electricity and gas markets in the 1980s and 1990s. They had unwittingly made an assumption about human behaviour – that consumers would leap at the chance to switch their energy supplier, constantly searching the market for the best deal. But in practice that didn't happen. Switching your utility supplier turned out to be one of those slightly irritating things that we all know we should do, but many of us don't get around to. Such everyday decisions have come to be at the heart of some of the hottest political issues of recent years: making competition work for 'ordinary people'; the cost of living; and the fairness of markets.

In Britain, even when people did finally get around to checking a website or calling a switching intermediary, large numbers still failed to switch. Many people weren't sure who their supplier was, weren't sure which tariff they were on, and struggled to find the key customer number they needed to be able to switch. If you haven't switched, don't feel too bad: you're not alone.

But in mid-2015 something changed. As a result of a new consumer power pushed by BIT, energy companies were required to make it easier for customers to access information. In particular, they were required to print on bills a QR code that summarised the customers' details, patterns of use and their current tariff (see Figure 26). In technical terms, this makes the customers' data machine-readable. In everyday terms, it means that all customers need to do to save some money is to scan the QR code with their mobile phone, and a switching site app can search the market for the best tariff for them. Instead of switching being a task that would take a few hours, it can be done in a few seconds.

You don't have to be a top economist to see why this seemingly small change is a game-changer. Before the change, utility providers could make much of their profits by quietly ensuring that switching providers was complicated and time-consuming. Those millions of customers who never shopped around, and were still on the same tariff they were years ago, could be quietly charged higher rates, and were very profitable for the companies. Those pesky few who did shop around – 'rate-tarts' as they are sometimes unflatteringly called – got better deals, though even they might find themselves baffled by the range and complexity of the available deals.

But as that friction is stripped away, consumers start switching much more easily and companies instead have to compete on other grounds.

This chapter is about how the massive expansion in data and transparency can make lives and markets work better. But ever greater data by itself is no guarantee of a better world. If the net result is that some people, governments or companies are able to predict the behaviour of others better than those people can predict it themselves, it might not be a world we like at all. Transparency and the democratisation of data is a partial solution, but it is only the first step. Human beings have a limited capacity to process information, and we need to factor this in. More data could just be more noise. To get the benefits of a data-rich world, we have to build it around people's mental capacities and around behavioural insights.

'Midata' – taking the friction out of markets

The puzzle about why so many people would save money if they switched supplier yet don't provides a window into how parts of modern economies work – or sometimes don't. Many energy suppliers make more money from their existing 'sticky' customers than they do from new customers, or from selling energy on the open market. As such, they have a strong vested interest in making sure that switching is both boring and tricky.

It is a powerful illustration of how important 'friction costs' are in many markets (see Chapter 3), and how, increasingly, many companies make much of their profit from exploiting these costs. This applies

1. Scan your bill

2. Switch & save

Figure 26. A stylised illustration of how having QR codes on bills makes switching easier. This illustration, together with an early prototype developed by one of the switching sites, was shown to Ministers in 2012 and helped make the case to wider, behaviourally based changes in the regulation of consumer markets in the UK and beyond.

not only to electricity and gas markets, but to many other everyday services such as mobile phones and banking products. Until recently, the UK's main six energy suppliers had more than 500 tariffs between them. For mobile phones, where there is a choice of networks, tariffs and handsets, the choices facing consumers run into the millions. These vast numbers make it very hard for a consumer to figure out what is the best choice for them.

In a classic economic view, this shouldn't much matter. Consumers should be able to sort through the options and, even without 'perfect information', the magic of the market should weed out the weaker and lower value offerings over time, while the better products and companies should thrive.

But in the world of human beings, not 'econs', consumers use mental shortcuts to make such decisions. Like all shortcuts, they are open to error. They are also extremely widespread, given that we are all human. For example, studies have shown that consumers make considerable and systematic errors in predicting how they will use their new mobile phones and the facilities on them. This means that often many of us choose tariffs that are not, in retrospect, the best ones for us.

These issues in turn affect nearly all consumers, with big implications both for the money in our pocket and how businesses treat us, though these issues particularly affect the most disadvantaged. In recent years, big businesses have become better and better at predicting what consumers will buy and use. Your phone company, for example, has a much better idea of what features you will use on your new mobile than you do. This puts you at a big disadvantage when choosing between the millions of alternative phone-network-tariff options available when it comes to renewal.

Fortunately, it turns out that there are things that governments, and companies, can do to help consumers, and in so doing make markets work better. The conventional policy response, by regulators and governments, is to prod and punish companies when their abuses of consumers becomes too extreme or, as a fallback, to directly regulate prices and conditions. Behavioural insights, however, take you to some very different solutions, and have helped identify how seemingly subtle changes in regulation can put the consumer back in the driving seat. In short, behavioural insights can help us understand how markets and societies work in a way that conventional economics has missed.

At the heart of this approach are measures that give consumers access to their own data in a more usable form. The idea is not so much that consumers will start analysing all these data themselves, though a few may do so. Rather, it is that access to these data enables switching sites and other intermediaries to act on consumers' behalf. This means helping people find better deals and prices; avoid foods that they are allergic to; improve their diets; and take more direct control over their own behaviour.

In their book *Nudge*, Richard Thaler and Cass Sunstein expressed a closely related idea in the acronym 'RECAP': Record, Evaluate, and Compare Alternative Prices. The basic idea was that companies should be required to give the prices and attributes of products in comparable, machine-readable form, so that consumers could make easier and more effective comparisons (see Chapter 3). In the USA, this approach was picked up under the more memorable phrase 'smart disclosure', with a push from Richard and Cass, and championed by the appointment of a director of Smart Disclosure in the US Treasury, Sophie Raseman.[1]

In the UK, we first had a go at pushing the approach to giving consumers access to data on a voluntary basis, since much of our work for the PM was about removing regulatory burdens on business, not adding new ones. Working with the business department, and with strong support from then Minister for Consumers, Ed Davey, we set up a special taskforce to progress the midata discussions.

We asked Sir Nigel Shadbolt – often described as the co-inventor of the world wide web – to head the taskforce discussions, bringing together businesses and consumer groups to create a common data architecture to enable consumers to get better access to the volumes of data held on them by businesses. Sir Nigel's right-hand man on the taskforce was BIT's Rory Gallagher, who then led BIT's work on consumer affairs and the day-to-day work on midata.

There were two major forms of data that we wanted to get moving more easily for consumers. First, we wanted to make it easier for people to be able to compare similar products, including their attributes and prices. For example, if you were trying to decide which mortgage supplier or credit card to switch to, you would want to rapidly compare not just the headline 'price' or interest rate, but also the penalties for late payments and early exit. This was the principal focus of the early RECAP idea. Second, we wanted to make it easier for people to get access to their own consumption data. This might include how much you use your phone and which features; how much electricity you use and when; or how often you end up using your overdraft.

The word we used to express this concept was 'midata'.[2] We hoped that at least some companies would voluntarily decide to facilitate better access for consumers to their own data, not least because of the extra functionality and services they could build around this. For example, if you were a credit card company you might re-envisage your role not just as a provider of credit, but as actively helping consumers with their consumption and spending choices. With better data flows, the card company could point out that you spend rather a lot on your energy and could save by switching; or that there was another supermarket that generally offered better prices and was just as close to home as your regular one.

After a year or so we concluded that in most sectors we were going to have to push a little harder to get the data into the hands of consumers. Most big companies weren't in a hurry to let their customers or rivals have their data – and certainly not if their customers might use it to get a better deal somewhere else. So we used a meeting with the PM, coinciding with one of Richard Thaler's visits, to make the case for stronger action.

Rohan Silva, who with Steve Hilton had championed the wider case for data transparency, was strongly supportive. The PM was uneasy about a blanket requirement for businesses to have to share consumers' data, but he was persuaded by the case for more modest moves in this direction. By happy coincidence, we bumped into the Chancellor after seeing the PM, and he too was open to the idea, not least because it looked as if it could fit well into a forthcoming Enterprise Bill.[3]

The midata clause was passed into law by the Enterprise Bill in 2013. It gave the Secretary of State for Business the power to require firms to allow their customers access to their own consumption data in 'machine-readable form'. This last phrase was critical. In many countries, the UK included, there is legislation in place to enable consumers to get, in written or 'legible' form, the data that firms (or public services) hold on them. For example, in the UK you could write to the supermarket giant Tesco and ask for the data they hold on you through your loyalty card. For £10, and after a reasonable delay, Tesco would send you a printout of this data. For most people this pile of paper will be of little use. Imagine instead that you could get access to this same data in machine-readable form, and much more quickly. If you had an allergy, you could feed this data into allergies.com, which could warn you to avoid the cookies you didn't notice had peanuts. Similarly saveonyourshopping.com might figure out which supermarket would be best for your particular habits; and carbon.com might advise you of the carbon footprint of your basket. In short, enabling consumers to access their data in machine-readable form could give them access to a host of 'choice engines' that make the comparisons that their busy lives, and limited cognitive capacities, make too difficult.

The midata clause did not immediately oblige all companies to comply. In technical terms, it was a piece of primary legislation that still required a Minister to secure secondary legislation if they wanted an industry or sector to comply. But this sword of Damocles had an almost immediate impact, encouraging at least some companies to comply before they were pushed.

Several of the big energy companies, despite growing public frustration about how their prices seemed to 'go up like a rocket and down like a feather', continued to drag their feet. Some moved to make consumers' data possible to download, but still rather difficult. As illustrated in Chapter 3, every extra friction can have a big impact. In the end, the PM's patience snapped. We introduced a requirement for the big companies to print the data as QR codes on bills, and drove for common application program interfaces (APIs) to enable consumers, with the help of switching sites, to compare and switch more easily. This also opens the door to enable consumers to opt for 'auto-switching', so that a site can check the market for the best tariff automatically when their contract ends and switch if a better deal is found.

The midata approach is a game-changer, with the potential to turn markets upside down. It makes it possible to move from a world of companies doing 'consumer management', to one in which consumers can do 'vendor management'. We have a long way to go, but midata is already starting to change the way markets work – and it is a change decisively driven by insights from behavioural science.

I'll have what she's having

Everyone remembers that famous scene in the movie *When Sally Met Harry*. Sitting in a diner, Sally fakes an orgasm to make a point, and to humiliate Harry in the process. Not being in on the joke, a fellow diner tells the waitress 'I'll have what she's having'.

As we saw in Chapter 5, human beings are very social creatures and are strongly influenced by what other people are doing. Sometimes disparagingly called the 'herd instinct', it's often a pretty rational, fast and effective heuristic to employ. Other people's experiences can be informative, and psychologically salient – that is, if we can find out about them.

Some markets have already been transformed by, and even built around, making it easier for consumers to find out about the experiences of other consumers. There's hardly a person in Europe or North America who has not used the feedback from other consumers built into sites such as eBay, TripAdvisor or Amazon. It is handy and clearly helps to attract traffic to the platforms that feature it, but does it change markets more fundamentally?

Michael Luca is a geek in the best possible sense. He's attracted to big data sets as others are drawn to ice cream or fine art. He's also an assistant professor at Harvard Business School. What really got us interested in him was a series of ingenious studies in which he picked apart how feedback between consumers in a real-world context changed how markets worked. Many claims are made as to why consumer feedback is important and how it might alter the behaviour of consumers, but very few good empirical studies have been undertaken.

In a detailed study of the restaurant feedback site yelp.com, Luca documented how a restaurant that got an extra star on customer satisfaction ratings would see its turnover increase by around 5–7 per cent in the following year. His particular ingenuity was to show how this rise in turnover was actually caused by the feedback, and not just that the feedback and increased turnover both simply reflected that the restaurant had got better.

He did this by a method known as a discontinuity design. Imagine a website that gives one- to five-star ratings for a restaurant. Beneath those star ratings is an exact average of all the feedback given, but the user doesn't see that – they just see the simple stars (or maybe half-stars). But imagine two restaurants, one that scores an average of 3.49, and another that gets 3.51. The first result gets rounded down to a three-star, but the second gets rounded up to a four-star, even though their underlying rating is all but identical. Luca used this hidden difference in the data to pick apart the true causal impact of the rating itself. He found that if you get a higher rating, your sales go up as a result.

Michael Luca's work illustrated how the ratings changed the nature of the market in more subtle ways. It showed how, as the coverage level of yelp.com increased in given areas, it disproportionately drove the growth of small, independent restaurants, whereas large chains were largely unaffected. In retrospect, we can see why. Imagine you are choosing a restaurant for lunch tomorrow. Chances are you have a good idea about the kind of food and service you will get in a familiar chain like Pizza Hut, but you know much less about the small independent pizza places around the corner. Is it worth taking a chance on one of the small independents? If you don't know anything much about them, maybe not. But if you could find out how others had found them – and that they liked it – you might try one of them out.

You don't have to be a behavioural economist to believe that having more information in markets is helpful. But the behavioural angle suggests why information about others' choices might be especially potent, and why the way it is gathered and presented will be very important:

▲ We are influenced by what others are doing.
▲ We are strongly inclined to reciprocate and to want to tell others about our experiences (while a classic view would assume that we'd just free-ride – reading the reviews of others but not bothering to share our own).

▲ We don't attend to multiple dimensions at once (we will attend to a simple star rating, but won't be very good at comparing lots of different types of information at once).

So where else could we seek to harness the goodwill and power of personal feedback? A good place to start is areas and sectors where large numbers of people have to make choices between providers; where the subjective quality of the service is important; and where it is currently difficult to get that information. Several sectors stood out to us as suitable for this approach – including large parts of the public sector.

Introducing transparent customer feedback to public sector 'markets'

When I was a young lecturer at Cambridge my department used to hand out feedback forms to students at the end of lecture courses. One of my older faculty colleagues kindly explained the forms to me. 'I try and have a quick glance through them, and you might want to do the same,' he suggested, 'you get the odd idea, but you won't get much from them.' After giving out the forms a couple of times, I soon saw what he meant.

The forms consisted of a series of two contrasting statements or descriptors with a long bar in between, with students encouraged to put a mark down to indicate their view of the lectures. For example, it might say 'reading lists were too short and inadequate' versus 'reading lists were too long and detailed', and students would mark the line somewhere in between, putting a mark about midpoint if they thought the reading list was about right.

So far, so good. But let's look at what *didn't* happen:

▲ The scales were not numerated, so it was difficult to turn the marks into averages or make quantitative comparisons (today, online slider scales can be easily quantified, but not so pencil and paper markings in the mid-nineties).

▲ Students weren't asked to give overall evaluative ratings, such as 'How satisfied were you with these lectures overall?'

▲ The information was not fed back to subsequent students, or even put into a form that enabled the faculty to compare the performance of lecturers internally.

Given that some of my lectures were on psychometrics and selection, I really felt we could do a bit better than this. So I got myself on the relevant committee and redesigned the forms. It wasn't complicated. I replaced the continuous lines with simple Likert scales (i.e. numbers from one to seven). The number of questions was reduced and simple overall evaluative questions were included. I also moved the questionnaires away from dual questions, such as where students were asked to choose between, say 'the lectures were very detailed' and 'the lectures gave a good overview' (i.e. two different dimensions in one question).

The impact of the new forms was dramatic on two counts. First, almost overnight far more students started filling them in. Second, they caused quite a stir among some of the lecturers. It was very easy with the new forms to work out scores for different lectures and lecturers, and the comparisons laid bare student dissatisfaction in a number of areas. This led to quite a few grumbles, but also to some discernible changes. Lecturers who had not updated their reading lists for many years suddenly did so. Quietly spoken lecturers started to speak up, or use a microphone. But there were still limitations. The committee was not, for example, in a hurry to publish the ratings.

Across sectors, professionals are generally uneasy about the publication of satisfaction ratings, and often performance ratings in general. The fact that students couldn't get access to the satisfaction ratings of their lecturers was not limited to my then faculty, or even my university. Across the UK, and indeed throughout the world, there were universities (such as Harvard) that collected detailed student satisfaction data, but in the vast majority of cases this information was kept private, at best to be used by lecturers to quietly refine and improve their courses. There were sometimes legitimate reasons for keeping the data out of the public domain. For example, in some American universities with continual assessment courses, there was concern that students might pressure lecturers to give more generous marks in exchange for higher satisfaction scores. Similarly, some worried that challenging courses would get panned, while simplistic ones would score well.

With the support of the Universities Minister, David Willetts, and his Special Adviser, Nick Hillman, in 2010–11 we pushed for all British universities to ask comparable questions on student satisfaction – and to publish them. There were two routes in. One was to get all universities to ask similar questions on their internal feedback questionnaires. This had the advantage of generating substantial amounts of data down to the level of individual modules and lecturers. But it was also likely to be subject to gaming, and potentially some of the issues that had been raised in the US system. Fortunately, we had another way of gathering the data, too, in the form of a national survey of students immediately after they graduated, called the First Destination Survey. This survey had been designed years ago, with its roots in the age of manpower planning, to find out what students from different courses had gone on to do, and whether or not they were employed. I never thought it was a great tool for its intended purpose: it was conducted six months after students graduated, so would often catch talented students having a year out and was too soon to find out where many would ultimately end up in the labour market. Yet for measuring student satisfaction with their course it was an ideal vehicle.

Today, any prospective student can, in seconds, rank universities and courses across the UK by student satisfaction. For most applicants this won't be the most important factor in their choice – they will still be predominantly interested in the subject, course content and grade requirements. But it will be a factor for some, and will certainly help to decide tie breaks.

In other sectors, however, the impact on your choices and behaviour as a result of the recommendations and subjective experiences of others could be far more important. Imagine you are trying to choose a care home for your mother. Would it be 'marginal' to you to learn that residents and their relatives in Home A warmly recommend it, while those in Home B would not? Similarly, if you had a choice of maternity hospitals or GPs close to where you lived, would it matter to you that one was recommended by previous patients and another was not?

In the public service reforms of the Blair administration we had pushed for recording and publication of patient satisfaction data, but it was not a battle we made much much progress with. Armed with the evidence from behavioural science, and Michael Luca's work in particular, it was a battle that could be revisited in the 2010 administration.

In early 2013, the commitment was finally made across a wide variety of clinical settings that patients would be asked a simple question: 'How likely are you to recommend our service to friends and family if they needed similar care or treatment?' Answers were recorded on a simple six-point scale. By late 2014, more than five million had given such feedback on the NHS. Similarly, around 1.4 million patients of GPs are now surveyed twice a year and asked 'Would you recommend your GP surgery to someone who had just moved to the area?' along with other more detailed questions about their experiences.

If you are moving to a new town and have a choice of local doctors, satisfaction ratings of existing patients won't be the only factor influencing your choice, but once made accessible it will influence the choices of at least some people. Let's suppose I'm a new student in Cambridge, looking for a GP to register with. I can now type my postcode into the NHS Choices website for GPs – as an example, I've just typed in the postcode where I lived out of college as an undergraduate (see Figure 27). I then click on patient experience to see how existing patients rate the service they get.

The site ranks practices by distance from the location I've put in by default, which is helpful. It turns out there are 22 GP practices within two miles of my old lodgings. The nearest, less than a third of a mile away, has an overall patient satisfaction of 88 per cent, which sounds

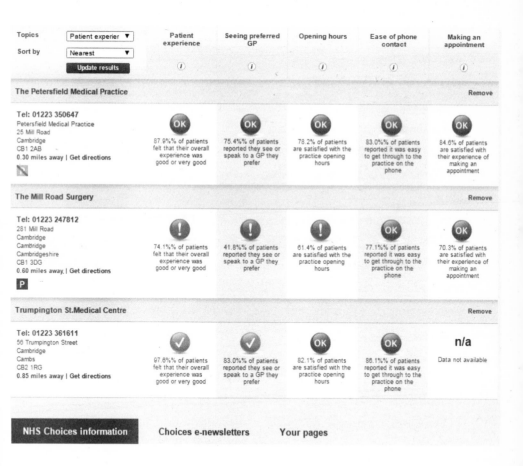

Figure 27. Patient experience data of a selection of GP practices within a mile of my old house in Cambridge (courtesy of NHS choices, March 2015).

pretty good, and is marked with an 'OK' symbol. It scores similarly respectably on a range of other factors such as whether patients get to see their GP of choice, the satisfaction with opening hours and ease of making an appointment.

Scrolling down, around 0.6 miles away there's a practice on the main road close to the shops and has parking. But its patient satisfaction scores seem to be quite a bit worse, with several of them marked with a red exclamation mark. Its overall patient satisfaction score is 74 per cent (versus 88 per cent for the closer practice) and less than 42 per cent say that they get to see the GP they prefer (versus 75 per cent).

Scrolling further down, I see there's a practice that has got a big green tick against its overall patient satisfaction rating. At this practice, 98 per cent of patients 'felt that their overall experience was good or very good'. It also does better on other ratings too, such as 83 per cent of patients reporting that they get to see the GP they prefer (compared with 75 and 42 per cent at the other two practices respectively). This practice is only 0.85 miles away, and it's in the direction of the university lecture theatres. Which would you choose?[4]

Separate regression analysis shows that a key driver of patient satisfaction in clinical settings is that you felt treated with respect and dignity. Some argue that what should really matter in clinical settings are clinical outcomes, such as survival rates, and that as such patient satisfaction ratings cause services to dwell on more superficial issues (such as doctors taking time to talk to patients and their relatives). But clinical outcomes can also be reviewed. For some patients the most important criterion is the proximity of the surgery, not clinical outcomes or satisfaction.

Satisfaction ratings, alongside other measures, drive improvements in services in two ways. First, some patients will use the ratings to help choose where to go, thereby driving faster growth among those facilities with better scores. Second, and probably more important overall, is that the ratings change the behaviour of staff and management in the facilities directly. NHS facilities are expected not only to ask the 'Friends and Family' question, but to display the results in the ward or facility they relate to. This creates direct feedback to staff and, as I noted in Cambridge as a lecturer more than a decade ago, it leads those who score poorly to think about what they could do differently to improve their scores. Indeed, several companies now offer to gather the 'Friends and Family' test questions for free, on the basis that when hospitals and practices get the data back they tend to want to know more about why some patients are unsatisfied and what they can do about it.

Nudging me, nudging you

Car thefts in Britain have fallen by more than 80 per cent since 1995.[5] Other forms of crime have fallen, too, but the fall in vehicle-related thefts is particularly spectacular. One key reason for this is simple: cars are much harder to steal than they used to be. It is certainly not that people are better at locking them – if anything, the data indicate that we are much more lax about locking our cars nowadays. The manufacturers have done the heavy lifting by adding immobilisers and other devices that have made cars much harder to steal.

But why did manufacturers make the change? In the UK, and a number of other countries, a major push came from the publication of data showing the relative theft rates of different cars. As behavioural scientists have shown, privacy and security are things most people don't consider until prompted.[6] Many consumers were shocked to learn just how easy it was to steal a car, and the publication of relative theft rates meant that this became a salient factor in their decision about which car to buy, and how much they cost to insure. The publication of that data nudged consumers, through their marginal choices, to nudge manufacturers to do better.

The reduction in car theft has helped to reduce other crimes, too. Car theft, and joyriding in particular, had become what criminologists call a 'gateway crime'. It was a fun sort of crime that you could try out when you were 14, with a couple of your mates, and for many young adults it became a stepping stone to more serious forms of crime.

This is an example of a particularly powerful form of nudging: nudging consumers in order to nudge manufacturers or producers. Its particular elegance is that it doesn't need very many consumers to change their behaviour (or manufacturers to think that consumers *will* change their behaviour) to be effective. At the same time, if manufacturers do respond, it means that for many consumers their behaviour doesn't have to change at all – they buy a car just as before, but the new model is harder to steal.

It is precisely this sort of 'double nudge' that is likely to deliver changes around some of the greatest social challenges we face. This includes solutions to what are sometimes called 'wicked problems' – deep and chronic policy challenges, such as obesity and climate change. Indeed, until recently, crime was considered one of these unsurmountable 'wicked problems', too. It is now at its lowest level since reliable measures started over 30 years ago.

Obesity

Consider obesity. It has been rising inexorably across the OECD nations for decades. Worldwide, obesity rates have roughly doubled since 1980, with around 200 million men and 300 million women now obese. In the USA, around a third of adults are now obese, a figure projected by some as likely to include half the population by 2030. It is also unevenly distributed, with higher rates among low-income groups, and among certain ethnic minority groups, such as African American and Hispanic women.[7] There are high-income countries with lower rates, such as France, but their trajectory is much the same as fatter nations such as the USA, the UK and Germany, albeit with a 20-year lag.

Behaviour change is often cited as the way forward, but the success of individual level behaviour change programmes are patchy at best, as any serial dieter will tell you. At the core of the problem is that much eating is 'mindless', as Brian Wansink, probably the world's leading expert on eating behaviour, puts it. Wansink's experiments have shown that people use a variety of external cues to decide how much to eat, and are generally surprisingly inattentive as to the actual amount of food consumed. In one of his most famous experiments, subjects were given a bowl of soup and allowed to eat as much as they wanted, unaware that in the experimental condition the bowl was secretly refilled from the base. Sure enough, these subjects ate far more than those whose bowls did not automatically refill. Similarly, subjects have been found to eat more if served on large plates, if the serving container is larger or even if the serving utensil is larger.

Introduce a distraction and we are truly lost. Think when you last bought some crisps or biscuits to eat while watching TV – the chances are you ate them all. If you put two biscuits on a plate, then you ate two biscuits; but if you brought the whole packet in, you ate the lot.

The power of mindless eating is illustrated by how poor people are at keeping track of what they eat. Subjects consistently underestimate how much they eat, even when asked to keep a detailed diary. As if in a fugue state, we magically forget the mid-afternoon snacks and the treats we ate while watching our latest box set on TV. But there is hope: we can nudge the nudgers to nudge us back – a 'triple nudge' (maybe we should call it a nudge sandwich).

Do you add up the calories, or salt and added sugar, in your shopping basket? I don't, and not many other people do. But what would happen if the supermarket did it for us? If your till or online shopping receipt told you how much fat, salt and added sugar there was in your basket, and how it compared to that of an average healthy shopper, might it change your choices? The evidence is that it would, particularly if you then said 'yes' when asked, 'Would you like us to prompt you for healthier choices?'

Retailers and producers, just like the car manufacturers, will soon respond to such choices. If consumers start to shift to slightly healthier or smaller desserts, retailers will start to offer more of them and reduce the unhealthier versions. As consumers, we in turn will find ourselves confronted with healthier choices as producers reformulate. Many consumers will hardly notice the change at all. We'll still be buying pizza and dessert, but these products will gradually become healthier, with less salt, less added sugar, and perhaps portions that are a little smaller.

The question then becomes, what is the initiating nudge that triggers this cycle? It is here that governments, consumer groups, or even enlightened businesses come in. At the start of the chapter we read about the midata and smart disclosure initiatives, nudges that are initiating such a cycle – the lighting of a fuse. Twinned with the rise of online shopping, consumers will soon be better informed than they have ever been. Importantly, this will be personalised, easy and can occur at the moment of purchasing (see Chapter 6).

In the offline world, improved labelling can also make a significant difference. Traffic lights and other visual heuristics are significantly more impactful than conventional calorific information expressed as numbers, and ongoing lab work by BIT and others has identified ways of significantly improving their impact still further. For example, a four-light traffic-light system leads to significantly lower calorific choices than a three-light system, and adding a human figure also improves impact. For most people, these more effective labels won't lead them to abandon ice cream for a bag of carrots, but they will nudge a significant number of consumers to shift to a slightly healthier diet within product-class choice – swapping the ice cream for frozen yogurt or a low-fat version. These changes will, in turn, drive product reformulation.

This isn't science fiction – it is already happening. There is evidence in both the USA and UK that, for the first time in a generation, child obesity levels have stopped rising, and are even starting to reverse, at least in the youngest age groups. In the USA, with a prod from the First Lady, a number of big retailers have moved to make healthy foods more available, especially in poor neighbourhoods; calorie labelling is spreading, including in fast food outlets; and suppliers have been expanding their low sugar products. Modest shifts in consumer patterns, such as away from sugary drinks, are being reinforced by product reformulation to reduce sugar, and these in turn are making it easier for consumers to eat more healthily, even when they are not thinking about it.

Personal theft: mobile phones

Returning to the example of crime, in 2014 BIT and the Metropolitan Police published a mobile phone 'theft index'. Against a general background of 20 years of falls in most types of crime, mobile phone theft has been one of few crimes to have risen. In the UK alone, around three-quarters of a million people per annum report a stolen phone. Just like car theft a generation ago, there are marked differences in the rate at which different mobiles are stolen, reflecting both their relative value and the ease with which their security can be cracked. Thieves know about these differences, and so do the police and manufacturers. The only people who didn't know were the consumers who actually bought them.

Once again, the basic idea was simple: analyse the theft data relative to market share and publish it in a simple-to-understand format to help inform consumers. As we sought to develop a measure, a number of mobile phone manufacturers were not happy at this prospect and, just like car manufacturers a generation earlier, lobbied hard for the data to remain unpublished. They argued, with some justification, that the data was far from perfect. Sometimes, for example, thieves would snatch a handbag unaware of which phone they were stealing. However, we were able to separate out thefts where the phone was visible from when it was not, clearly demonstrating that thieves were strongly favouring the theft of some phones over others. Similarly, some manufacturers argued that the numbers partly reflected the value and attractiveness of different phone types. This, of course, was true, but that didn't diminish the finding that value affects the theft rate. For these reasons, it took a while to get the data published, but with the backing of the Home Secretary, it did finally happen (see Figure 28).

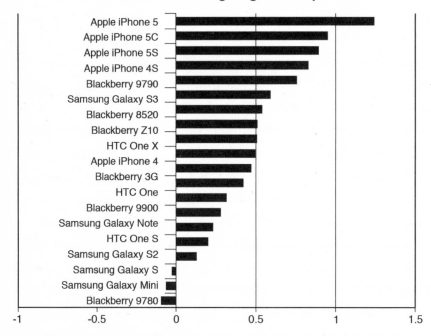

Estimated excess targeting of smartphones

Figure 28. The relative theft rate, or targeting, of different brands of smartphones relative to the average theft of mobiles in the UK in 2013–14. A value of 0.5 implies that the mobile is 50 per cent more likely to be stolen than an average mobile.

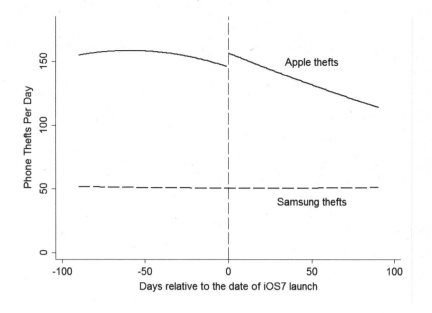

Figure 29. Thefts of Apple iPhones, relative to Samsungs, over the 100 days before and after the launch of iOS 7.

We knew two important things. First, that consumers don't think much about security unless prompted to do so. The headlines in response to the publication of these data will have changed this at least somewhat, increasing awareness of the risk of theft in the minds of some consumers (and the concern of one manufacturer in particular was testament to this). If you were buying a mobile for your 12-year-old, might it influence your choice between two rival models once you discover that one was twice as likely to be stolen?

Second, and importantly, we were able to show that innovations by manufacturers to make a mobile more secure have a demonstrable impact on the chances that it will be stolen. It seems that thieves figure out pretty fast whether a new model is hard to 'crack', and choose softer targets instead – or, in some cases, give up completely (cf. the reduction in motorbike thefts in the wake of laws requiring motorbike helmets to be worn, in Chapter 3). This effect can be seen, for example, when Apple introduced the more secure iOS 7, with a marked fall in the theft rate in the period following the launch in 2013 (after a brief surge immediately after the launch, see Figure 29). Thieves figured out that it was harder to crack.

Publishing the data in a simple and accessible form reinforces this trend. The data provide a nudge to consumers to choose, or pay more for, more secure models that are less likely to be stolen, and will make their personal data more secure if it does get stolen (nudge 1). The shift in purchasing by consumers provides a nudge to manufactures to make their products more secure (nudge 2). The retailers and manufacturers then highlight these more secure features, and encourage consumers to adopt more secure practices themselves (nudge 3).[8]

Just as for car and other crimes, this triple nudge is likely to have a wider impact on crime more generally. Having more secure mobiles, and less theft of them, cuts off a gateway to other crimes, such as identity theft, and also shrinks a route into crime for potential offenders. As our mobiles move from being just phones to our wallets and our identities, this is especially important. It is a nudge not only to reduce crime, but to create a safe platform for our economy and evolving society.

Information you can understand

The modern world is full of information: data made transparent for consumer and citizen benefit. Food labels are ever more widespread. Car adverts and showrooms have information about performance and economy in standard formats. Financial products, like mortgages and credit cards, are required to display the costs and charges in comparable forms.

Often regulators and governments have required this information to be made available as part of a deal with industry: a sensible seeming compromise between doing nothing, thereby failing to protect consumers, and direct regulation of prices or products, a potential burden on industry and deadening hand on innovation. But often too little attention has been paid to the exact form in which information is presented. This 'detail' can make all the difference between transparency that informs consumers and transforms markets, versus one that has no effect or even confuses consumers more.

One example of what *not* to do can be seen in the area of financial products. In many countries, regulators and industry have converged, insisting that products come with extensive 'warnings'. These range from the wording on advertisements that say 'market values may go up or down', to thick pages of caveats and warnings about the risks attached to mortgages and other financial products. Yet many consumers have been found to interpret such warnings or caveats as implying that the products must be *safer* because the financial regulator has somehow 'checked them out'.

Complexity is a particular enemy to effective consumer action. Standard annual percentage rates (APRs) were introduced to help consumers compare financial products, and their display is mandated by the European Union. However, add in initial interest rates, and fees, and consumers struggle to make any sense of it. In a recent study by the organisation Which?, less than half of consumers were able to identify the cheapest of five five-year mortgage deals given these three pieces of information. Removing the mandated APR figure and replacing it with one that showed the total cost of the mortgage for the first two years, and the proportion of those able to identify the cheapest rate rose from 48 to 70 per cent. The proportion able to rank all five correctly rose from 3 to 36 per cent.[9]

In contrast to complex financial information and statutory consumer warnings, simple star-rating systems have been found to have significant impacts on consumer choices and on producers, as illustrated by Michael Luca's work on restaurants. Similarly, simple star ratings for car safety, such as those showing that many early SUVs performed poorly relative to other types of cars, led to clear shifts in consumer purchasing, and to rapid adaptions and improvements by manufacturers. Such NCAPs (New Car Assessment Programmes) have behind them a series of separate tests, but the headline result that really influences consumers is published as a simple overall star rating, with a maximum of five stars being awarded.

The way the information is displayed matters, too. Food labels that are printed in green (as they are for many US products) will tend to give the impression of healthiness, regardless of the actual levels of sugar, fat and salt contained. Posters and leaflets in restaurants with calorie information, often favoured by fast food outlets, are arguably less deceptive, but on the other hand they are almost never looked at. A field study by Christine Roberto of the Harvard School of Public Health found that less than two in a thousand customers actually looked at the posters, counted as looking at them for three seconds or more, or picked up one of the leaflets. In general, such information has a much bigger impact on consumers if it is presented in a simple and intuitive visual heuristic, such as coloured traffic lights over the relevant numbers (where red means unhealthy), or a simple star rating.[10]

For complex or mathematical information, presenting it in a form that humans – rather than econs – can understand can be a difficult challenge, even if the ultimate results look like 'common sense'. Gerd Gigerenzer and his colleagues, for example, have spent a lot of time and effort seeking alternative ways to present probabilities – seemingly simple numbers that both professionals and the general public often misunderstand. They were able to demonstrate that, by presenting the same information in the form of 'natural frequencies' instead of probabilities, experts and non-experts were much more likely to understand it. Natural frequencies – such as a visual depiction of how many people who have been screened for a cancer will actually develop the disease, and the number who will be helped by a clinical intervention – seem to be much better suited to the way that most people think about the world. Using this approach, they were able to increase the number of clinicians correctly interpreting risk and screening data for breast cancer from 10 to 46 per cent.[11]

This basic effect was observed in Chapter 3 where we noted BIT trials that showed that consumers would buy more expensive but better value appliances when the label clearly showed the lifetime running costs. For the majority of people the most expensive thing they ever buy is not an appliance, or even a car, but their home. With this in mind, one of the early interventions of BIT was to refashion the UK's recently introduced Energy Performance Certificate (EPC). Following the principles above, the EPC was radically simplified, and potential purchasers were instead shown on the first page the estimated costs of running the home for three years (along with actions that could be taken to improve the home's energy efficiency).

A recent analysis of more than 300,000 transactions concluded that the new EPC ratings have had a significant impact on house prices. Compared with similar dwellings rated EPC G, those rated a more efficient F or E sold for approximately 6 per cent more, those rated D sold for 8 per cent more, those rated C for 10 per cent more and those rated A or B sold for 14 per cent more. The authors estimated that moving an average UK home from a G to E, or from D to B, implied adding more than £16,000 to the sale price of the property.[12] This is strong evidence for the new EPCs working – the transparency of the information has not only helped many house buyers decide whether it is cost-effective to insulate their homes, it has fed through to house prices, too. The transparency of the information has subtly changed the market, and might even edge us towards saving the planet.

Shaping better nudges, with better data

We have seen how behavioural science can shape how, and when, data is presented to create an especially powerful class of nudging – what we might call 'behaviourally shaped informing'. But the relationship is two-way. Data science is also shaping and enhancing the power of nudges. We will explore more about this in Chapter 10, but let us have a glimpse into this world.

Many businesses, and occasionally governments, have dabbled in the art of segmentation. Advertising agencies and political pundits often classify people into different groups, sometimes adding an evocative name to catch the segment, such as 'soccer mums' (argued to be a key segment in the Clinton campaign); 'Generation X'; or the 'aspirant working class'. These segments are often based on underlying data that splits the population up by socio-economic group, age or attitudes in an attempt to identify key population segments that might be subject to a more tailored campaign or promotion. With the help of ethnographers and marketers, products and services could be developed especially for these segments. Clients would pay handsomely for this impressive-sounding advice. 'This branding has been adapted to appeal to the Generation X male' is just the sort of line a sharp CEO might be expecting to hear.

But there is a problem with many impressive-sounding segmentations: they don't predict much. Often they are developed by a creative, focus-group exercise rather than by hard analysis of the data. Segments can sound plausible and convincing – what is called surface validity – yet have more in common with a horoscope than a serious predictive model. Even if they are based on real data, such as socio-economic profiles and clusters of attitudes from survey data, this doesn't mean that they differentially predict what those people will do when faced with a real product choice, or whether they pay their tax on time. It was precisely this low predictive validity – that attitudinal clusters were generally rather poor predictors of behaviour – that led many psychologists to lose interest in the study of personality types in the 1970s. In contrast, it was found that behaviour predicts behaviour. In other words, a person who was regularly late last week will probably be late next week, regardless of what paper they read, the party they vote for, or the flavour tea they say they like.

This means that the most valuable data is often behavioural: it's not what the person says, but what they do. For example, many millions of dollars have been spent on plausible segmentations of American adults by US political campaign teams to identify who is most likely to vote for, or donate to, them. But often the most powerfully predictive data is incidental behaviour, such as whether the person opens the email, clicks on a link, or how fast they respond. Similarly, a pretty good start for figuring out if they will vote for you, or give you money, is their past behaviour – if they've done it before.

Armed with this knowledge, it is possible to build behaviourally based segmentations: that is, based on behaviour rather than attitudes or standard socio-economic variables. Moreover, in a world rich in data, it is then possible to see how these behaviourally based segments respond to different messages or nudges.

Let's put some flesh on this. In Chapter 5 we saw how certain messages, based on how we are influenced by the behaviour of others (social), boosted the payment of tax. In short, pointing out to late taxpayers that 'most people paid their tax on time' and you are one of the 'small minority yet to do so' led to around a 15 per cent (or just over 5 percentage point) increase in the number who paid up without further prompting. This nudge was found to be effective across many traditional population segments. It was slightly more effective among men (who tended to be more likely to be late payers), and slightly less effective among those who had been late payers in previous years, though it still had a highly significant impact (see Chapter 6 for further discussion). Still, it turned out that there was one particular group for whom this generally very effective message not only did not work, it actually backfired. Furthermore, this happened to be an especially important group to the Revenue

Service: those who owed a large amount of tax. Among the top 5 per cent of debtors, using this nudge led to a *fall* in payment rates of around 25 per cent (from 42.4 to 31.9 per cent paying without a further prompting), and among the top 1 per cent of debtors it led to an even greater drop of 35 per cent (from 39.3 to 25.7 per cent paying without further prompting).

Fortunately, we were able to use systematic testing to identify other messages and nudges that did work in this rather important population segment. It turns out that highlighting the fact that not paying tax means we all lose out on vital public services like the NHS, roads, and schools' was highly effective with this group, though it was much less effective than the social norm nudge for the majority of the population. Working with HMRC, we found that this public service plea, framed in terms of loss (i.e. 'not paying' means that ...) led to an increased payment rate of 8 per cent in the top 5 per cent of debtors, and an enormous 43 per cent increase in payments among the top 1 per cent of debtors (from 39.3 to 56.3 per cent paying without further prompting). In other words, for the top 1 per cent of debtors, who typically owed more than £30,000, changing one line of their reminder letter from one that used social norms to one that referred to the loss in public services led to more than a doubling of payment rates without further prompting.

In retrospect, it's not difficult to tell a story that makes sense of this remarkable result. If you are in the top 1 per cent of debtors, and probably pretty rich, perhaps it doesn't mean much to you that most people pay their tax on time – you think you are special, and in terms of tax debt you are! At the same time, when you owe more than the average salary of a teacher or nurse, it is literally true that your not paying it has real consequences for public services. But this finding was far from obvious *before* the results came in. It was only possible to refine and tailor the messages in this way on the basis of randomised control trials (RCTs) across tens of thousands, and sometimes hundreds of thousands of people, and by carefully mapping the behavioural responses on to the different characteristics, or segments, across the population.

Such tailored nudging is only possible in the context of large amounts of data, and a system able to gather and analyse it. It is an approach that is becoming an integral part of the digitally enabled commercial world. Some governments are also starting to develop such tailored approaches, too, though very often the ICT systems of the public sector are not yet 'smart' or data-rich enough to go there. Indeed, in some public services and countries, statutory barriers exist to prevent such tailored approaches almost entirely.

We shall return to the ethical issues raised by such data-shaped behavioural nudges in Chapter 11. But regardless of whether you think these are frightening, or a wonderful development of personalised services, you should be in no doubt about one thing: using 'big' and behavioural data to tailor and shape nudges is potentially very powerful. That's why it is so important to make sure that power is in the right place, which to me means in the hands of citizens or consumers themselves.

Conclusion: data transparency plus behavioural science can reshape markets, and often do a better job of it than conventional regulation

The use of data to inform consumer choices is a long-standing policy tool. It is, in some sense, the most basic 'nudge' of all – informing people without constraining or mandating their options. Behavioural insights have given it a further push from three directions.

First, behavioural studies have shown that much of the information put out by commercial players, and sometimes regulators, is deeply confusing to consumers. For this reason it has become a key battleground for consumer groups, and one that has pulled some governments into the world of behavioural science whether they wanted to go there or not.

Second, there is a growing recognition that how and what information is presented is key to its impact. Better information – presented in a timely and human-friendly form – can have dramatic impacts. Such interventions can trigger 'double' or 'triple nudges', prompting manufacturers and producers to change what they do, and in turn to prompt further consumer change. Interestingly, some of the most useful and powerful information is that of the experiences of our fellow citizens in areas, from healthcare to consumer durables. In this new world, switching sites and new forms of 'choice engines' become critical.

Third, we have seen how the use of big data, combined with large-scale experimental methods, can in turn shape nudges – by both governments and businesses – to be much more personalised and powerful.

Big data, mixed with behavioural insights, is a potent force. With consumers and citizens in control, it can open the door to personalised services and products that we have only begun to glimpse. But in the hands of unscrupulous business or corrupt government, it can lead to consumer detriment and manipulation. This is why smart disclosure is so important. For regulators, governments and good businesses smart disclosure can be a route to higher productivity and quality, lower regulatory burdens, and markets that serve citizens and consumers better.

As it happens, my older son has just applied to university. One of the criteria he used to narrow his choices was student satisfaction. Rightly or wrongly – rightly, I would say – it certainty swayed his choice. It wouldn't have occurred to him that a decade ago he wouldn't have been able to get this information at all.

CHAPTER 8

▲

A DIFFERENT APPROACH
TO BIG POLICY CHALLENGES

Behind the shiny black door of No. 10, and no doubt the grand columns of the White House, crises flow like casualties in a hospital A&E department. Some days it's relatively quiet. On others, they seem to flood through the door and the emails cascade. These crises can range from a report on a failed care home to an international incident. Often they are triggered by the media reports of the day – the single biggest block of desks and people in No. 10 is not the Policy Unit, tucked away on the second floor, but the sprawling Press Office on the ground floor. Issues also regularly arise from the wrangles between departments, or between the political elements and ideas that make up a government, whether a formal coalition or not.

Despite the much discussed influence of the 24-hour media cycle, many of the decisions facing a Prime Minister, and the major departments of state, reflect deep-seated challenges. Endless documents, slide packs and notes fly back and forth around Whitehall, filling Ministerial red boxes to overflowing at the end of most weeks.[1] Though the popular perception of politicians is that they are self-interested and even lazy, the reality is that most Ministers in government face punishing workloads.[2] While most civil servants go home on Friday nights, Ministers face a weekend of papers and submissions to work through. Their offices and departments will be waiting on Monday morning for the 'box returns' – the scribbled views and answers on all the policy choices and options they were given to work through over the weekend. For Prime Ministers, it is even more intense. The famous red box sits on the desk of the PM's Principal Private Secretary just outside the PM's study in No. 10, filling up every day with notes from the private office staff and key political advisers.

In a combination of scribbles in the margins, and headline bullets on the face of the note with their distinctive initials underneath, Prime Ministers can give a steer on the options presented, and these lines echoed through the system. On other occasions we and other staff would meet the PM in person, either huddled around on the miscellaneous set of chairs that always seem to accrue in the Prime Minister's curiously modest study (the famous site of 'sofa government') or, if other Ministers and departments were involved, in the Cabinet room next door with its famous coffin table and rich sense of history. Most of all, there were the endless meetings with colleagues in and around No. 10: in and out through the link door to the Cabinet Secretary's grand room (much grander than the PM's study), in my own tiny room in No. 10, and – most frequently, in the corridors, the lobby of No.10, and Whitehall itself.

In such a world, there's often not the time, nor the patience, for the answer to be 'more research needed', let alone a randomised control trial – though perhaps there should be. Some of the decisions relate to communications, but most do not. Do you want to legislate? This is the issue, and these are the options. Minister A thinks X, the Chancellor thinks Y, we think Z – do you agree with our line? It is these sorts of questions, bolted at the end of an endless stream of notes, that fill a Prime Minister's box and much of their lives.

If the work of the Behavioural Insights Team, and sister units like it across the world, was to have an impact it needed to have something to say and to add to this flurry of notes and decisions. Such policy advice was always central to our work. The deeper test of BIT was never just about a few clever tweaks in letters to encourage people to pay their tax on time, important though that may be. Rather, it was about bringing a more sophisticated and realistic account of how real people live, behave and make decisions, and the implications of this for policy. If the Nudge Unit was to survive in the vortex of No. 10, it had to offer advice and solutions to the PM and other Ministers that was distinctive, and value adding, from all the other advice that poured in through the myriad meetings and river of paper that flows across Whitehall and into the PM's red box.

The curious case of electronic cigarettes

Rory Sutherland is a larger than life character. He's one of those people who positively embraces eccentricity and, with a twinkle in his eye, seeks to push a story or an idea to the point where you're not really sure if he's serious. In organisational psychology, he's what is sometimes called a 'plant' – a person you deliberately keep around to produce crazy ideas. Many of these ideas might be completely unworkable, but occasionally one of them will turn out to be brilliant, or at least the spark of something that could be made brilliant. You can see why the advertising industry, where he's based, wants to keep him around. On the other hand, you might have to listen to quite a bit of nuttiness.

As it turns out, I went to college with Rory, though I hadn't seen him for many years until we started BIT. He dropped by to see us very early on, when we were still at Admiralty Arch, the grand building that looks towards Buckingham Palace. The craziness of Her Majesty's Government having a Nudge Unit was just his sort of thing, and he was clearly delighted we'd mysteriously appeared in the usual grey of government. I remember peering at him trying to work out why he was so familiar, and whether he was actually nuts, before I remembered our distant days at Christ's College, Cambridge. I hadn't known him very well. He was arty and posh, and I was a natural scientist and not very posh. Occasional trips to a dusty library versus 30 hours in the lab. Different worlds.

At some point Rory produced an 'e-cigarette'. Back in 2010, these were still very rare. I think he'd got his on a recent trip to Japan. Almost as an aside, he waved his e-cig and proclaimed that maybe these were a good thing.

Whatever else he had to say, I thought Rory might be right about e-cigs. In general, it is much easier to break a habit, or shift a behaviour, by introducing a substitute behaviour rather than simply extinguishing it, as generations of lab-based psychologists had discovered (see also Chapter 6). This is especially true for addictive or compulsive behaviours. Rather than just trying to quit, you're generally better off identifying the 'trigger' then introducing a new and paired behaviour to be associated with it, effectively swapping one habit for another less harmful one. Provided e-cigarettes were actually safer – an important 'if' – they seemed much more likely to work as an effective substitute given their similar feel, movements, and perhaps even physiological effect to a cigarette.

With this in mind the team started digging deeper. There weren't many studies, but early lab work did seem to show that at least the better brands of e-cigarettes were effective enough to eliminate smokers' cravings over a two-week trial. It turned out that they had some curious advocates, too. John Britton, a passionate and leading medical expert on smoking, as tough an evidence-based expert as one can find, assured us that across the world there had at that time been only a single death that had been arguably linked to an e-cig – and that was a home-made device used by a man who had already

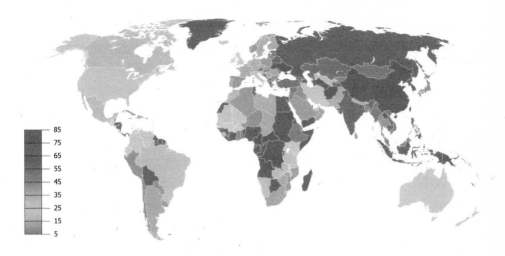

Figure 30. Prevalence rates of smoking (male) across the world. In Anglo-Saxon countries, more than 10 per cent of all years of healthy life lost are as a result of smoking – and smoking rates are much higher and rising elsewhere.

been a heavy smoker for many years. Perhaps more surprisingly, it became clear – over coffee at No. 10 – that even the UK's anti-smoking group ASH was leaning in favour of e-cigs.

However, not everyone agreed. The public health sector, or at least those that had come across e-cigs, were far more uneasy. Many there had long memories of the battles with tobacco companies. People still remembered the long disputes with, and denials of, tobacco companies about the dangers of smoking. Scepticism was further fuelled by historic hollow claims about the effectiveness of filters and the development of 'low tar' and 'lite' cigarettes. Even in 2010, many governments had already banned (or were starting to ban) these new e-cigs as yet another trick of the tobacco industry.

It wasn't a clear call. Policy decisions are often like this. Prime Ministers and Ministers, with the aid of their advisers, often have to make decisions in the face of incomplete evidence. We looked hard at the evidence and made a call: we minuted the PM and urged that the UK should move against banning e-cigs. Indeed, we went further. We argued that we should deliberately seek to make e-cigs widely available, and to use regulation not to ban them but to improve their quality and reliability.

As it happens, the first publication of the young Nudge Unit was to be on health behaviour, to be published in New Year 2011 – Steve Hilton was rather taken with the idea that the document itself could harness the public's own New Year's resolutions to live more healthily. The publication included a section on the case for e-cigs, but in the last-minute negotiations over the text that characterise policy development and publication in Whitehall, the Department of Health insisted we take the section out. We agreed on the basis that the issue would be picked up in their own harm-reduction strategy for smoking.

The battle really begins

We reasoned that while nicotine was addictive, the evidence indicated that the biggest danger from smoking came from the carcinogens in smoke. Of course it would be better if you could get people off nicotine, too: nicotine is thought, for example, to prime addictions to other drugs, such as cocaine. On the face of it, e-cigs could reduce smokers' exposure to harmful carcinogens, and could act as a plausible substitute to help them quit smoking altogether.

However, even if we went down this route we would still need to make sure that these products were as safe as possible. They were appearing on street corners shipped in from the other side of the world. How could smokers know what was in them, not least if there was enough nicotine to make them effective. After all, if smokers endeavouring to quit tried them, and then went back to smoking because they didn't get rid of the cravings, then that was potentially worse than not trying to quit at all. At the same time, what was to stop them being sold as the latest craze to 11-year-olds?

We deliberated whether we could regulate e-cigs like foodstuffs or electronics, but eventually concluded that our best route might be a 'light-touch' medical route to regulation. The inverted commas are appropriate here because, as anyone who deals with regulation will know, 'light touch' is not necessarily the default instinct of regulators. Nonetheless, we asked the body that regulated medicines in the UK, the Medicines and Healthcare Products Regulatory Authority (MHRA), to develop as light a touch regulation as they could – just enough to make sure that e-cigs didn't have other toxins, and that they had enough nicotine in them to be effective. Their head was very helpful, and I felt greatly encouraged that we could get it right. The MHRA were confident they could do it, keeping the regulatory costs low and still making sure they'd be widely available through supermarkets and garages, not just pharmacies (rather like nicotine patches). This was in 2010–11.

Here's the thing about life in the centre of government – and maybe most large organisations. You're really busy. You think you've got a decision and a plan. The wheels are set in motion, and you turn your attention to other issues. But other people have other plans.

The public health sector might have been caught unaware by e-cigs and our rapid action in 2010. But through 2011–12, significant sections of the policy community, and particularly the public health sector, started to turn against e-cigs in earnest. The Chief Medical Officer moved from being on the positive side of neutral to firmly against. Pharmaceutical companies that made nicotine patches and gum weren't too pleased about the new competition, and started lobbying against e-cigs. The argument also wasn't helped by big tobacco companies, who moved from being bemused and slightly hostile observers, to becoming actively interested in the products and even, it was rumoured, buying up some of the e-cig companies. Furthermore, the slightly dubious behaviour of some e-cig companies in some countries, with rumours that they were being sold outside schools, didn't help their cause much either.

By the time the proposals came back from the MHRA, they didn't look quite like the light-touch regulation we had in mind. The issue was also becoming a European matter, with many countries arguing for a ban, or at least very heavy regulation. Faced with the backlash in the public health sector, one of the UK's largest retailers withdrew e-cigs from its shelves. Despite our early efforts, we were losing the battle. We were heading towards heavy restriction of e-cigs in Europe, where they might only be available from pharmacies, and possibly only on prescription. Some wanted to go further still, and to follow the Australians towards an outright ban, or availability only possible under tight medical supervision. Even the MHRA was concerned that the European position would go too far.

There's behavioural literature on expert judgements, and it's not pretty reading. Philip Tetlock has documented how, very often, political and policy experts aren't very good at getting it right.[3] In particular, experts who have strong views of the world, with clear-cut but rigid theories, tend to make predictions that turn out to be wrong. In contrast, experts who make more accurate predictions tend to have much messier views of the world. They change their minds when new evidence comes along. They're often full of doubt, so they don't make great pundits on TV. But they're more likely to get it right, because the world is, after all, a complicated place. The question was, who was who in this discussion? Perhaps we were the ones being dogmatic and simplistic in this debate – in Tetlock's analogy: the stubborn 'hedgehog'.

With Tetlock's warning in mind, we looked again at all the data we could find. In particular, we wanted to consider the actual behavioural evidence on the rates of quitting smoking in the UK since 2010–11 when e-cigs first hit the market. The evidence was striking. After a long period of decline in the successful quit rates of smokers, the quit

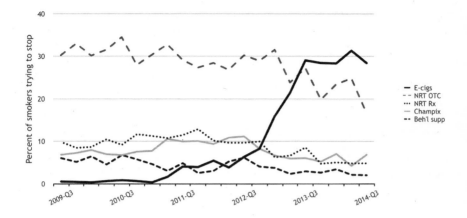

Figure 31. Aids used in most recent attempt to quit smoking: UK data from 2007 to 2014. From 2013, e-cigs overtook over-the-counter NRT as the most popular route to quitting – and have been associated with a higher success rate of quitting.[4]

rate rose from 4.6 per cent in 2011 to 7.2 per cent in 2014. Looking behind these headline figures – at how smokers were quitting – the story seemed pretty clear (see Figure 31). There had been little change in the proportion of smokers quitting through over-the-counter, or prescription, nicotine replacement patches or gum (known as NRT – nicotine replacement therapy). Indeed, in percentage terms, the proportion of smokers quitting using over-the-counter NRT had drifted down from around 30 to 25 per cent, and those quitting through prescription NRT had fallen from around 10 to 5 per cent. In contrast, the proportion of smokers quitting through the use of e-cigs rose from less than 5 per cent in 2011 to around 30 per cent by mid-2013, to become the biggest single channel to quitting. It was compelling evidence. In simple terms, e-cigs had created a new and attractive channel for smokers to quit, and they were doing so in their hundreds of thousands. *Make it easy and attractive ...*

One concern was that e-cigs might pull in non-smokers, but, again, the numbers did not suggest this. There was a tiny fraction of non-smokers who had used e-cigs, but this number was similar to that of non-smokers who, perhaps surprisingly, sometimes used NRT (for example, the BBC's *Sherlock Holmes*). There was also the concern, voiced particularly in the USA, that e-cigs were being used by some smokers instead of quitting. With two million e-cig users in the UK, and around 12 million in the USA, it was clear that there was a growing population of smokers who were using a mixture of e-cigs and smoking. But the evidence still suggested that this was still better than just smoking, and more importantly, the rising quit rate strongly suggested that the overall effect was positive.

We took the evidence back to the PM and the Cabinet Secretary. As it happens, David Cameron was one of the only people in No. 10 who had been a smoker, and had once even tried an e-cig (he wasn't especially impressed). We took the decision to stick to our line: to ensure that, for now at least, e-cigs should be widely available; to push for light-touch regulation to ensure that they were free of other toxins but had enough nicotine to satisfy smokers' cravings; and to legislate to ensure that they were not to be sold to under-18s. Available, but safe, was to be our line.

Based on behavioural and other evidence, and with the help of a new Public Health Minister and our European and Global Issues Secretariat (EGIS), this is the line we took and pushed and more or less secured in the UK and Europe. It is a situation we continue to watch. Depending on your assumptions, estimates suggest that from 20,000 to 200,000 extra smokers are quitting a year as a result of the availability of e-cigs in the UK alone. It is difficult to be completely sure about the precise effect, since other changes, such as restricting the visibility of tobacco products sold in stores, also occurred over this period, though estimates of the impact of this change are much smaller than that of e-cigs. We also cannot be sure what their impact would be in other countries that have less aggressive tobacco control than the UK. Nonetheless, the pivotal gain from e-cigs seems to be that they make quit attempts more frequent and more likely to be successful.

The evidence also suggests that, unlike conventional information campaigns to encourage quitting, e-cigs appear to be encouraging increased quitting in all socio-economic groups. For higher socio-economic groups, smoking rates fell 2 percentage points from 2008–9 to 2014 (from around 15 to 13 per cent). For lower socio-economic groups, they fell 4 percentage points (from around 29 to 25 per cent) – a bigger absolute fall but proportionately similar. The net effect, given the extensive harm caused by smoking, will be to reduce health inequalities. E-cigs seem to be able to help people quit across all levels of society, perhaps because they operate with the grain of behaviour and habits rather than operating on the basis of 'health education' or conscious persuasion.

In crude terms, smoking knocks an average of ten years off the life of an average smoker, but quitting before the age of 40 eliminates almost 90 per cent of this elevated risk. We can use this to estimate roughly the number of years of life saved by the increased quit rates resulting from e-cigs. Taking a mid-level estimate from above of the number of extra smokers quitting, and taking some conservative assumptions about the impact on individual quitters, suggests that e-cigs are currently saving around 100,000 years of life per annum in the UK alone.[5] The advisory health body NICE uses a soft cut-off of around £30,000 ($50,000) per year of life saved in its recommendation of a new drug as being effective. In other words, if e-cigs were a new drug, we'd have been prepared to pay around £3 billion per annum, or $5 billion, to achieve an effect this big. That is quite considerable.

As with much of policy, this is an unfinished story. In July 2014, the World Health Organisation published a report concluding that countries should pursue a 'two-pronged regulatory strategy – regulating ENDS [e-cigs] as both a tobacco product, in accordance with the provisions of the WHO Framework Convention on Tobacco

Control, and as a medical product'.[6] They did not recommend a ban, but for many countries regulating e-cigs in this way would dramatically curtail their availability. On the other hand, the report noted:

> Whether ENDS fulfil the promise or the threat depends on a complex and dynamic interplay among the industries marketing ENDS (independent makers and tobacco companies), consumers, regulators, policy-makers, practitioners, scientists, and advocates. The evidence and recommendations presented in this report are therefore subject to rapid change.'

We might note how this market and its effects play out fundamentally depends on behavioural factors discussed throughout this book. It is possible, indeed likely, that further refinements of the restrictions on e-cigs will be necessary, such as if their producers push the boundaries of their marketing to attract younger vapors (are bubble-gum flavoured e-cigs really aimed at adults?). Similarly, if evidence starts to build that e-cigs are more harmful than currently believed, further regulatory change may be necessary: at least their contents and effects are now monitored.

Yet one of the most interesting twists to the e-cig story may be yet to come. E-cigs offer, perhaps for the first time ever, the prospect of eliminating (or even banning) smoking altogether. With a plausible, and seemingly safer substitute in place, the public health community might want to ponder whether e-cigs, however ambivalent they feel about them, might enable societies to get rid of smoking for good. Given that smoking is the leading cause of preventable deaths in the USA and many other countries in the world today, this would be a remarkable achievement.

In a finely balanced policy argument, e-cigs have become widely available – in the UK at least – because of an argument made on behavioural science principles. The success rates for attempts to quit smoking are now at the highest level they have been recorded in recent times in the UK. But across the world, more than 480,000 people currently die of smoking-related causes every year. Though time will tell, the initial indications are that by helping people quit – and possibly opening the door to a future outright ban on smoking – e-cigs may prove to be the biggest boost to public health in a generation. Even more extraordinary, much of the public health bodies would have blocked them.

Back to work

The young man nodded, 'yeah, sure'. The jobcentre adviser had checked he didn't mind me sitting in on the session. In fact, he barely seemed to notice me seated to one side of the adviser's desk in the large open-plan office. Their conversation seemed to follow a familiar pattern. She asked him what jobs he had looked for since they'd last met, and he told her. She alerted him to a new training option that he might want to apply for. She led, and he followed, except on the one occasion when she forgot to ask him to sign one of the forms, and he reminded her.

It was a slightly depressing experience. The office was modern and pleasant; gone were the glass barriers and dehumanising queues of the jobcentres of the seventies and eighties. The adviser did her best to be upbeat, but she had a tight schedule and a role to fulfil. The young man, perhaps no more than 18 or 19, was compliant and polite, but also listless and passive. He was only a year or two older than my own son, and it reminded me how much of life seemed to depend on the throw of the dice.

The visit to the jobcentre was to help us better understand what really happened in this everyday part of the great apparatus of state. Several members of BIT – Rory Gallagher, Sam Hanes and Alex Gyani

– had been dispatched to spend time in jobcentres to think about whether behavioural insights might help get people back to work faster. It felt like one of our toughest assignments. Could we really get people back to work faster, without addressing their formal skills or what was happening in the labour market, with a few BI-inspired 'tweaks' to the process?

The team had learnt early on that a healthy dose of ethnography – a 'method acting' approach to policy – was an essential ingredient in translating BI-inspired ideas into the real world. The work in jobcentres was to prove a good example of just how essential this was, not least since most of us had barely stepped in one before.

One of the ideas that I was keen to pursue was whether we could do something about the 'weak ties' and low confidence of many of those that found themselves caught in unemployment. This was based not only on the BI literature, but also the literature on social capital (people's networks and norms). Back at the office in Whitehall we looked at how jobcentres might bring together small groups of the unemployed with those who had got jobs, the idea being to boost the morale of those still looking for work, while strengthening their connections to those in work, since by some estimates as many of 80 per cent of jobs are filled by word of mouth.

A week or two later, Rory explained that it was not going to happen: apparently it was too difficult to arrange the meetings and most jobcentres didn't have suitable rooms anyway.

Often seemingly good policy ideas fail for such reasons of practicality. Some jobcentres do have rooms that they can use for training or other purposes, but not always. Similarly, jobcentre advisers work on tight schedules. Carving out the time to call around previous jobseekers and making appointments could take an hour or more of time that the advisers just didn't have. Even losing a few minutes could make a difference. Time was a valuable asset.

One issue that stood out for us was how jobseekers had to show they were looking for work. A central idea behind welfare policy over recent decades is that claimants have to show that they are actively looking for work, an idea borrowed from the 'active welfare states' of the Nordic countries and vigorously pursued by the Clinton administration in the USA and by governments in the UK and many other countries. In practice, 'active welfare' means that the unemployed are asked to prove that they are really looking for work. In the UK, this means jobseekers showing that they have looked at three job vacancies at least over the previous week or two. So the jobseekers typically come in clutching a local newspaper with three jobs ringed to indicate the ones they had looked at.

Even though there is good evidence for active welfare policy overall – the more people look for jobs, the faster they get back to work and the lower the overall unemployment rate – we had doubts about the details. From a psychological point of view, the requirement to look for at least three jobs introduced a strong 'anchor', and one that most experts would agree was far too low. If you are to find a job, applying for three vacancies every two weeks is very low – most jobseekers should be thinking more like 50 or more. Even more problematic, we thought, was the focus on the *previous* week, rather than the *coming* week.

A growing body of work suggests that if you prompt people to think ahead about how, when and where they will do something they are much more likely actually to do it. For example, if you want to encourage someone to vote, it's much more effective to prompt them to make a plan about when and how they will get to the polling booth than simply appealing to their civic duty (see Chapter 6).

We decided to test this type of 'implementation intention' approach to see if it could help get people back to work faster. Rather than advisers asking jobseekers what they had done last week, we encouraged them to ask what they would do next week, and to prompt the jobseeker on specifics such as 'what day and time is good for you to search?'; 'what kind of jobs will you look at?'; and 'how will you go about it – online, in the paper, or through friends?'.

We also asked advisers to get jobseekers to write down their plans in a diary-like booklet that they would keep and bring back next time. (Advisers expressed concern that many jobseekers would lose these but almost none did.) We also built into the intervention a few other changes that we thought might help. We reduced the number of forms jobseekers had to read and sign on the first visit to the jobcentre, thus allowing more time to be spent from the outset on focusing on job search. We sought to give jobseekers a stronger sense of progress with a short checklist of all the steps between that stage and getting a job, with many of the tasks being ticked off even in the first session.[7]

To get some of these changes in place, we had to get permission to 'break the rules'. This was far from straightforward, even coming

Easy	Cut the paperwork in the first session, to enable the main focus to be on getting the person back to work.
Attractive	Create a sense of progress through a checklist that jobseekers can tick as they complete tasks, with many achieved during the first session. Support the motivation of jobseekers through (optional) exercises that identify what they are good at.
Social	Move computer screens to the side, and focus on the person. Encourage jobseekers to write down their plans for themselves, as a form of personal commitment.
Timely	Encourage jobseekers to plan ahead, with advisers prompting them to think about what, when and how they will carry out their job search activities in the week ahead.

Figure 32. Summary of the key changes to how jobcentres worked with the unemployed to help get them back to work faster.

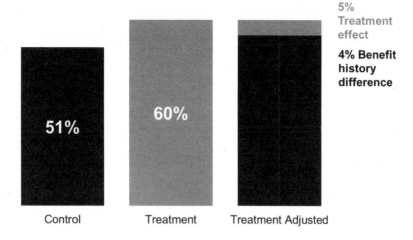

Figure 33. Per cent of jobseekers off benefits at 13 weeks in the control and treatment groups. The third column controls for individual differences that might have accounted for some of the differences.

from 10 Downing Street, but getting that permission helped to motivate and persuade the advisers that it might be worth trying out our suggested new approach. The initial trial was run in a jobcentre in Loughton, Essex, on the outskirts of London, partly chosen because the centre operated over two floors. Jobseekers were randomised between the two floors, with one floor getting the new procedure and the other getting the old. Our outcome measure was to be the number of new claimants off benefit at 13 weeks after starting, since this was the key measure used by jobcentres across the UK.

Several months and a couple of thousand jobseekers later, we nervously awaited the results (we were reliant on the Department of Work and Pensions to independently gather and analyse the data). Much to our delight, the intervention seemed to have worked: 60 per cent of jobseekers who went through the new procedure were off benefits at 13 weeks, compared with 51 per cent of the control group.

Still, we're a suspicious lot and we worried if any other differences could have crept into the two groups that might have affected the results.

With the help of analysts in the Department of Work and Pensions, who had access to the detailed data, we applied a variety of statistical controls to remove any other individual differences that might have led to the treatment group getting back to work faster. These controls, we concluded, could explain some of the effect but still left a substantial and significant impact of around 5 percentage points, or about an extra 10 per cent of people getting off benefits faster.

The result was very promising. The Minister for Employment was certainly pleased, even if his department had started off rather uneasy about the trial. Visiting the Loughton centre, he noticed how the restructured process seemed to prompt a much more natural and active conversation with the advisers, commenting to the press that the intervention 'put the personal back into Personal Advisers'. The department went from hostile to keen, and the wheels started to turn to roll out the new approach across the country.

It is important to remember that many results are never replicated. Indeed, as one group of researchers have famously – and unpopularly – documented, as many as half of all published results are subsequently shown to have been 'false'.[8] With this in mind, we were keen to get a second, larger-scale test of the new approach before it was fully adopted as national policy.

To do this we used an approach known in the (geek) trade as a 'stepped wedge' design. We identified a region of the UK, in this case Essex, that was ready to adopt the new approach. But instead of introducing this to all the jobcentres in the region at the same time, we worked with the managers to gradually introduce the new approaches to different centres randomly at the beginning of each month. This gradual introduction meant that, over a number of months, each of the centres spent some of the time with the old and some with the new procedure, effectively acting as their own control. If you can picture this, you can see that at the start none of the centres are following the new procedure, but they gradually 'step' in one at a time until they have all switched over (with the 'wedge' above forming the control).

It was hard to keep this step-wedge trial protected, and to maintain department interest, when they were already focused on the wider roll-out as well as the other endless changes in the system. Again the randomisation was not totally perfect, in that some of the centres that introduced the changes were deemed administratively 'not ready' and had to be given extra time to make the changes and so statistical controls had to be added to take out any effect that might have arisen with respect to these centres. This is one of the prices to be paid for doing empirical work in the real world. Unlike in laboratories, field trials sometimes have to incorporate pragmatic compromises, and the researchers have to use statistical controls to iron out the imperfections, rather as engineers had to correct the blurry lens of the imperfect Hubble Space Telescope.

Fortunately, when the results finally came in, the effect was very close to that of the original Loughton RCT. Our best estimate was that the revised approach led to a rise of around 2 percentage points of jobseekers off benefits at 13 weeks (cf. 5 percentage points in Loughton), and even after applying full statistical controls.[9]

By early 2014, the new procedure had been rolled out across the country. Unlike changing a letter, changing the procedure and habits of 25,000 jobcentre advisers is a big task. To do it, we had to rely on a 'train the trainers' approach, with BIT members (especially Alex Gyani) training the first generation of advisers, and with them going on to train their colleagues. At the centre of the new procedure was the job plan booklet that jobseekers would fill in and keep, and built within it the use of implementation intentions, a sense of a journey and progress, and the implicit self-commitment of the jobseeker filling out the plan for themselves, albeit supported by the adviser.

From mid-2013 to late 2014, unemployment in the UK fell by more than half a million, from 2.5 million to less than two million. The fall was almost entirely due to the reduction of people on Jobseeker's Allowance, which fell from around 1.5 million to around 950,000, its lowest level since before the 2008 crash. At the same time, unemployment rates stalled across the rest of Europe.

There will be many factors in the dramatic reduction in unemployment, a lot of which had little to do with BIT. But as a result of the Loughton RCT and Essex step-wedge design, we are pretty confident that the BIT/DWP intervention did make a difference. Our estimate is that the new approach trimmed around five to ten million days off benefit claims in the first year alone, by getting the people who pass through Jobseeker's Allowance back to work around two to four days earlier on average. In cash terms this equates to around £50–£100 million in direct savings.[10] In human terms, it is much more: it is people's pride and lives back on track faster, and advisers who can justifiably feel that they are making a difference.

Interestingly, detailed analysis suggests the approach most helped those jobseekers who tended to be 'disorganised', a group that advisers previously found particularly difficult to get back into work. For those who were highly skilled and well organised already, the 'my job plan' approach simply laid out what they would have done anyway. But for those who had previously struggled to organise their time, and who most likely would have been left behind even by the rising tide of renewed economic confidence, it made – and continues to make – a significant difference.

Since introducing this 'planning' approach to UK jobcentres, BIT has worked with both Australia and Singapore to test similar interventions. In Australia, Rory and Alex worked with the government of New South Wales to see if we could get injured workers back to work faster. Using similar approaches to the original work in the UK, they found that injured workers got back to work 27 per cent faster – within 90 days. In Singapore, BIT worked with the Ministry of Manpower to develop an enhanced version of the intervention. This led to an increase in those back in work at three months from 32 per cent to 49 per cent – an even larger effect than our original trial.

If I had to choose one area of BIT work that I'm most proud of, it would probably be getting people back to work faster. It is a lot harder to operationalise than changing a tax letter to encourage people to pay on time, but it is arguably more important and directly impactful on people's lives. We know that extended unemployment is deeply damaging, leading to economic 'scarring' in the form of lower earnings even when people do get back to work, a scarring that can mark entire generations. We also know that unemployment has big impacts on well-being that far exceed those that result from the loss of earnings (see Chapter 9).

The impact on advisers was almost equally as interesting. Many jobcentre advisers have been in their roles for years: many of those we met had been doing the job for twenty years or more. In staff surveys, they tend to report relatively low engagement and satisfaction compared with many parts of the civil service. But in Loughton, in the wake of the intervention, staff satisfaction scores soared. We don't know for sure whether this increased satisfaction followed as a result of the improved outcomes, the changed approach, or just because of a Hawthorne effect, but in some ways it doesn't matter.

By using a more realistic model of human behaviour and motivation, in conjunction with the staff of jobcentres across the UK (and now other countries), we have been able to get hundreds of thousands of people back to work faster. It's helping not only to heal the economy more quickly; it's also healing lives.

Kick-starting an economy

It was tough running a small business in 2010. Robert was a small builder and much of his work had dried up. The larger house builders that had filled most of his order book had stopped building.

Commissions from private clients were almost as bad. People were worried about job security and were putting off the extensions they might have planned. Stagnating prices and failing house builders meant that there were bargains to be had in the form of small sites that were 'shovel-ready' to build on, but there was no way a bank was going to give him a loan to finance the purchase of building materials that he would need. Reluctantly, he let one of his employees go and kept the others on part-time.

By late 2009, the UK economy had shrunk by 7.2 per cent. It was the most severe recession in living memory. At the same time, most of Europe was also in, or sliding towards, recession. Customers were less likely to buy, banks didn't want to lend, and the government was committed to cutting spending and the deficit. Economic fear stalked the land. For the first time in at least a decade, more businesses were closing than opening. In 2009, 41,000 more UK businesses shut than started up.

For the Coalition Government of 2010, the top priority – along with containing the budget – was stimulating economic growth. Indeed, without growth there was little chance of sorting out the country's enormous budget deficit anyway. One area that we thought behavioural insights might add value was around financial products and markets. Could we help to get enough money and confidence back into businesses so that they would start to invest and grow once again?

Getting money flowing

The shock waves from the 2008 near-collapse of the financial system had revealed deep weaknesses and left perilous cracks in the economy. These reached from economy-wide issues of lack of finance and liquidity for businesses, to ongoing concerns about levels of personal debt. On the former, a key priority through 2010–11 was the lack of finance getting through to small businesses. The paradox was that while many businesses were complaining that they could not get finance, overall large businesses were holding unprecedented levels of cash, running to hundreds of billions. Despite the Bank of England pumping huge amounts of extra cash into the economy through the big banks, this cash and liquidity was somehow failing to make its way to small and medium businesses.

BIT was asked to work with the Department of Business (BIS) and Treasury (HMT) to see if there were any other, more behavioural angles that might help unlock the issue. Part of the problem was structural (the big banks patching up the holes in their own balance books), but another was also a matter of 'animal spirits' – the sentiments and fears of business people across the country that reinforced a cycle of risk aversion and contraction.[11]

One approach was to open up new channels of finance. We noticed how small businesses, such as the key sector of small builders and tradesmen, didn't really trust or like the big banks, and it wasn't clear the big banks liked them much either. Using the principles of 'make it easy' and 'attractive', we looked at where else such small traders might go other than the banks. One option was to get behind the newly emergent trend of peer-to-peer lending, through releasing extra finance and a light regulatory framework, which was duly put in place. Another, more uniquely BIT approach, was to see where else small traders and businesses would go to and trust on a regular basis and see if we could get these players to act as channels of finance. For example, we noted that most tradesmen would make very regular visits to hardware and lumber yards, and to hire centres. We therefore reached out to the larger chains in these sectors to see if we could persuade them also to become lenders, using the knowledge and relationships that they already had with these tradespeople.

At first, the reaction was pretty negative. 'We don't want to be a bank!' said a senior executive of one of the UK's largest trade counter firms as we sat around the table at the first-floor meeting room in No. 10. We knew that this company alone held cash reserves of around £1 billion. 'Why should we use our cash like this, as opposed to expanding into central Europe?' It took a while to persuade them that this might make sense, including helping them calculate the returns that they might get on such loans. A key point was that they often had better information about their customers than a bank. They knew their businesses better, and, more importantly, the guys at the counters often knew them personally. Most tellingly, they were already in the business of 'lending' to these small businesses in the sense that they would let them head off with a pile of building materials on account, so why not lend them money, too, not least since much of it would end up spent in the store?

With the help of BIS, we modified programmes to make it much easier for firms like this to get access to additional cash that they could use to lend to small businesses, gearing their own cash to achieve decent returns. Despite the climate of fear, we showed them how such loans to small businesses could achieve results at least as good as they could get from 'expanding into central Europe'. But making the change rested as much on a mindset shift in the heads of the relevant chief execs as it did on a structural change to state funding.

Similarly, extensive efforts were made to encourage large firms to engage in supply chain finance. While Rolls-Royce, with its brand name and cash holdings, might be able to borrow from banks at 2 per cent, its many suppliers might struggle to get banks to lend to them at less than 10 per cent, if at all. But if Rolls-Royce were to underwrite the loan, in effect telling the bank that they would be paying the small business for its work in a specified number of days, the small business could now borrow at rates comparable to that of Rolls-Royce.

The amount that flowed through such schemes was ultimately modest compared with the £100s billion that flowed through the mainstream banks, but for many businesses at this key time it was the difference between life and death. It also had another important aspect, which was to keep pressure on the conventional banks to sharpen up their act, because it created an awareness that there were alternatives to them. Indeed, some of the alternative financing initiatives that were started in this period have continued to grow, and are now emerging to become significant players in a more diverse financing market, an important legacy of this period in its own right.

Behavioural insights had, and continue to have, impacts on the personal finance market, too. Work on behavioural finance had already helped to shape thinking about consumer information, including explaining loans in standard terms (such as APRs), as well as exploring the limits of such approaches (see previous chapter on data and transparency). A key battleground, pushed forward by BI work, was the enhancement of cooling-off periods, and particularly those targeting the burgeoning growth of store cards. Inside the financial regulator, not least driven by their recruitment of the behavioural economist Stefan Hunt and others, the regulator moved for decisive reform of payday lenders and personal banking, based heavily on the results of well-designed studies of behavioural impacts.

Boosting confidence and the take-up of schemes

Behavioural insights thinking had impacts on other aspects of growth policy, too. The drive for growth led to a clutch of new government schemes to support businesses, but often these weren't taken up. The Prime Minister and other senior figures were often exasperated and puzzled by why so few businesses took up these new forms of support, even while they were complaining about the lack of finance or support. Within BIT we concluded that at least part of the problem was that businesses didn't really understand the schemes, and often had never even heard of them. This mattered not just to the businesses directly affected – the ones that the schemes were aimed to help but that weren't taking them up – but also to the wider business community through the impact on business confidence, or Keynes's 'animal spirits'. Even if your business seems all right, with money in the bank and enough orders coming in, if you sense that other businesses around you are in trouble and there is no help at hand, then you will hold back. You won't take on that extra employee, or invest in new equipment, if you think other businesses are in trouble.

With this wider set of concerns in mind, we looked for ways of persuading more businesses to take these growth-related schemes, and also to more generally increase awareness that the schemes existed. BIT argued that we could add messages to existing large-volume emails and letters already being sent out to businesses by other government departments, rather than developing stand-alone campaigns for each new scheme. The biggest communicator with business, by a large margin, we argued, was not our business department (BIS), but our tax department, HMRC, which sent out hundreds of millions of communications every year. We argued that we should use these other channels of communications for new purposes, and especially to drive the awareness and take-up of growth-related schemes.

There was one major problem: HMRC was concerned about the use of their channels for non-tax purposes. Officials within the department wrote to its Ministers and Permanent Secretary warning that it risked straying outside of its statutory remit. The Permanent Secretary, or Head of Department, Lin Homer, also had practical concerns. If other government departments were allowed to add messages to HMRC communications, would this detract from the core messages relating to tax? And what if businesses, confused about who they should call, flooded the HMRC helplines? When you are running a massive department responsible for gathering hundreds of billions of pounds, you are right to be wary about some smart-arse idea from No. 10 throwing grit into your machine. No one will thank you when its cogs start to jam (see also Chapter 2).

Fortunately, Lin and her Ministers did allow us to run a few trials to test the hypothesis. Working with HMRC's own newly established internal BI team, led by Rohan Grove, we designed a series of short emails that informed businesses about a particular growth-related scheme alongside the normal information about tax. The results were dramatic. Not only did the emails lead to a cascade of extra traffic and applications to the business growth scheme, they also, if anything, increased click-throughs to HMRC's own tax information. The results, tested over a series of trials, proved decisive. Importantly, they convinced HMRC to allow a wider use of their channels to increase uptake of other government schemes.

The success of later government growth-related schemes, such as encouraging businesses to invest in broadband and thereby expanding their online presence and ability to trade across the world, owed much to the use of these new channels. Huge spikes in uptake followed each email. We were also able to show, in a similar way to examples seen in earlier chapters, which messages work better than others and for who for example, messages that indicated that the business was in some way 'chosen' or identified as suitable for the scheme were much more effective, whereas certain government or marketing 'brands' added to the email made it less likely to be opened. What we cannot quantify is the impact on business confidence more widely, including on those who didn't actually use the extra support, but who were made aware that it was going on. This is the subject of ongoing work, but for now we can only speculate.

This is how it often is in real-world policy. Sometimes we have to use the best of our knowledge and take a view. What we do know is that 'animal spirits', such as business confidence, optimism and gut feelings, matter greatly to what businesses and consumers do. As Keynes put it, 'a large proportion of our positive activities depend on spontaneous optimism rather than mathematical expectations ... a spontaneous urge to action rather than inaction, and not as the outcome of a weighted average of quantitative benefits multiplied by quantitative probabilities'.[12] In other words, businesses' decisions are based on mental processes that are far from perfect, and in times of recession and doubt, much of policy is really about moving this sentiment. It may seem strange to think about it this way, but often the billions of pounds spent on schemes from tax breaks to quantitative easing (the printing of money) is more about sentiment than direct effect. If we think it's getting better, or that someone has a plausible programme that might work to boost growth, then this itself can become a self-fulfilling prophecy, or at least one that will amplify the impact of the programme itself.

Not winning every battle

BIT did not win every argument. Even Prime Ministers sometimes don't get their own way, so it's to be expected that, even with his support, we wouldn't either.

When approaching a problem, it is good practice to deliberately consider as wide a range of options as possible. In the design world this is sometimes referred to as the diamond: a designer should initially develop as many possible ideas as possible – the first, expanding half of the diamond. Only later should they seek to whittle down the ideas – the second, contracting half of the diamond. As such, many ideas and options were left on the cutting room floor of No. 10, and rightly so. Others made it into notes or proposals but fell along the way in the face of other considerations: practical constraints; opposition from departments; or sometimes because of political concerns.

Some of these ideas were worked up in detail, but still fell at the last hurdle. This does not mean that they were wrong to fail, but it is instructive to get a sense of why they did.

The most common reason for an idea to fail was a blurry mixture of practicalities and departmental resistance. For example, on more than one occasion we had a go at adding prompts on to the letters that went to the 12 million people receiving winter fuel allowances, only to be told that it was too difficult, too expensive, or too late. There's no doubt that there were complications involved, but disagreements between the department and the centre over the department's budget settlement were probably a bigger factor in their lack of cooperation. (In 2014, with the help of Oliver Letwin, we did finally get a prompt on to the envelopes at least – it led to an immediate and sharp increase in visits to the energy regulator's website about how consumers could switch to better deals.) We lost similar battles with the energy department over the structure of their Green Deal finance scheme; with the Department for Communities over changes to right to buy in social housing (though this finally fell into place in early 2015); with the Department of Health over simplifications around organ donation; and the HMRC and welfare departments over reducing fraud and error in benefits.

Sometimes battles are lost because Ministers take a political judgement that they do not want to pursue an idea. This may be because they don't think it fits with their own political or ethical beliefs, or because they are uneasy about how the public or media might react. This is sometimes called political interference, especially by those on the losing side of the argument, but to me it seems right and proper – it's democracy in action (see Chapter 11 for further discussion).

We found some departments much harder to make progress with than others, at least in the early years of the 2010 administration. For example, their was one particular policy area that the Liberal Democrats were keen that we apply behavioural and other evidence-based approaches to, and had added a line to that effect in the original Coalition Agreement. As it happens, it was an area with good grounds for thinking that such approaches would work. Together with the relevant lead in the team at No. 10, I drafted several shortlists of such ideas. But despite a number of conversations with political advisers and senior officials in the relevant department, we made little progress for several years, even with the support of the PM. It probably didn't help that the political advisers in that department weren't big fans of Steve Hilton, and perhaps coincidentally the department did eventually warm to the approach after he left, at least around some issues.

Other ideas that fell on political grounds in 2010–15 included those around illegal immigration (to break the implicit collusion between rogue employers and illegal employees); healthcare (such as clarifying the wishes of patients approaching end of life); social inequality (encouraging people to bequeath benefits to later generations); and changes to incentives to encourage employers to take on the long-term unemployed (in effect, offering a money-back guarantee to take on a young, unemployed person).

I don't begrudge these defeats. We did have many wins. Ministers are the ones who get elected, and kicked out if the electorate don't like what a government does. They work insane hours, labouring over decisions that will generally be met with derision from one side or another, and for careers that often end in what some will regard as failure (removal by the Prime Minister, scandal or the electorate). As we shall discuss further in Chapter 11, someone needs to make a final decision about which nudges are acceptable and which are not, and this should be someone other than the 'nudgers' themselves.

Conclusion

The publication of a cool trial result, such as how adding a line to a letter can encourage more people to pay tax or join the organ donor register, can attract quite a bit of media and academic attention. Yet much of the activity of BIT was, and continues to be, focused on policy: the day-to-day decisions that Prime Ministers, Ministers and officials make.

The battle over e-cigarettes illustrates a classic type of policy: deciding what the position should be on whether to allow or restrict an activity or product, ultimately expressed through regulation and law. The second example concerned a much messier area, sometimes known as operational policy: how policy should be translated into practice by tens of thousands of public servants and, in this case, by the millions of unemployed people passing through the benefits system as they try to get back to work. The third example provided a glimpse into policy where the levers of government are even more indirect: trying to kick-start a stalled economy. It's for individual businesses to decide whether to invest or hunker down; for banks to decide whether to lend or not; and for consumers to decide whether to spend or save: but nudges can affect some of these decisions.

The line between these methods of government and private sector action is far from perfect. For example, many of the questions around e-cigs will rest as much on how sellers decide to operate, while the operation of the economy is, at least to some extent, affected by the rules that regulators set. The three examples give a glimpse into the world in which BIT, and other central units, operate.

There were many other policy areas on which BIT offered advice within No. 10 and the Cabinet Office. Our ability to make an impact was greatly enhanced by the support of the political advisers to the Prime Minister such as Rohan Silva and Steve Hilton, and to the Deputy Prime Minister through his political advisers, Polly Mackenzie, Tim Colbourne and others – and of course in direct conversations with them and notes written. Absolutely critical, especially after the departure of Rohan Silva and Steve Hilton, was the ongoing support of the Cabinet Secretary, Sir Jeremy Heywood, whose deft skills and all-seeing eye touched almost every area of British policy.

Unlike with a controlled trial you can't always be sure of the effect of the policy decisions taken. In the case of getting people back to work, we're pretty confident of the positive effects because of the trials we ran before the changes went both national and international. Further changes are now under way which we think could have even bigger impacts. We're also pretty confident that we made the right call on e-cigs, with thousands of years of life already saved as a result. On economic growth, it's harder to nail down the precise effects. We do know that we managed to drive big uptakes in specific government schemes, from funding for business advice to broadband, and helped to get new forms of lending established, but it's very hard to isolate the impacts of these particular interventions on the wider increase in business confidence and the dramatic turnaround in the UK economy. Critics might argue that the increase in confidence would have happened anyway, or be entirely due to other factors.

Many such issues continue to pass through government in-trays and Ministerial boxes. Some are driven from inside government itself, and many by public demand. Is there more that can be done about the cost of living, to promote social mobility, or address mental health? What to do about new forms of crime, such as cyber-theft or bullying, illegal immigration, or obesity? Should we introduce taxes on unhealthy foods? Should we legalise certain drugs? Many of these issues are choices for society, as markets, technology and preferences evolve, with strong business and special interest views arrayed around them.

The key challenge for behavioural scientists is whether our approaches can identify solutions to these challenges that traditional analysis may have missed. For example, if frictional factors are so important, would world trade increase, and prices fall, if online shopping always showed shoppers the best equivalent price across the world (or at least within the EU or North American Trade Agreement area)? How much of the lost billions to fraud and error in tax and benefits systems is a result of self-interested 'laziness' rather than active fraud, and could this gap be closed by simply making it easier to do the right thing?

Perhaps the most important but subtle change on policy brought forward by the work of BIT was around method and mindset. After three or four years of the Nudge Unit, alongside the normal discussion of costs and benefits, of politics and economics, notes into the PM and Ministers increasingly contained the language of behavioural insight. The Minister for Government Policy, Oliver Letwin, and his staff at No. 9 Downing Street were – and continue to be – perhaps particularly important. Letwin, like the Cabinet Secretary, Jeremy Heywood, had oversight across policy areas. After many meetings with BIT in attendance, he soon had a pretty good grasp of BI approaches himself. He would often direct departments and policy teams across Whitehall to consider behavioural approaches, or point them in the direction of BIT. By 2014, this was true of much of the Cabinet. Policy decisions are the lifeblood of government, and through it the ideas and approaches of behavioural insights have started to spread widely through the branches of government.

Even with a No. 10 email address there's still no guarantee that recommendations will be followed. But enough of our recommendations and our way of thinking got through to make a significant difference. Sometimes proposals need the right time or opportunity and to resonate with the sentiments of the time. Some are still working their way through the system now. And some of those ideas that were left on the cutting room floor after the battles of Whitehall may yet see the light of day, if not in the UK, then in other governments and contexts across the world.

CHAPTER 9

WELL-BEING

Nudging Ourselves, and Each Other,
to Happier Lives

*Gross National Product counts air pollution and cigarette advertising,
and ambulances to clear our highways of carnage. It counts special locks
for our doors and the jails for the people who break them. It counts the
destruction of the redwood and the loss of our natural wonder in chaotic
sprawl. It counts napalm and counts nuclear warheads and armored cars
for the police to fight the riots in our cities. It counts Whitman's rifle and
Speck's knife, and the television programs which glorify violence in order
to sell toys to our children. Yet the gross national product does not allow
for the health of our children, the quality of their education or the joy of
their play. It does not include the beauty of our poetry or the strength of
our marriages, the intelligence of our public debate or the integrity of our
public officials. It measures neither our wit nor our courage, neither our
wisdom nor our learning, neither our compassion nor our devotion to
our country, it measures everything in short, except that which
makes life worthwhile.*

ROBERT F. KENNEDY, UNIVERSITY OF KANSAS, 18 MARCH 1968

Elaine is a commuter. Door to door, her journey into work takes around one hour and 40 minutes each way. Compared with many of her fellow commuters, Elaine is a newbie: she's been doing this commute and job for less than five years. When she gets on the train, it's already half full of other commuters. On the plus side, she and her family live in a good-size house with a nice garden, and certainly a lot bigger than they could afford if they lived in London like many of her friends. It's tiring, and sometimes she and her husband talk about moving, but the job pays well and the kids seem happy. It's one of those trade-offs that you make in life.

I've a lot of empathy with people like Elaine because I'm one of them: my own commute takes about an hour and 20 minutes each way. Elaine is one of those already on the train when I join it at Cambridge, coffee in front of them, trying to catch a few extra minutes of sleep if they can. When I started working for Tony Blair in 2001, my wife and I thought about moving back to London, but we decided against moving into a three-bed flat from the house we had in Cambridge with our two young boys for what was supposed to be only an 18-month stint in government.

Was Elaine 'right'? Were we 'right'? Is the long commute worth it to live in a big house with a nice garden or would we all be significantly happier living in smaller accommodation nearer to work? The evidence from the science of well-being suggests that most people *would* be happier with the shorter commute and the smaller home. It looks like the extra income and living space don't make up for the grind of the long commute, not only for the commuter but for their partner as well.[1]

It turns out that the same mental shortcuts that help us get through life, and occasionally trip us up, get used in the big decisions in our lives, too. When comparing a house with a garden with a city apartment, we think of summer days and the kids playing on the lawn. Faced with this choice, it seems a no-brainer. But there are other aspects of the choice that may be less salient, that may have a big impact, too, such as how the commute might mean that we'll miss the kids' bedtime and the chance to read to them. And maybe the garden will take more time and maintenance than we think; time that could instead be used to take the kids to a nearby park or the zoo.

These types of decisions, at personal and societal level, are the focus of this chapter. It's no coincidence that many of the leading behavioural scientists study well-being and happiness too. From Daniel Kahneman to Danny Gilbert, Elizabeth Dunn to Paul Dolan, all have converged on the fascinating intersection between behavioural science and well-being, though often from very different starting points. At the heart of this intersection is a startling question: do we actually know what makes us happy?

If we believe the data from the new science of well-being, it looks like we often get it wrong. We buy expensive presents for our kids that they rarely play with, when they – and we – would probably be happier if we had spent the money and the time on doing something with them. We stretch ourselves to buy a fancy car, but then find six months on that it sits in the traffic just like any other. And we choose the longer commute and the bigger house, when actually we'd probably have been happier in a smaller place with more time at home. It is also likely that some of our collective decisions – at community and national level – are equally off track.

The implications for how we live our lives, for business and for governments, are great. That is what this chapter explores, and it turns out to be a curious and radical journey. It was also a question, alongside the other work of BIT, that the Prime Minister wanted pursued.

Early roots

People have long thought about well-being – the subjective experience of happiness and positive emotion. In philosophy and religion it is strongly linked to the notion of a good life – but is not necessarily the same as it.

For Aristotle, the pursuit of 'eudaimonia' – let's call it happiness for the moment – was the ultimate objective in life, since all other goals, be they material or spiritual, were a means to this end. He saw it as a distinguishing feature of humans that we could use our reasoning to choose actions that would attain this state: seeing through momentary pleasures, or discomforts, to fashion a life of virtue, intellectual curiosity and friendship, and through these attain a deep sense of what we would call well-being. Happiness was not just a fleeting mental state, but 'an activity of the soul', and one that took a lifetime to achieve: 'for as it is not one swallow or one fine day that makes a spring, so it is not one day or a short time that makes a man blessed and happy'.[2]

Though more than 2,000 years old, Aristotle's thinking has stood the test of time. It is echoed in the thinking of John Stuart Mill, whose notions of happiness were rooted in higher virtues. But it was Mill's godfather, Jeremy Bentham, who is perhaps best known for pushing the idea of happiness into the modern age.

Bentham was one of a number to advance similar ideas during the eighteenth century, including Francis Hutcheson,[3] David Hume and William Paley.[4] But Bentham has become perhaps best known because of the directness – some would say oversimplicity – of his case. He argued that happiness should be the guide for how an individual should live his life, and also the guide for what government should do. He proposed using a 'felicific calculus' – or 'hedonics' – by which we could scientifically determine the amount of pleasure gained or lost from a specific activity, and could make political decisions based on it.[5] As Bentham put it, 'pleasures then, and the avoidance of pains, are the ends that the legislator has in view'.

Benthamite utilitarianism ran into problems on two fronts. The first was philosophical. His felicific calculus appeared to imply that it could be right to subject one person to great unhappiness, if this gave great pleasure to everyone else. The second problem was practical: how could a person, or government, empirically measure happiness? The first class of problems have kept philosophers happy, if no one else, for a good 200 years. But without an answer to the second question – measurement – the whole debate had to be left to philosophers in their armchairs.

Measuring well-being: from GDP to SWB (subjective well-being)

In 1937, Simon Kuznets presented the report *National Income, 1929–35* to the US Congress, which contained the initial idea of a single measure of economic progress. This measure became known as Gross Domestic Product (GDP), and was designed to capture the economic activity of an entire country. Since the Second World War, GDP has been used to measure and compare countries' economic growth, but has also been used as a proxy for how well off the country's citizens are. Though far from perfect – GDP figures are based on a wide variety of inferences that are often subject to revision and change – GDP has become extremely prominent, and is perhaps the most widely reported statistic of our time. Political careers, elections and even the trajectory of the economy itself can be affected by the quarterly ups and downs of GDP.

Yet GDP is a very limited measure of the well-being of a country. As Robert Kennedy famously put it, almost as an aside in a speech mainly on Vietnam in the late 1960s, GDP has other limitations. GDP is a measure of what we do in the real economy, or our material output. To the classic economist, this ought to be more or less the same as what we value or what makes us happy, since rational economic actors (econs) in well-functioning markets should only enter into deals that increase their utility. But there are big problems with this assumption.

First, there are many subjective judgements about what counts as output. For example, large swathes of the grey economy are generally not counted. GDP figures are perpetually subject to adjustment according to what gets included. For example, in 2014, the UK's Office for National Statistics, along with some other national statistical agencies, decided that GDP should include estimates for the value of the sex and illicit drug trades (and contributing to the extra bill the UK had to pay to the EU on account of its higher GDP!). Yet GDP does not include volunteering, the value of our time bringing up our children, or the natural and other capitals that often get depleted by growth. The clean-up of major oil spills counts as GDP growth, yet the depletion of the oil and the carbon it releases does not feature.

Second, even in a modestly expanded classic model, the net result of individual 'rational' actors' choices can lead to a reduction in utility or well-being. The overexploitation of the commons is a simple example – everyone overgrazes and destroys the commons. A more subtle example, offered by Tibor Scitovsky in his classic text *The Joyless Economy*, is where the economic decisions made by some actors inadvertently create wider consequences, or spill overs, that can result in much lower well-being overall. Consider if people start buying flat-pack furniture because it is much cheaper and does the job just as well as individually manufactured pieces. Even if just a few people do this, it may be enough to put the skilled producers of hand-made furniture out of business, a choice not made by the craftsmen, and arguably to the detriment of many consumers. Similarly, think how many people bemoan the loss of traditional high streets and stores while still choosing to do their weekly shop at out-of-town superstores.

A third issue, fundamental to this book, is that we're not 'econs'. Viewed through the lens of behavioural economics, the assumption that we *do* what makes us happy, looks very shaky. If we're interested in well-being, we'd better measure it directly – and certainly not presume that GDP is a good measure of it (though it might contribute to it).

But while many experts acknowledged the shortcomings of GDP as a measure of societal well-being, they couldn't see a better alternative. To many philosophers and policymakers, the measurement of subjective well-being seemed so insurmountable as to render the discussion of it little more than idle gossip. Fortunately, more than half a century of work by psychologists and social researchers has gradually chipped away at this most basic of problems.

Not the concern of governments?

It is a long road that has brought governments and societies, and the UK in particular, to the point that well-being features as more than a rhetorical flourish in speeches. While advocates of the well-being agenda often like to quote the famous words of the American constitution about 'the pursuit of happiness', one can argue that the prime intent and practical application of these words was that government should largely stay out of the way and allow citizens to find their own routes to happiness. The role of government was limited to creating the conditions for citizens to find happiness – and certainly not to find, or define, it for them.

In the UK there have been several attempts to incorporate subjective well-being measures into national statistics and policy. Shortly after the election of the Labour government in 1997, officials in the environment department suggested that well-being measures be added to their indicators of quality of life. Though initially agreed to by the Minister, Michael Meacher, he later backed off their use when he saw the actual survey results, reputedly declaring 'people cannot be that happy!'. After what had been seen as a long and tough period under the previous government, with high levels of poverty, inequality and public services in need of investment, how could it be that so many Britons said they were satisfied with their lives?

Five years later, after I first joined government, we published a discussion paper by the Prime Minister's Strategy Unit exploring the issues more widely. *Life satisfaction: the state of knowledge and implications for government* was a paper I had suggested be written before I joined the Strategy Unit in 2001, though at that time its then head, Geoff Mulgan, was sceptical (he has subsequently become a powerful and vocal advocate of the promotion of well-being). In truth, it was a paper we published at the margins of the main work we were doing. In case there be any doubt, the paper had prominently printed on every page 'this is not a statement of government policy', and though it would have been submitted to his box, it was not a paper that our then Prime Minister Tony Blair read, at least to my knowledge.

Nonetheless, the 2002 paper attracted considerable external interest and was one of the most heavily downloaded papers that the PMSU ever produced. It offered a signal that policymakers were interested and helped encourage others in the academic and policy world that it might be worth taking seriously. Economists such as Richard Layard entered the fray, and even the then Head of the Treasury, Sir Gus O'Donnell, made it clear that he thought it was a serious and important agenda.

But, politically, it failed to attract any serious interest. None of the main parties, nor any Minister, staked a claim on the territory. One reason may have been that few were sure of what the policy implications of well-being might be. Another reason was simply the fear of ridicule.

It was not until the run-up to the 2010 election that David Cameron, by then the new leader of the Conservative party, began to talk about well-being. It was Cameron, albeit encouraged by Steve Hilton, who raised eyebrows by talking about whether the UK should take a leaf out of Bhutan's view of the world and consider not just

GDP, but Gross National Happiness, too. For some this was just part of Hilton's rebranding of the Conservative party, but it turned out that Cameron was serious.

Well-being goes mainstream

On 25 November 2010, the press corps were assembled in the Treasury for a major speech and announcement by the Prime Minister. Several hundred commentators, journalists and experts were in the room, and behind them were several TV crews. The Coalition Government was barely six months old and the tired scepticism that sinks into the press pack had yet to take full hold. Even so, this was a speech that the Press Office within No. 10 would rather the PM did not make. In particular, they were worried that talking about happiness at a time of austerity and a weak economy would be subject to ridicule.

I had been working on the speech with Steve Hilton, and with the Office for National Statistics (ONS), on the announcement details for weeks. Up to the last minute I wondered if it might get pulled. But there we were, on 25 November, with the Prime Minister about to announce publicly that the UK was committing itself to the large-scale measurement of subjective well-being and its systematic consideration in policy.

The run-up to the event had picked up many of the tensions around well-being. We had originally planned to have Daniel Kahneman join us, but a combination of diary pressures and his questions about how exactly our national statistician proposed to measure well-being (the details of which would have been lost on the lobby journalists) meant that at the last minute we switched to the Canadian economist and well-being expert John Helliwell. Helliwell's extensive analyses of cross-national differences in well-being were certainly influential on my own thinking. The evening before, as I mentally ran through the sequencing of the event, I recalled John

Figure 34. The Prime Minister announces the programme on well-being in HM Treasury, flanked by the then Cabinet Secretary, Sir Gus O'Donnell.

getting a group of policymakers in his native Canada to stand and sing 'If You're Happy and You Know It' at the start of a presentation. There was a serious point behind it – singing with a group of others makes you feel happy. I pictured the look on the PM's face, recorded for posterity by five camera crews, as John tried to get the entire battle-hardened press corps and upper echelons of the Treasury on their feet to sing. I called him at his hotel in London, just to check. 'Oh, yes', he explained, 'I find it always goes down very well!' Best not on this occasion, we agreed. (I apologise for posterity for this YouTube sensation that never was.)

The seniority of the line-up was as significant as the announcement itself. On one side of the Prime Minister sat the Head of the civil service, Sir Gus O'Donnell, on the other the national statistician, Jil Matheson. The heads of our political, administrative and statistical systems were standing together to say that there was a real gap in how previous governments had thought about the objectives of policy and it was time to get serious about subjective well-being.

The speech made the argument that economic growth was important, but not as a means in itself:

> ... economic growth is a means to an end. If your goal in politics is to help make a better life for people – which mine is – and if you know, both in your gut and from a huge body of evidence that prosperity alone can't deliver a better life, then you've got to take practical steps to make sure government is properly focused on our quality of life as well as economic growth, and that is what we are trying to do.

In his speech, the PM set out three commitments. First, the Office for National Statistics was formally asked to develop and implement large-scale measurement of subjective well-being. Second, the Treasury was asked to revise the Green Book that sets out the calculus behind decision-making to incorporate impacts on well-being. Third, all government departments were asked to consider the impacts of new policy on well-being.

Measuring subjective well-being

Generally speaking, on a scale of 1 to 10, how satisfied are you with your life, where 1 is very unsatisfied and 10 is totally satisfied? Take a moment to answer this question. What number did you come up with? Did it take you long?

Psychologists were working on how to measure well-being long before the PM's speech. Back in the 1950s, particularly in the USA, surveys were asking people questions similar to the one above. In parallel, a large psychiatric literature developed that showed that unhappiness, ranging from serious psychiatric conditions to everyday misery, could be reliably and consistently measured. Screening questionnaires, such as the Langer-22 and Goldberg's General Health Questionnaire, showed that, contrary to the widespread view at the time, people seemed able and willing openly and honestly to answer questions about their emotional and psychological state of mind. As such, the preponderance of questions about physical symptoms in the early questionnaires, such as about having trouble sleeping, and physical aches and pains – gradually gave way to much more direct questions about how people felt.

By the seventies and early eighties, a number of cross-national surveys emerged that asked questions about respondents' happiness and life satisfaction, such the Eurobarometer and the World Values Survey (WVS). The data showed marked and stable differences between countries. But as this data came through, new methodological questions were raised. One question was whether linguistic and cultural differences led respondents to interpret happiness differently. The easy conclusion was that national differences were measurement error, rather than anything deeper. Policymakers were also sometimes dismissive because of the lack of responsiveness of the happiness data. For example, in the USA wasn't it puzzling that, despite 50 years of economic growth, major events and even wars, average levels of happiness never seemed to change very much. Subjective well-being measures looked like a broken dial on the dashboard – they didn't seem to respond to anything that politicians were doing, so after a while no one looked at them any more.

Yet for those researchers who scratched beneath the surface, well-being measures were not so easy to dismiss. Ronald F. Inglehart, who led the WVS, showed that linguistic differences did not seem able to account for the differences in happiness in European countries.[6] German, Italian and French speakers were all much happier in Switzerland than their fellows in Germany, Italy and France. The measures also stood up well to other kinds of testing. People's ratings of their own happiness and life satisfaction were found to correlate highly with ratings of their happiness by people who knew them; their ratings were consistent (reliable) over time; and correlated with the independent ratings of strangers given the opportunity to watch them.[7]

Still, even among psychologists important arguments about how to measure well-being continued. The behavioural scientists Kahneman and Tversky had shown that people systematically misremember how painful or pleasant an event, or sequence, was. In one survey they asked patients exposed to an unpleasant medical procedure to report their level of discomfort throughout the whole procedure. They then later asked them to rate how unpleasant the event had been. It was found that what drove the overall rating was not the average or total level of discomfort, but peak experiences and the level of pain at the very beginning and end of the procedure. The results fitted perfectly with psychologists' studies of memory, such as people's ability to remember a random list of words. People disproportionately remembered the words at the beginning of the list (primacy effects); the ones at the end (recency effects – just as you can remember the last few words of what was said to you); and words that stood out as especially salient or graphic. These findings led Kahneman and others to argue that truly accurate measures of well-being needed to be experiential – recorded in real time – rather than relying on a retrospective answer to a question such as 'generally speaking, are you happy with your life?'.[8]

Another critique of subjective well-being measures is that their very subjectivity means that it is not obvious what the anchor point to the scale is. In physics, scientists can anchor scales to fixed points, such as temperature in centigrade being fixed to the freezing (or triple point) of water as zero degrees and boiling point at one atmospheric pressure as 100 degrees. But when someone says they are about an 8 out of 10 for life satisfaction, what are they comparing this to?

This leads to a subtle and important critique of well-being measures – that they are subject to a sort of false consciousness. Sometimes known as the happy slave problem, the argument is that people in objectively terrible circumstances might say that they are happy, though any rational person looking at their circumstances would say that their conditions are unacceptable. This has led some well-known figures, notably the Nobel Prize-winning development economist Amartya Sen, to be wary of subjective well-being, instead arguing that objective or 'capability' measures should be used – such as access to education or healthcare.

Interestingly, this is not a problem limited to subjective well-being. It is an issue that the hard end of psychology has been wrestling with for more than a century in the form of subjective impressions of how bright a light or loud a sound is. In the study of perception, it led to the conclusion that much of how we see the world is in contrasts, or relativities (see Chapter 1).

Big questions

The questions raised by these challenges go much deeper than measurement: they bear on who and what we humans are; how we see and feel the world to be; and the choices we make in our lives. But to answer these questions we have to get out of the philosopher's armchair.

Let us start with the 'happy slave' challenge. Suffice it to say, closer inspection of the data suggests that the happy slave problem has often been overstated. Ed Diener, for example, highlights how certain population segments have extremely low levels of life satisfaction. Prostitutes in developed nations typically report life satisfaction scores of 2 or 3 on a 10-point scale, well below typical answers of 7 or 8. Similarly, the data repeatedly show that people with lower incomes tend to be less happy. This is true at both individual and national level. Average levels of life satisfaction tend to be above 7 in most developed nations, but at around 5 or below in most developing nations (see further below).

This is not to say that there is no evidence of relative positions in society affecting well-being. There is evidence that people who live in neighbourhoods where they are less well off than most of their neighbours report lower life satisfaction than would be expected on the basis of their income alone. But this does not mean it's measurement error. We are actually made less happy by being constantly reminded that we're less affluent than our neighbours.

A key question is whether well-being is one or many different things. Studies have shown that, in general, people who report higher levels of happiness also report higher life satisfaction, less anxiety and so on. Nonetheless, there is evidence that different measures do tap into subtly different aspects of well-being, and are affected by slightly different drivers. A simple everyday example is when parents are trying to get their children to do their homework, or when a carer is looking after a sick relative. In such circumstances, the person is unlikely to say that they feel happy, but may well say that what they are doing feels worthwhile. This has led many leading figures to the conclusion that good measures may need to tap into several aspects of well-being. Marty Seligman, for example, argues that these should include a range of positive emotions, but also a sense of meaning, engagement and accomplishment. For others, such as John Helliwell, these wider measures are nice to have, but a simple measure of life satisfaction gets you a long way.

In sum, at first approximation measuring subjective well-being turns out to be very hard in theory, but relatively simple in practice. People seem able to give a rapid answer to a question such as 'generally speaking, how satisfied are you with your life?' – just as you probably could a few moments ago. As Helliwell, Diener and others have shown, such measures seem to be pretty reliable (i.e. stable over time), and to have both surface and predictive validity. But human emotions and experiences have facets and complexities that are not bounded by a single question, and, where resources allow, there is merit in seeking to measure these, too.

From academic to official statistics

In the wake of the PM's speech in November 2010, we worked to move the measurement programme forward. Despite a tough spending round, money was found to fund a measurement programme led by the Office for National Statistics. The programme contained two key elements. First, a measure of subjective well-being was to be developed and fielded, plugging a specific gap in our measurement dashboard. This was to be done rapidly so that the data would begin to be gathered within a year. Second, the ONS was to consider and develop a more balanced measure, or dashboard of measures, to stand alongside existing headline measures, notably GDP.

The core insight was simple – high-profile conventional measures of social and economic progress, notably GDP, had serious flaws. In the wake of the OECD Stiglitz report, the ONS's chief economist Joe Grice led a review that concluded that most of the measures Stiglitz et al. recommended statistical agencies should gather had already been collected in the UK. However, one clear omission was good data on subjective well-being, a conclusion that both ONS and those of us then at No. 10 reached.

It was felt important that the work to develop the exact well-being measures be led independently of the political process. The ONS was given the space and the resources and embraced the task with vigour. They conducted a national consultation on what citizens thought well-being and progress were about. On the well-being measure specifically, they assembled an expert advisory group and commissioned reviews from leading experts on the range of existing measures. The technical

discussions about which measure, or measures, of well-being should be used were at times heated. As discussed above, there were some passionate differences of opinion about whether to go for more evaluative (e.g. life satisfaction), hedonistic (how happy are you?), or 'meaning' and flourishing measures (related to the concept of flow). There were also arguments about which questions would be used even within a given category, such as the pros and cons of the standard life satisfaction question versus a 'ladder of life' question that asked people to assess their lives relative to others.

The final conclusion was that four questions – or experimental measures – were included in the national survey (see box), while a wider range of more detailed questions was included in smaller sample supplementary surveys. To minimise bias from previous questions – for example, people tend to report lower well-being if they have previously been asked a series of questions about politics – the well-being questions were put early on in the survey, just after the factual questions about age and other demographics.

The first full year of data was released in the summer of 2012, and since then the ONS has published dozens of further updates and analysis. Despite the concerns of the No. 10 Press Office, virtually all of these releases have attracted widespread and thoughtful public interest. In late 2014, the well-being measures officially became national statistics, shedding their experimental status.

The drivers of well-being

Let's suppose that a government or Prime Minister was really serious about trying to systematically increase not just growth, but well-being. The first thing they would need to do, alongside figuring out how to measure it, is to work out what factors actually drive it.

I won't attempt a comprehensive review here but instead summarise some of the key factors that we know about. In broad terms, there are three types of factor that appear to influence differences in levels of well-being, almost regardless of how it is measured. These are: individual constitutional or personality differences; material factors; and social factors, including personal relationships. We will look briefly at each of these.

A sunny disposition

We observe every day that some people seem blessed with more positive outlooks on life. In contrast, others seem prone to darker outlooks, or to seeing the negative side of life. It turns out that most of us seem to have a sort of set point or anchor for our well-being, and this helps to explain why we tend to give a similar answer to how satisfied we are with life when asked the same question a decade or more later.

Evidence from twin studies suggests that there is at least some genetic basis for this difference. Identical twins, even when adopted and raised apart, have more similar levels of reported life satisfaction than non-identical twins.

Part of these individual differences are thought to lie in cognitive style, whether rooted in genes or upbringing. This is especially manifest at the negative, or sad, end in a tendency to interpret events in a negative, internally attributed way. For example, if a passing car splashes a pedestrian, most people will swear at the car and blame the driver. But some pedestrians will instead blame themselves (I was stupid to walk so close to the kerb) and even to generalise this (I'm always so unobservant). Of course, most events have multiple causes. Psychologists have shown that most of us have a strong tendency to interpret the world through self-serving biases – i.e. we tend to take credit for things that go well, and blame others and the situation when things don't. It seems that, to some extent, these biases help to keep us happy.

Differences in psychological outlook, or positivity, also show their hand through the choices we make in life and the circumstances in which we end up. For example, happier people tend to be more attractive to others, and may find others more helpful to them and more likely to do business with them.

These individual differences in outlook explain a lot about the individual differences in well-being across populations. They also in turn have impacts on other outcomes. For example, retrospective studies have shown that those with a more positive outlook on life as young adults are likely to live around a decade longer than those with a more negative outlook.

As of now, there's not much that policymakers can (or should) do about genetically rooted differences in well-being, but a lot of the constitutional differences also relate to upbringing and ways of thinking that are malleable and open to change. For example, the way parents and teachers encourage children to look at life's inevitable upsets can greatly affect how they respond and feel about them. Cognitive therapy can also help, in effect encouraging people to reshape how they interpret the world.

Material factors

Some popular, and even religious accounts, posit that material factors are irrelevant to people's subjective well-being. This might be true for Tibetan monks, but is not for most people in the world.

Even a cursory glance at the relationship between levels of subjective well-being and income strongly suggests that money does buy at least some happiness.[9] The correlation between the two, at national level, is around 0.8 – or about as strong a relationship as is found in the social sciences. A similar shaped curvilinear relationship is found within countries, with the rich consistently reporting greater life satisfaction than the poor. Of course, correlation does not imply causation. It is likely that at least some of this relationship is mediated by other factors, such as better healthcare and education in richer countries or places. It is even plausible that some of the differences in income are partly driven by well-being, rather than the other way around, at least within some populations. It is much less likely that individual level differences in outlook, or positive psychology, can explain national differences in GDP, though some have suggested it.[10]

There's more to material and environmental factors than income, of course. There is increasing evidence that having access to green spaces, expanses of water and other manifestations of nature boosts our well-being.[11] Another key factor appears to be what you do with your wealth. In the words of a wonderful paper by Elizabeth Dunn and others, 'If money doesn't make you happy, then you probably aren't spending it right'.[12] For example, it appears that you should buy your kids experiences, rather than things, if you want to make them and yourself happier.

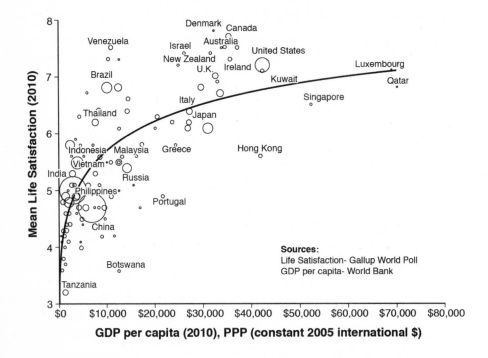

Figure 35. Average life satisfaction versus GDP by country. The size of the points indicates population size. (Based on original plot by Angus Deaton using Gallup data.)

Importantly, people often habituate to many material goods and circumstances, a process known as hedonic adaptation. When you first get your new car, it is a real source of pleasure, but after six months of sitting in traffic just like in your old car, that early buzz has substantially faded away. Such adaptation was famously argued by Richard Easterlin to be the leading contender for why Americans' happiness had failed to increase since the 1950s despite steady increases in GDP, coining the term the Easterlin paradox. Easterlin concluded that the increase in material well-being creates an increase in aspirations, which negates the expected positive impact on happiness. (A rival, or complementary interpretation, posited by figures such as Richard Layard, is that since the Second

World War the increases in well-being from greater wealth have been cancelled out by the unhappiness caused by other changes, such as the deterioration of social relationships – see below.)

It is not just income per se that makes a difference. Human well-being, and indeed that of other mammals, is strongly affected by a sense of control. In old, and not very nice, experiments where two monkeys are strapped into chairs and one has to press a button to prevent them both getting a small electric shock, the yoked monkey – the one that gets just the same number of shocks as the one whose button works – fares much worse. Similarly, people in insecure employment appear to have much lower life satisfaction than those with similar incomes but with more job security. It also appears that the lower mental and physical health of people at more junior levels in large organisations is driven by lack of control, not just lower pay.

The impact of material factors on well-being points to a set of policy tools and interventions that are familiar, particularly to those on the left of politics, such as poverty reduction. But the well-being literature also brings some new twists, suggesting that factors such as control and access to the natural world play an important role over and above income per se.

Social factors

The third bundle of factors concerns how we relate to those around us. This is perhaps the area where the well-being literature is most disruptive and challenging to contemporary policy.

We are profoundly social beings, so perhaps we should not be surprised that our relationships with others is so important to our well-being. How many movies and TV series pivot around a pay rise as compared with those about a relationship – will they ever get together?

When we look across the literature, again and again we find that the quality of our relationships with others appears to have an enormous

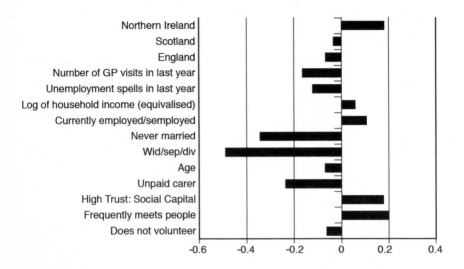

Figure 36. Analysis from the British Household Panel Survey showing the relative impact of various socio-economic variables on life satisfaction. Note the large associations with social variables. (Cabinet Office internal analysis; with thanks to Paul Oroyemi and Ewen McKinnon.)

impact on subjective well-being. To illustrate this, consider Figure 36. The bars that stand out are almost all about personal relationships.

Being widowed, separated, divorced, or never married appears pretty bad for your well-being (though note the causal issues above). In contrast, seeing others regularly, volunteering and feeling that those around you can be trusted are all strongly associated with higher well-being. A large body of evidence suggests that these associations are at least partly causal – supportive social relationships provide emotional and physical nurturance, with effects that are manifest on our mental and physical well-being.[13] As Aristotle again noted in *The Nicomachean Ethics* more than 2,000 years ago:

> Being loved, however, people enjoy for its own sake, and for this reason it would seem it is something better than being honoured and that friendship is chosen for its own sake.

The effect of personal relationships is so powerful that researchers have found that just getting subjects to keep a diary for a few weeks is enough to lead to demonstrable improvements in their health and well-being, such as improved immune system functioning.[14] Similarly, many people are surprised at the relatively high level of well-being in Northern Ireland relative to other parts of the UK. But what is often forgotten is that most people's day-to-day experience in Northern Ireland is of living in strong and vibrant communities, even if historically these have sometimes been in conflict.

The large impact of unemployment also relates in part to social relationships. Researchers have long noted that unemployment is bad for your life satisfaction and for your mental health.[15] But what is striking is just how great the effect is. Using statistical controls, we can show that the negative impact of unemployment on well-being is much greater than can be explained by the loss of income alone. Unemployment involves far more than loss of income: it also brings with it a loss of social contact and meaning.

Even at work we see the powerful effects of social relationships. According to diary and experience sampling studies, time spent with the boss is generally among people's least happy. On the other hand, having a good relationship with your boss is associated with dramatic increases in life satisfaction: rating your relationship with your boss just a single point higher (on a 10-point scale) has the statistically equivalent effect of a 30 per cent increase in your pay on your life satisfaction.[16] And it's not just your boss. People who say that they work with a best friend report work engagement scores around seven times higher than average.[17]

The impact of social relationships on well-being suggests a significant rebalancing of policy, business practice, and perhaps even the priorities in our own lives.

Policy implications

Many people are under the general impression that if you are Prime Minister, President or CEO, if you give the instruction for something to happen then it will. This is often not the case, particularly when the request is unusual or counter to the habits of the organisation.

In the case of well-being, we found that the rare parts of the system that were interested in well-being pushed ahead, and the rest did the bureaucratic equivalent of raising an eyebrow. The most rapid progress happened on measurement and data. But we found it much harder to get progress on policy.

In order to reach out to departments we ran a series of workshops with senior civil servants across the major departments of state, to get them to think about when and where a well-being viewpoint might lead them to different policy conclusions. People really enjoyed the sessions, just as they had those we had run on behavioural approaches, but then they went back to their departments and carried on their work largely unchanged. A key difference was that behavioural insight tools, such as MINDSPACE and EAST, could be applied to whatever Ministers and departments were already trying to do, as we've seen in earlier chapters. In contrast, a session on subjective well-being wasn't just a new tool – it was a new objective.

Because of this relatively slow progress the PM asked Lord O'Donnell, who had recently retired from the civil service and Cabinet Secretary role, if he would lead a more detailed review into the policy implications of pursuing subjective well-being as an overt objective. To keep it independent, we asked the Legatum Institute to host and support it. The Legatum Institute already published a cross-national annual prosperity index, which was unusual in that it combined both material prosperity measures with a wider range of indicators such as personal freedom and quality of relationships. Gus rapidly assembled a Commission, including the economist Richard Layard;[18]

Martine Durand, chief statistician at the OECD; the sceptical but brilliant Angus Deaton from Princeton; and me, albeit wearing a non-government hat. In parallel, we pressed forward with some policy interventions from inside the Cabinet Office, particularly around volunteering, workforce well-being and the use of data.

The O'Donnell–Legatum report was published in March 2014, in London and Berlin, the latter reflecting the growing interest of the German Chancellor Angela Merkel. The emergence of German interest in the well-being agenda also helped move it away from being just a curiosity of the British.

We need to recognise that it is still early days for the well-being agenda. As such, apart from the measurement agenda which is now well advanced, the rest of this chapter is as much about what governments and organisations should do, or might do, rather than what they have already done. Most of the interventions have a strong behavioural, or nudging element.

A users' guide to a happier life – 'de-shrouding' well-being

In addition to creating robust measures of well-being in the UK, the ONS and chief statistician took a leading role in encouraging other national statistical agencies and the EU to adopt comparable measures. We can increasingly compare not only life satisfaction across nations, but also the proportion of people across the EU who feel that what they do in their lives feels worthwhile. Denmark tops the EU with 91 per cent, scoring 7 or higher on life satisfaction, while in Bulgaria that figure is only 38 per cent. The UK sits, alongside Germany, at just above the EU average at around 72 per cent. Denmark also topped the rankings for feeling that life is worthwhile, at 91 per cent; the UK again just above average at 82 per cent, but with Greece trailing at the bottom at just 48 per cent.[19]

While there is always much interest in the headline figures, the real value of the ONS survey is that its large sample size – more than 100,000 people a year – enables far more refined analysis than has ever been possible before. The UK survey is designed to enable representative samples for every local authority area in the UK, as well as producing nationally representative results on a quarterly basis. These data can be cross-tabulated with other data to answer a host of policy questions (see below), but perhaps even more importantly they can be used by citizens to inform their own life choices.

Imagine you are a 17-year-old trying to decide on a career. If you hunt around, you may well be able to find data on how much the average car mechanic earns relative to a forester, a teacher, or a lawyer.

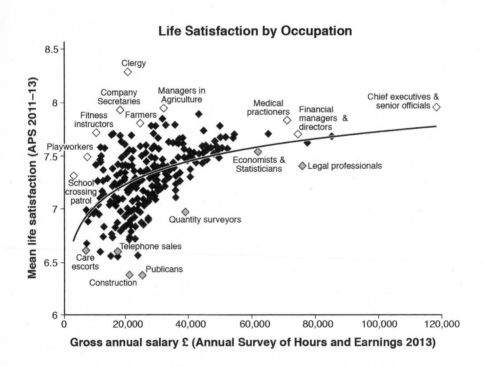

Figure 37. Life satisfaction versus earnings by occupation among UK workers, 2013 data. (Analysis by Cabinet Office analyst Ewen McKinnon.)

But wouldn't it be good to know how satisfied people are in such professions, especially having controlled for other factors such as educational attainment, earnings or gender? Do 45-year-old lawyers or teachers feel that the things they do in their lives are worthwhile? You can ask a friend of your parents who are in those professions, if they have one, how they feel, but are they typical? But imagine if you could ask hundreds and thousands of people?

When this graph was published in early 2014, it caused great interest – and especially among publicans and the clergy. Of course, it doesn't necessarily follow that a given 20-year-old will be assured a life of bliss in the Church, nor one of despair as a publican. But it was still an eye-opener for many to discover that while pubs might be a great source of satisfaction to their customers, they weren't much fun to run. Similarly, it's pretty interesting, and not necessarily obvious, that farmers and fitness workers report significantly higher life satisfaction than construction workers and surveyors, despite the latter generally earning quite a bit more, or that lawyers earn more than medics, but are quite a bit less satisfied with their lives.

Similarly, imagine you are trying to decide where to settle with your young family. Where is a nice place to live – not just the quality of the housing stock, but a place where people are happy? Or maybe you're trying to decide whether to have children early or late: are people who have children early in their career happier than those who wait – or maybe on average it makes no difference?

These aren't just academic questions: they are real questions that most of us face in our lives. As psychologists have shown, people are often surprisingly poor at predicting what will make them happy.[20] The answers to such questions, even in rudimentary form, are generally 'shrouded attributes', as the economist David Laibson has put it. Of course, the 'right' answer for any individual to any of these questions will depend on many factors, lots of which may be highly personal and specific. But in the absence of time machines that enable us to speak to our future selves, learning from the experiences and feelings of others is a rich and potentially useful guide to our own likely experiences and feelings.

It is not for government to make these choices for people, or even to produce the citizens' 'trip adviser for life'. But governments – and potentially others – can help to generate such data, as the UK's ONS has shown. They can, in the words of the 2010 Coalition Government, help find '... intelligent ways to encourage, support and enable people to make better choices for themselves'.

Mental health and character building

It was noted above that individual differences in well-being are, to some extent, a function of how we think about the world. Governments have long been involved in shaping the curricula of schools, and schooling has in turn been steadily extended over the past century. Churches, business, parents and schools all have a hand in shaping what young people learn and think. Probably for as long as there have been human societies, each generation has sought to shape the thinking of those who follow and vice versa. Societies based on fishing or farming need different skills and temperaments from those living in times of conflict and war.

We know so much more today than even a generation ago about how the way we raise our children affects their temperament and their ability to face life's inevitable hardships. When we praise a child for their effort, rather than their ability, we instil in them a theory of mind that success in tasks, and the mastery of skills, is something that can be acquired through focus and effort. In contrast, if our feedback keeps linking their performance to inherent ability, when they struggle in the face of difficulty they will give up instead of striving harder.[21] It is now thought that such patterns of thought, and mental resilience, not only affect how well a child will go on to perform at maths or music, but also ultimately affects their attainment and subjective well-being in later life.

I believe it is irresponsible for us not to take this literature seriously. In 2013, we held a seminar on resilience at No. 10 with Marty Seligman, Angela Duckworth and other leading figures, including a previous Head of the Policy Unit and education lead at No. 10, James O'Shaughnessy, who had gone on to reach a similar conclusion. Though we should tread carefully and not latch on to a universal formula for all, we should be systematically testing ways of building mental resilience, 'grit', and 'hardiness' in our young people – and indeed developing skills around self-control, mental planning and 'metacognition' (thinking about how to think). Early results from teaching mental resilience skills to teenagers have shown promising results, including reductions in childhood depression. However, the results of many of these early programmes have been found to fade out after a couple of years – not bad, but not good enough. Such programmes have often been a small add-on to the normal curriculum, rather than fully integrated into it. The next generation of programmes are better integrated, and the results are eagerly awaited.

This is an agenda that is about supporting parents as much as schools. As the parenting expert Stephen Scott has long argued, we know exactly how to make a troubled young person – and we've a pretty good idea of how to avoid it, too. It's astonishing that until very recently, while we have provided parents-to-be with lots of support and information about childbirth, we have given them almost no help at all with what comes afterwards. Working with Steve Hilton and the Department of Health, we supported the development of a raft of short video clips that parents-to-be could choose to download or have sent to them before and after birth that would provide advice on topics that ranged from how to bathe an infant to how important it was to talk to and 'mesh' with the child. More than £400 million was also found to support a massive expansion of the 'troubled families' programme, aimed at identifying and helping the 120,000 most troubled families in the UK. The objective was not just to reduce the difficulties created by such families to their neighbours, or the extensive costs across a range of services that they incurred, but genuinely to help turn their lives around and especially for the sake of their younger children.

Very often, the adults in such troubled families had mental health problems, and these were rarely diagnosed. These conditions played the role of both cause and effect: a mother with severe depression struggled to control her teenage children, but her depression was in part generated by the difficult circumstances she found herself in.

Addressing mental illness more generally is another strong implication of looking at the world through a well-being lens. It is estimated that only around a quarter of mental illness is ever treated, and, when it is, it is generally after considerable delay. As Richard Layard puts it: 'If you have a broken leg, you will be treated within three hours, but if you have a broken spirit, you'll be lucky if you will be treated within three months, if at all.'[22] Interestingly, when people who are well are asked about how unpleasant it would be to have different illnesses, and what they would pay to prevent them, they systematically underestimate the negative impacts of mental illness.[23]

Ironically, for those who do come in for treatment, especially for anxiety and depression, arguably we then overmedicate. In the UK alone, there was a 165 per cent increase in antidepressant prescriptions between 1998 and 2012, with almost half of that rise in the last four years alone.[24] That's 40 million prescriptions a year in a population of 60 million, albeit noting that many of these will be repeat prescriptions. Levels of prescribing also vary greatly between GP practices, from less than 75 prescriptions per 1,000 patients to over 300 prescriptions per 1,000 patients. It is estimated that around a third of this variance is accounted for by actual variance in depression, but much of the rest is accounted for by factors such as the readiness of GPs to prescribe in general (there is a strong correlation between high prescription rates of antibiotics and antidepressants, for example), and population and GP characteristics (for example, more are prescribed in practices with more older people, though ironically less by older GPs).

Across political parties in the UK there has been support for a significant expansion in access to psychological therapies, notably cognitive behavioural therapies (CBTs). The advantage of CBT is that, while it works about as well as drugs in the short-term, it works considerably better in the long-term because it addresses the underlying patterns of thought that lie behind depression. This leads to a significantly lower relapse rate over a ten-year period, and saves money and angst in the process. A promising next step looks to greatly expand the quality of, and access to, computer-assisted CBT. Early indications are that such approaches can increase access to effective therapy fivefold while using the same number of trained therapists.[25]

But ultimately there are limits to how far we can and should seek to improve population well-being by changing the thoughts in our heads, and certainly by turning all unhappiness into a clinical condition. The roots of a more satisfying and fulfilling life must also lie in the life itself, and the choices we make for ourselves and the society around us.

Community

Focusing more on the importance of social relationships is one of the key implications of looking at the world through a well-being lens. Not only do relationships have a huge impact on our well-being, we appear to systematically underestimate how impactful they are. In particular, we tend to underestimate how much pleasure we get from being nice to other people.

In one of my favourite field studies, Elizabeth Dunn gave out $20 to people. She asked half of them to spend it on a treat for themselves, and other half to spend it on someone else. After completing their task, she asked them how they felt. Those who got something for someone else felt considerably happier than those who had bought themselves a treat. However, when a similar range of people was asked which of the two conditions would make them happier, the majority thought it would be getting a treat for themselves.[26]

Numerous studies have now shown that acts of giving money or time – i.e. volunteering – are associated with significant increases in subjective well-being. Regardless of absolute income, those who give more to charity as a per cent of that income are found to be happier. Volunteering has a similar effect, and also appears to create positive well-being spillovers to the wider community: even if you personally don't volunteer, if you live in a community with high levels of volunteering your well-being will tend to be raised.

The Prime Minister was always intuitively supportive of the idea that relationships and community were important to well-being, and to society more generally. This was a central idea that lay behind the 2010 speech, and subsequent speeches, as well as his and Steve Hilton's notion of the 'Big Society'. But the 'Big Society' message was stumbling politically. In 2012, I spoke to the PM and our then Civil Society Minister Nick Hurd to see if I could persuade them to use a BIT-style approach to stimulating social action. The idea was to use both the 'how' of behavioural science and the tough experimental methods we had shown to be effective in other areas. With support from the No. 10 lead, Michael Lyons, they agreed, and with £40 million of Cabinet Office funding, a Social Action Team was established modelled on the BIT approach. (I wish we'd had that kind of money when the BIT started!)

Virtually all the previous results on the positive impacts of volunteering and community action came from cross-sectional data, where we cannot be certain of the causal direction. The Social Action Team gave us the opportunity to test this hypothesis more systematically, and to figure out which forms of social action might be more effective.

The flagship scheme, of the UK's National Citizenship Service (NCS), provided an early test of impact. The NCS programme, introduced from around 2011, gives 16–18-year-olds the opportunity to conduct several weeks of volunteering, including engaging in a local community action project. Participants were asked the four ONS well-being questions before their involvement in the programme and

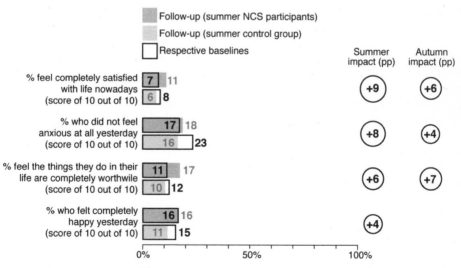

Bases: 3,035 summer NCS participants; 1,710 summer control group; 1,243 autumn NCS paticipants; 1,391 autumn control group

Figure 38. Impacts of the UK's National Citizenship programme on the well-being of participants relative to matched controls. The figure shows the impact tested both over the summer, and in a slightly shorter autumn version. (From the independent evaluation by Ipsos MORI, 2014.)[27]

three months after, and the results were compared with a matched cohort of young people engaged in other activities over the same period. The results were striking.

The young people engaged in NCS showed significant increases across all the measures of subjective well-being, and particularly in life satisfaction and reduced anxiety (see Figure 38). They also showed marked increases in their confidence in 'trying things that are new to me' (+12 points); disagreeing that 'how well you get on in this world is mainly a matter of luck' (+9 points); and agreeing that 'I stay calm when I face problems' (+9 points). NCS participants also subsequently reported more extensive social connections with people from different ethnicities, religions and social backgrounds – an overt objective of the social mixing built into the programme.

Powerful though the results from the NCS evaluation were, the controls were matched rather than strictly randomised into the programme. We therefore worked with the new Social Action Team on a series of true randomised control trials testing the impact of different forms of out-of-school programmes for children aged 10 to 16. These showed significant increases in a range of soft skills, and modest but significant impacts on well-being.[28]

One of the characteristics of modern life, particularly in Anglo-Saxon countries, is that we have often used our wealth to avoid other people. Households have become smaller, and even within households we often spend less time together than previous generations did, such as over meals or even watching TV. Wealth and technology have given us new choices to be able to watch and do what we want, when we want, without having to negotiate with others along the way. It is a very effective way to dealing with what Hirsch called 'the economics of bad neighbouring' – why risk interacting with your neighbours since there's bound to be some who you really dislike.

But this convenience can also cut us off from the satisfactions of relationships, and in ways that sometimes become deeply entrenched.

More than one in ten people describe themselves as lonely often or most of the time. While this has long been recognised in older people – around a third of the over 65s report that the TV is their main source of social contact – surveys suggest that loneliness is as common, possibly more so, in younger people. Robert Putnam, author of *Bowling Alone* and almost certainly the world's leading expert on social capital, once quipped in the mid-2000s that it was unclear whether the internet would evolve into a 'fancy TV or a fancy telephone'. The former would act to increase social isolation (the more hours of TV you watch, the more impoverished your social networks), whereas the latter would connect us even better with our friends and relatives. The answer, it appears, is both. For many people, technology has enabled stronger and more extended networks, but for a minority – including a significant number of younger people – it is a pale substitute for more direct personal interaction. Young people, in the UK at least, are more likely to report feeling lonely than any other age group.

It turns out that there's a fairly similar set of conditions for the formation of satisfying and supporting relationships both in the virtual and the real world. Enforced interaction is not a winning formula – being squeezed together on the Underground just leads to withdrawal: avoid contact and certainly don't talk to others. In contrast, what does work are spaces and places that create opportunities for social interaction but that enable people to maintain a sense of control over who and when they meet others.[29] The coffee machine in an office is a simple everyday example. If you feel like a moment of sociability, you can stroll over and get yourself a cup. But you can also see who is there – if it's Bert from accounts who you don't really want to talk to, you can walk on by.

Armed with this knowledge, communities, businesses and even governments can subtly reshape environments, real and virtual, to foster more satisfying and supportive relationships. School gates, as the internet social entrepreneur Tom Steinberg once observed, create a natural environment for parents to gather and get to know each other, and we should make this a virtue, not just an accident. Streets and buildings can be designed to create spaces where residents can pause and gather. Street parties can be made easy. Communities and activists can organise 'neighbourhood directories' of residents' interests.[30] Technology can lower the barriers to collaborative consumption so that we don't all need to buy a ladder or a drill that we only use once a year. More importantly, it can lower the barriers and intrusiveness to helping our elderly neighbours, or even just organising a football kick-around for the kids on the street.

The data suggest that our well-being is also boosted by access to the natural environment. This overlaps with, but is not the same as, the more well-rehearsed (and important) green agenda. In terms of carbon, it makes no difference whether a tree is planted in a suburban street or a woody copse a hundred miles away. But in terms of well-being it makes a big difference. Designing cities and streets that enable people to see greenery and glimpses of 'nature' is a straightforward way of boosting well-being.

But can we really nudge people and communities to become more sociable, and, even if we could, would it affect population well-being? The short answer seems to be 'yes'. In a test of the wider approach, the Cabinet Office funded a programme called Community First, which provided small grants for projects run by local people designed to boost community action and well-being. It also built on a programme of training for 20,000 community organisers, based loosely on the Chicago model in which President Obama was schooled. The Community First funds were used by communities to get together more often, such as organising street parties, clubs and social activities. Organisers also worked to foster and mobilise their communities to address local issues, though which was entirely up to them. Three years on, we used the new ONS data to see if there had been any impact on well-being. We found that the Community First areas, compared with socio-economically matched control areas showed significant increases in life satisfaction, happiness, feelings that life was worthwhile and significant reductions in anxiety.

Income, work and markets

As mentioned earlier, there is a strong association between GDP and well-being. Though the causal relationship is complex, you'd have to be a brave soul not to think that growth contributes in some way to our subjective well-being. Economic growth gives people choices.

Sure enough, time budget studies show that people work fewer hours than they did 50 years ago, both in terms of hours in paid work and hours spent doing chores at home. What do we do with all this time? A very big chunk of it is spent looking at screens – around 3 hours a day for most people. On a more positive note, most parents spend more time with their kids, freed from an extra hour every day of washing and cleaning.

Yet, as we have seen, we are not necessarily very good at judging how spending our time will make us happy. Survey data suggest that we should spend more time with others (see above), but also that we might be well advised to spend more of this hard-won time going to museums and cultural events (especially with our friends); exercising more; and engaging our curiosity and learning.

The curvilinear relationship between income and well-being is interpreted by most researchers as implying that, at the margin, an extra pound or dollar will bring more well-being for low- than high-income groups. As such, leaving aside the effects of inequality per se, policymakers (and firms) might work harder to boost the incomes at the tail end of the distribution. Yet the effects of income are dwarfed by the devastating effects of unemployment on well-being. This goes to the heart of an old policy conundrum: whether to focus on boosting the income of the out-of-work versus more actively pushing jobseekers into employment. In as far as this is a real trade-off, the well-being literature decisively suggests that the priority should be getting people back into employment.

What is perhaps less well rehearsed is the impact of the quality of work itself. There is a small industry of experts who argue that employers should seek to enhance the 'engagement' and satisfaction of staff in order to boost productivity and the performance of the firm. There are some great examples of how this can be done. Mike Norton of the Harvard Business School has built on Elizabeth Dunn's work to explore how firms that give their workers small bonuses that they have to spend on co-workers can boost both the satisfaction and productivity of workers. It appears to do this because giving makes us feel good and because the gift nudges us to connect with our fellow workers more. The increase in productivity from being put in a better mood is in turn partly because positive moods encourage more creative and open thinking. If you are going to see your doctor, for example, you might want to offer them sweets before they have to make the diagnosis – researchers have found that after being given sweets (which puts them in a better mood), clinicians considered more alternative diagnoses and were more likely to correctly identify the correct one.[31] We also saw earlier how having a good relationship with your boss not only increases your work satisfaction, but dramatically boosts your life satisfaction, too. All this hints at how changes in the character of work may be one of the best ways of boosting life satisfaction in general.

I don't think this means that governments should start passing new laws that bosses should be nicer to their workers, or should require bonuses for workers to buy each other gifts. But I think what we are starting to see, and that governments or other intermediaries could catalyse, is prospective workers being able to find out more about the satisfaction, and frustrations, of existing workers. Figure 37, which shows the life satisfaction of people in different professions, gives a glimpse into this world, as does the steady growth in 'best place to work' guides and competitions. I believe these are a really important development, subtly changing the pressures on firms to improve the quality of working life without state intervention. Firms that want to get the best workers will need to compete not just on salaries – indeed, perhaps less on salaries – but more on the aspects of the workplace that make all the difference between a job and life you love versus one you hate.

Let's push this argument one step further. Much of our consumption is based on predictions about what will make us happy, and it turns out that we're often not very good at these. But one thing that the internet and online feedback has enabled, combined with our deep human urge to share our experiences and learn what others think, is that it is starting to subtly reshape our choices. Better-informed consumers don't just mean better functioning markets in the classical sense of lower prices or choosing lower fat desserts (see Chapter 7). It also implies the reshaping of consumer markets more deeply.

Imagine a world in which consumers are more aware that experiences tend to boost their well-being more than things; where they choose forms of consumption that are more social; and where workers choose the firm with the best boss and most collegiate atmosphere over the highest salary. For businesses that embrace and anticipate this change, it will mean growth and success; for those that fail to notice or adapt, it will mean decline. The de-shrouding of the drivers of well-being – all those quirky books, increasingly based on hard science of what really makes us happy – will reshape and direct markets. Forget GDP: better-informed consumers will reshape markets and economies for themselves. It is the ultimate double nudge.

Governance and service design

One of the commitments of the PM's November 2010 speech was that we would build a consideration of subjective well-being into the heart of policymaking, specifically including a revisiting of the Treasury's 'Green Book' that sets out how to make policy.[32]

The Treasury was lukewarm and never particularly fond of being given a direction from No. 10 under any administration. It took a firm push from, and a stormy meeting with, the then Cabinet Secretary, Gus O'Donnell, to get the Treasury to move forward on revising the Green Book. The revisions had two aspects. The first was to set out how subjective well-being could, and should where possible, be used as the utility measure in policy cost-benefit analysis. The Green Book already had some discussion on how policymakers should seek to factor in all costs and benefits, such as impacts on carbon emissions or loss of natural habitat, even if it was difficult to monetise them. In principle it was a modest and logical step to seek to express the rate of return on an investment in terms of increased life satisfaction, not just pounds or dollars saved.

The second change to the Green Book was more subtle, but quite radical – and with strong behavioural roots. One of the principal methods of valuation, particularly of 'goods' that are hard to price directly, is to ask people what they would be prepared to pay for that marginal improvement or change. For example, if you were trying to work out whether it was worth spending a few billion on a faster train link, a new bypass, or a revamped museum, you might ask a sample of people about what they would be willing to pay, such as for a daily journey that was ten minutes faster. But the behavioural and well-being literature tells us that we should be very wary of such estimates. People think that if they win the lottery their life satisfaction would soar, whereas if they were to lose the use of their legs their lives would be ruined and they would be bitterly unhappy. As such, people say that they would pay a lot for an improved chance of winning the lottery, and a great deal to reduce the chance of becoming paralysed. Yet empirical studies of lottery winners and paraplegics show that, after a couple of years, their life satisfaction is only modestly raised or lowered respectively.[33] This discrepancy arises because the framing of the question makes us prone to error. We focus on all the things that not being able to walk would stop us doing, but tend not to notice all the things we would still get to enjoy, like the taste of good food, the smell of a fresh spring day, or seeing our kids grow up. This focusing error in turn throws our estimates of willingness to pay.

An alternative is to seek to derive more direct estimates of the impacts on subjective well-being, and to use these to derive our valuation. For example, you might seek to measure directly how much people's life satisfaction is affected by a shorter commute, or having access to a museum, and calibrate this against how much it would cost to raise their well-being by a similar amount through other measures (such as higher pay). With all credit to the Treasury, they did commission and publish such a review in 2011 as a complement to the Green Book,[34] though internally they remained sceptical about how much weight to put on numbers derived.

Beyond the technical aspects of Green Book policymaking, which in reality passes most of the world by, the well-being agenda has more direct implications for the governance of nations, companies and communities. As mentioned earlier, our well-being is greatly affected by autonomy and self-control. This can be seen in laboratory experiments through to explaining national differences in happiness and life satisfaction: countries with greater or increased freedoms show higher levels of subjective well-being, even having controlled for GDP.[35]

Regardless of the objective outcome, people value and derive well-being from a sense of control over the process that led to that outcome. When they lose that sense of control, and instead feel that things are being done to them, it has demonstrable effects on their physical and mental well-being. An early example of this from my own work was the impact on GP visits in a population of 2,000 people living on a housing estate that was threatened with demolition, then apparently reprieved, but then re-threatened. Even without a brick being touched, the seasonally adjusted consultation rates tracked the events like a mirror.[36] Similarly, people prefer products and designs that they have had a hand in creating, even if experts rate them as less effective, and prefer websites that show them what they are doing, such as when searching for flights, holidays or partners, to ones that don't, even if they take longer.[37]

The argument is often made that governments, and businesses, should allow people to make spending decisions for themselves on the basis that individuals are often better informed about their own preferences and personal situations. For example, people with long-term conditions should be given direct control over their care budgets so that they buy forms of care that suit their needs and lifestyle, rather than having such services delivered letter-box style in a generic and unchangeable form. A reading of the behavioural literature leaves the impression that we might be less good at making those judgements than classic models imply, particularly in the face of complex and unfamiliar products such as pensions or finance – though noting that experts sometimes don't do much better. However, adding in an analysis of well-being suggests that the act of choosing, or at least some control over the process, may have a direct and substantial value in itself.

On the other hand, the whole point of behavioural and mental shortcuts is for our brain to spare us from overload. Do you really want to be asked about every option that might be available for every product you buy? Or for your doctor to keep asking you about what you think the best treatment should be? In 2007, as part of the process leading up to the handover of power from Tony Blair to

Gordon Brown, we held a one-day deliberative forum in Downing Street with 60 members of the public to test various ideas on public service reform. A strong theme in the ideas presented was around empowering service users, but most of the public weren't very keen. 'I want my doctor to know what's the right thing to do' was a common refrain, 'I don't want to be choosing my treatment – I want my doctor to do that.' On the other hand, when the issue of surgeries' opening hours arose, it was a different reaction entirely. People felt very strongly that surgeries should be open longer to enable them to choose a time for an appointment that suited them.[38]

One powerful route out of this conundrum, without wandering into the treacherous territory of willingness to pay, is to use domain-specific satisfaction measures to help nudge choices. This means asking users of services how satisfied they were with them, or whether they would recommend them to others. Service providers can then look at what drives this satisfaction and adjust their services accordingly.

When this idea was first floated with respect to public services, it was met with considerable professional unease. Doctors, for example, argued that what should really matter was the quality of the clinical care – whether the patient got better or not – not whether they were 'satisfied' by the quality of food or whether the doctor held their hand (see Chapter 7). The Canadians were early adopters of measures of citizen satisfaction with public services, but the surveys were kept generic and not directed at specific named service providers.[39] Similarly in the UK, it took more than a decade of argument to introduce satisfaction ratings into public services, but, since 2010, millions of people have given and used such feedback.

Focusing on well-being in services makes you think much more about treating people with respect and dignity. To take another example of the Social Action Team projects, we expanded volunteering in a large teaching hospital, built on the back of a survey asking staff: 'What are the things that you would like to do for patients, but just don't have time to do?' A year later, with 2,000 volunteers, these things were getting done – from having the time to talk to having someone to help settle the patient back in at home. Patient satisfaction soared. On the back of this result, hospitals across the country are now taking up the approach, with 78,000 volunteers by early 2015.

The well-being literature may not be ready to guide legislators about the detailed design of constitutions and democracies, but it is starting to reveal interesting empirical clues. For example, there is evidence from the new larger surveys that higher levels of local devolution, and fiscal devolution in particular, is associated with significant increases in well-being. Similarly, the low level of life satisfaction in the former Soviet Union countries does not appear to be attributable to GDP levels alone. Whether documenting such differences will provide enough of a nudge to persuade the people of war-torn Ukraine or the Middle East to choose one path or another is an open question, but it is certainly an intriguing one.

Conclusion

It turns out that the same mental shortcuts that we use to decide what to have for lunch, or whether to fill in a form or leave it until tomorrow, also affect our judgements about the big decisions we make in our lives. The job we take; where we live; and who we marry are at least partly based on mental shortcuts that are prone to error. We often misremember what made us happy in the past, and predict incorrectly what will make us happy in the future. In short, behavioural insights raise profound questions about *what* we are trying to achieve, as well as *how* best to achieve it – both for ourselves and within governments.

For some this is a rather unsettling discovery. For classic aleconomists it is potentially devastating, but it does not imply that we are somehow helpless, or that we should sit back and let experts and politicians make our decisions for us. It does mean that we should understand ourselves, and look out for areas where we are prone to predict incorrectly, just as we learn that water often looks deeper than it appears or check our blind spot when driving.

For policymakers – both civil servants and politicians – the well-being agenda is deeply disruptive. It subtly shuffles the sense of what is important, and potentially undermines some of the tools they have previously relied on. Perhaps the biggest shift it brings is to highlight the profound importance of social relationships, and emphasises the importance not just of 'hard' outcomes but the extent to which citizens have control and leverage processes along the way. Of course, cracking cancer is important, but from a well-being point of view don't loneliness and mental health look strangely under-resourced, too? We want our kids to leave school able to read and write, and to get well-paid jobs, but don't we want them to have acquired the psychological resilience and skills to enjoy satisfying and meaningful lives, too?

Finally, let us return to Elaine and her long commute. A couple of years ago, on a visit to the Booth School at Chicago to see my friend and colleague Richard Thaler, I met a young professor called Nick Epley. He'd conducted a study to get commuters to do something really radical – not to give up their commute, but to talk to their fellow commuters.

For those of you who are fellow commuters, perhaps even commuting now as you read, this prospect may fill you with horror. Even the thought of speaking to your fellow travellers may be enough to make you look nervously around. That was certainly the reaction of many of the subjects in Nick's study. 'People will think you are mad!' argued many, or, 'How do I know they won't be a bit odd?' As their immediate emotional reactions give way to a more reasoned, 'thinking slow' response, many argued 'but I need my commuting time to work!'

Still, when the subjects did finally take part in the study, something amazing happened. First, nobody thought they were mad when they started talking to their fellow commuters. And they did talk quite a lot: on average about an extra 20 minutes a journey. Second, their subjective well-being increased markedly. It turns out that changing a commute into a more social experience makes it much more pleasant, and eliminates most of the negative effects documented elsewhere. Third, they got just as much work done as they had before. So much for that excuse.[40]

I love this study for a number of reasons. It is a beautiful example of how we incorrectly predict our well-being, but it also empowers us to do something about it. Personally, I do now make a point of talking to people more on my commute, and often try and coordinate my journey with one or two colleagues who do the same route. Sometimes I feel a bit guilty about the few minutes of work I'm not doing, but then I remember Nick's results and consider that I probably would have been looking out of the window or reading the paper anyway. But it also opens the door to important ideas for policymakers, and indeed train operators, especially when set alongside the other studies that show the importance of personal control and the factors that lead to positive social relationships – as Robert Frost put it, 'good fences make good neighbours'. Trains and buses often now have 'quiet carriages', where people are politely asked not to use their phones and to respect those who want to read or work. But why not also have 'talkative carriages', for those who'd like to chat. Indeed, I've always thought a great experiment for someone to try would be to have a carriage labelled 'sport', and perhaps another labelled 'politics'. If you wanted to talk about last night's game, or maybe next week's election, you could do so. But if you just wanted to work, you could pick another carriage.

This might seem frivolous, but it illustrates an important point for policymakers. The cost-benefit analysis of a given action, such as building a new high-speed railway line for billions of pounds rests heavily on how you value people's time, and specifically the time saved. If you can find a way of changing the subjective quality of that time, the cost-benefit analysis changes dramatically, too.[41]

In sum, I don't think any of us quite know where the behaviourally based exploration of well-being will take us, or quite how radical it will be. Many national governments, and businesses, are now starting to measure well-being and take it seriously. Indeed, some have explicitly made it their number one priority.[42] From a political perspective, the emerging well-being literature can be cherry-picked to find something for everyone. Those on the right choose to highlight the powerful role played by personal relationships, volunteering, freedom and control, and even organised religion (people who go to church are happier, though it's the attendance rather than the religious belief that makes the difference).[43] In contrast, those on the left may choose to highlight the higher well-being returns to boosting income at lower income levels, the negative impacts of unemployment, and the role the state can play in reducing risk.

But regardless of what governments and firms do, the science of well-being is already starting to change people's behaviour. This alone will reshape markets and tip elections. Policymakers and CEOs who think the well-being agenda is no big deal have not even begun to understand it.

▲

CHAPTER 10

WHAT WORKS?

The Rise of
Experimental Government

There's an idea that's been around for decades for how to reduce crime. It's simple, intuitive, politically appealing and has a nice behavioural- sounding edge. Why not bring teenagers who are getting in trouble into prisons to see the life that they are sliding towards? It could serve as an early warning about where their behaviour is taking them; jolt them into thinking about the choices they are making; encourage them to study harder at school; and generally 'nudge' them away from a life of crime. In so doing, it would help prevent crime, save others from becoming victims and save a lot of public money, too.

It is such a great idea that it has been proposed by a number of rising political stars, and tried by a number of governments. Across the USA alone, this 'scared straight' approach has been used on such a scale that it can be delivered for just a few dollars per child. There's just one problem: it doesn't work. In fact, a number of evaluations have shown that such 'scared straight' programmes make it more likely that kids will end up in a life of crime.1

It's interesting to reflect on what's going on from a behavioural or psychological perspective. In favour of the programme: it is dramatic and likely to catch the young person's attention ('attract'). It also should help visualise and identify with the future, breaking through our 'present bias', just as showing people digitally altered slightly older images of themselves helps them identify with their future selves and encourages them to save more for pensions. However, it has a number of flaws, too. The future that is being shown is of

Schoolchildren in north London taught lessons on life behind bars

Children put in handcuffs and prison van in anti-gang drive

Handcuffs: pupils are handcuffed and put in a prison van (Picture: Glenn Copus)

Figure 39. 'London schoolchildren are being taught how it feels to be handcuffed and are shown how small a prison cell is in a bid to steer them away from gangs ... They want to challenge assumptions that prison life is all about "watching Sky TV". Pupils aged 11 and 12 at Newman Catholic College in Harlesden took part in a pilot of the scheme, which will now be rolled out across other schools in Brent' (*London Evening Standard*, 18 June 2014). It would seem that nobody involved had read the extensive systematic review the previous year concluding 'programmes like "Scared Straight" are likely to have a harmful effect and increase delinquency relative to doing nothing at all to the same youths' (see text).

prison and a life of crime, not of college and hard work. It is signalling that this is a route chosen, or taken, by many people, bringing in the powerful force of social norms or 'social proof' in a negative direction (just as described in Chapter 5). As it turns out, the downsides are stronger than the positive aspects, and the net effect is that the child is more likely to offend – and by up to 60 per cent according to some studies.

The real tragedy of the 'scared straight' story is not that it doesn't work – lots of good ideas don't work – but that it is one of the very rare examples of where a programme has been tested to see *if* it worked – but then the results ignored. The fact is, across many areas, governments, businesses and individuals spend billions year after year on things about which we have no idea whether they have any positive impact, and sometimes carry on doing them even when they have been shown to do harm.

The God Complex

Around cabinet and boardroom tables across the world, there's a familiar dynamic. Recommendations and data are shared, and, ultimately, decisions have to be made. Those around the table, and the senior advisers who sit behind them, did not get to these positions by saying 'I don't know' or 'I'm not sure'. Leadership needs to be shown.

Those who have worked in such circles will recognise the sentiment 'it is better to be decisive and wrong, than uncertain and right'. Decisiveness, confidence and a clear vision is seen as a recipe for re-election as a politician, and to calm nervous shareholders as a business leader. Yet while it may be good career advice, and especially if you plan to spend much time as a TV pundit, it's ultimately a terrible way to run a country or a business. In short, it's a recipe for squandering millions.

If it is results we're after, our leaders – and all of us – need a different strategy. We, they and their advisers, need to get used to saying, 'I don't know – but I know how we can find out.' We can test, learn and adapt.[2] And we can do it fast.

Most people understand the basic idea of an experiment, or can at least dimly remember it from science at school. But when most people leave school, they leave behind the idea of experiments. They go on to learn skills, facts and professions. They learn the way that things have always been done, and that seem to work. Yet learning that something seems to work doesn't tell you why it works, or whether an alternative would work better. In fact, it's possible that it doesn't work at all, or at least works no better than doing nothing.

It turns out that our brains are great at telling us stories, and especially ones that make us feel better about ourselves. If we believe that taking lots of vitamin C wards off colds, we'll tend to notice all the times that people had vitamin C and didn't get sick, and especially notice those times when someone got a cold and hadn't taken lots of vitamin C. Yet we'll tend to miss all those people who didn't have much vitamin C but didn't get sick, and see those who did have vitamin C and did have a cold as 'unlucky' or stressed out. In short, we have what psychologists call self-serving, and confirmatory, biases: we tend to believe things that fit in with our prior beliefs and reject those that don't.

One consequence of these biases is the 'God Complex', the tendency we all have to believe that what we think and do is right. Doctors, teachers, politicians – we all assume that what we're doing is effective. This God Complex does serve a useful purpose. You really don't want your surgeon opening you up and then freezing with doubt. A teacher won't last long in front of a classroom of boisterous kids if she keeps stopping to ponder if she is doing the right thing.

There are a few exceptions – people who do pause to wonder if what they are doing actually works. One such man was a doctor named A. L. Cochrane. Archie Cochrane had, at his core, what most professionals would consider a flaw – he was riven with doubt. As a young man he became a prisoner of war, and because of his medical training found himself treating tuberculosis victims at a POW camp in Elsterhost. As he later wrote:

> I remember at that time reading one of those propaganda pamphlets, considered suitable for POW medical officers about 'clinical freedom and democracy' ... I had considerable freedom of clinical choice of therapy: my trouble was that I did not know which to use and when ... I knew there was no real evidence that anything we had to offer had any effect on tuberculosis, and I was afraid that I shortened the lives of some of my friends by unnecessary intervention.[3]

In contrast, while still a prisoner, Cochrane managed to persuade his captors to get him a food supplement rich in vitamin B and was

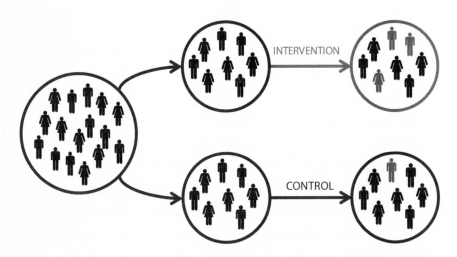

Figure 40. The basic idea behind a randomised controlled trial (RCT). Subjects are randomly allocated to either the intervention (or 'treatment') group, or the control group. Any differences that then arise should be attributable to the intervention.

able to show that its addition to the diet greatly helped many of the sick prisoners. It was a lesson he took home with him after the war: not just that food supplements might greatly help a sick prisoner, but that medics needed to question even their most established practices and to actively test whether they were really helping – or harming – their patients.

Through the 1960s and 1970s, Archie Cochrane and his colleagues started testing, on an ever-expanding scale, whether the practices of the medical profession actually worked. On many occasions such testing was criticised as being unnecessary, and even unethical. Yet when the results came in, just like the meticulous statistics of Florence Nightingale from a century before, Cochrane's work often showed that the established medical practice was ineffective, and sometimes counterproductive, from the treatment of pregnant mothers, to removing tonsils, to keeping patients with heart disease in the hospitals of the time rather than just sending them home.

The shock waves from Cochrane's and his colleagues' restless search to improve the evidence base behind medical practice ultimately extended the lives of millions of people across the world, and helped reshape the character of medicine itself. It led in Britain to the creation of the National Institute for Health and Care Excellence (NICE) in 1999, which is dedicated to collating the evidence of the effectiveness of different medical treatments and drugs. Their work also led to the Cochrane Collaboration, a global network of collaborators spread across more than 120 countries dedicated to summarising the results of experimental medical evidence across trials into rigorous systematic reviews.

But while Cochrane's experimental methods transformed much of healthcare, many professions and the world of policy itself remained largely unchanged.

Not pretending to know the answers

When you take your child to see the doctor, you have good reason to think that the treatment they suggest is well evidenced and will be effective. But when you drop your child off at school, what makes you think that the way they will be taught mathematics has any evidence behind it? In medicine, there are more than 200,000 good quality trials of the effectiveness of different medical interventions, but across education, criminal justice, social welfare, and most other policy areas combined, the number is in the hundreds at best.[4]

Explanations for this yawning discrepancy that point to inherent differences in the professions do not stand up. There is nothing fundamentally different about comparing the impact of varying 'treatments' in maths tuition on attainment, or punishments on reoffending, versus comparing treatments to heart disease on

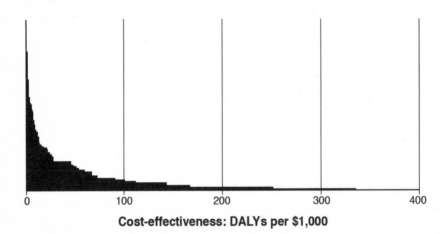

Cost-effectiveness: DALYs per $1,000

Figure 41. The relative cost-effectiveness, in Disability Adjusted Life Years (or years of life saved or freed from disability) per $1,000 spent. A few programmes, such as de-worming kids or mosquito nets, are incredibly cost-effective, saving hundreds of years of life per $1,000. About half are reasonably cost-effective, saving between 5 to 50 years of life for every $1,000 spent, but a long tail of around a third of programmes have almost no impact at all. (courtesy of Toby Ord, Oxford)

years lived. Ethical differences also don't offer a very convincing explanation: is it really credible to say that systematic testing of medical treatments are ethically acceptable where the outcomes are measured in life and death, but that such methods are not to be used to test the efficacy of welfare or education (see Chapter 11 for further discussion)? The dirty secret of much government policy, and professional practice, is that we don't really know if it is effective at all.

There is one area of government expenditure that does have much better evidence of its effectiveness: overseas health aid programmes. For example, Figure 41 shows a plot of the relative effectiveness of different programmes on years of life saved in the developing world. As you can see at a glance, while some programmes are incredibly effective, the range of cost-efficacy is very great indeed. As Toby Ord, a philosopher from Oxford, has pointed out, if you were to choose any two options from this range of programmes at random, the average difference in their cost-effectiveness would be around a hundredfold. To put this another way, armed with the knowledge in this graph, a policymaker could in principle cut the health aid budget tenfold and still have ten times the impact than someone choosing between the programmes without this evidence.

BIT showed that experiments don't have to be big and expensive

The 'randomistas' working in international aid programmes have proven that large-scale evaluations can be of great value, and have helped target aid much more effectively. However, they have had an unfortunate side effect of creating the sense that evaluations must be large-scale, time-consuming and expensive. This is not an attractive package for your average policymaker. As one Minister snapped when an official suggested that their grand idea might first be tested in the form of a trial, 'I didn't spend a decade in opposition to come into government to run a "pilot".'

For the Behavioural Insights Team in our first year of life we faced a deeply sceptical audience. Randomised controlled trials (RCTs) weren't really Steve Hilton's thing, or that of the Prime Minister, but without solid evidence we were never going to be able to persuade the sceptical heads of departments that this was more than a novelty. You might be able to wheel in the PM to win an occasional battle, but most of the time he can't be with you. If you really want to achieve impact on a large scale, as psychologists have studied, it's *conversion* not *compliance* that you're after. For conversion, you need to persuade and convince, not force and insist. We also had to persuade ourselves: how could we really know that some neat ideas developed from lab experiments with North American students would really work in the real, nuts and bolts world of government policy and practice?

We therefore made an early choice to seek out areas well suited to low cost, rapid RCTs. This was one of the reasons tax letters were of such early interest: as well as offering the potential of helping to bring in unpaid tax to help with austerity, HMRC was ideally suited to rapid, low-cost trials. We didn't need to set up an expensive separate measurement system to test whether a letter worded one way or another was more or less effective, since HMRC already had systems in place to track who responded and paid. We still had to get their approval, and in the early days to do the randomisation on a manual basis – literally pulling out letters and replacing them with alternatives – but it still offered the prospect of running a trial and getting results in a matter of months, and sometimes weeks.

The results of these early trials not only showed that behavioural insights could be effective, but also showed people across government that trials could be rapid and low-cost. Within a couple of years, the tiny Nudge Unit team had conducted more RCTs than the centre of British government had done in its entire history. It raised the question, even if a particular policymaker didn't care for nudging, why not use the rapid RCT approach to find better ways of doing things?

The rise of digital government reinforced the argument. Many people vaguely know that the likes of Google and Amazon have learnt to run almost perpetual trials on their sites, testing small variations in presentation and content to see if one form or another led to more click-throughs, often known as 'A/B testing'. At the same time, UK and other governments were seeking to move many services online, but, unlike Google and Amazon, their habit was simply to do a single version of the new digital option, perhaps because that's how the old version used to be.

BIT started to seek out digital interventions within the public sector that could be used to test multiple variations of approach. One such intervention was to test alternative forms of a webpage designed to help people quit smoking. Within a period of a few weeks running up to the main campaign, we were able to test more than 20 alternative pages and thereby refine the site to make it significantly more effective in helping smokers quit (see Chapter 6 for more detail). Similarly, we tested variations of webpages to encourage young people to get careers advice, or to encourage people to join the organ donor register.

The organ donor campaign provides a nice illustration of the approach. In Britain, everyone has to renew their car tax every year. It was an early example of digital government, since the website and transaction also checked that the car was insured and roadworthy (by checking that the car had a valid MOT). We managed to secure agreement that after people had completed the main part of the transaction, the website's final step would be to refer the applicant to a 'thank-you' page that would ask if they would like to join the organ donor register. One question was what message, if any, might stand alongside the button asking people to join the register?

Figure 42. Eight alternative messages to prompt joining the organ donor register.

Traditionally, policymakers would have asked a few people, perhaps employed a creative agency if they had some spare cash, and then plumped for their best guess. Instead we brain-stormed a range of ideas, each based on one or more behavioural effects, and then rather than go for one tried out a range of alternative options in parallel on the website. We then left it to run for a few weeks until more than a million people had used the site, or around 135,000 for each of the different versions of the webpage. The eight options we tried are shown in Figure 42.

Have a look at the messages yourself and see if you can guess which one would be most effective. It's not obvious.

The first is the 'control' – it just says 'Thank you. Please join the organ donor register', with the 'join' button below (1). The next three all have the same extra message, telling people something that is true: 'every day, thousands of people who see this page decide to register' (social), but one has no image (2), one has a picture of a group of happy, healthy people such as might be joining the register (3), and the other has the brand of the organ donor register. Each of the remaining four tests a variety of other messages: expressing the benefit of organ donation in terms of loss (5) or gain (6); reciprocity (7); and the implementation-intention gap – most people say in surveys that they intend to join register to become donors, but just haven't got round to it.

The main point is, even if you were an expert in the behavioural sciences it's very hard to know which of these messages would prove most effective. Indeed, there's good evidence to think that several of them should work. But, importantly, the designers of the site and organ donation programme didn't *need* to know: they (and we) could test the variations and *find out what works* best.

Seventeen million people renew their car tax every year, so if only 1 or 2 per cent saw this page and joined it would add hundreds of thousands to the register. But would the extra message make any further difference? The results are shown in Figure 43.

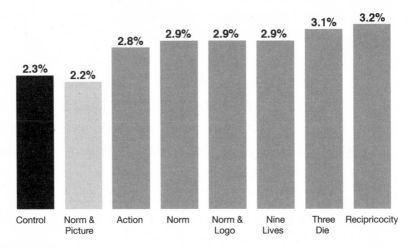

Figure 43. Per cent joining the organ donor register by alternative message seen.

As Figure 43 shows, adding the page led to 2.3 per cent of people completing their car tax payment to join the organ donor register. Almost all of the messages were slightly more effective than the control, with the best performer proving to be the message that employed reciprocity: 'If you needed an organ transplant, would you have one? If so, please help others.' This message boosted the numbers joining to 3.2 per cent – or 39 per cent higher than the control group. This is equivalent to around 100,000 extra people joining the register a year compared with the control.

In some ways, equally as interesting is that the social norms message with the photograph was actually, if anything, *less* effective than the control group. When we asked a number of leading behavioural scientists and policy experts which of the eight webpages would be most effective, many of them chose the page with the image. It is usually the one that the largest number of policymakers choose, too. It was a perfectly sensible hypothesis: we know that people will pay more for credit when the offer letter includes a photo of an attractive, smiling woman, and will be more than twice as likely to sign up to charity payroll giving with a photo of a colleague making the ask in the email. But in this case, the photo didn't work. It might be because it distracted people from the message, or perhaps it was just the wrong photo. But if we had simply plumped for that webpage with the photo, we would never have known that there were lots of better options. We might even have concluded that the webpage had been a great success (after all, hundreds of thousands of people would still have been joining the organ donor register).

BIT also showed that such trials could be run on major areas of expenditure. In 2013, in work on how to boost economic growth we noted how many firms, who appeared to have great potential but whose growth was slow or stalled, did not seek advice despite evidence to suggest it might help them. One of our conclusions was that firms often did not seek advice because they had no easy way of finding out whether such advice would be helpful, or which advisers might be particularly good or bad. We therefore worked up a scheme with the Treasury and business department to offer businesses 'Growth Vouchers' for several thousands of pounds that could be used to pay for advice, but on the condition that the business gave feedback through a public platform on whether the advice was helpful and good value (see also Chapter 8).

Once again, we also wanted to know whether the advice itself, and vouchers, did actually boost the growth of the businesses. To date, the only evidence we could find showed that businesses that took up similar schemes tended to grow faster, but it was plausible that those businesses that were well organised enough to apply for the grant might have grown faster anyway. The best way to be sure was to randomly turn down some of the businesses that applied and qualified, and see what happened.[5] With the help of the Treasury, and the slightly nervous support of Business Ministers Lord Young and Matthew Hancock, the scheme was set up as a true randomised controlled trial. The trial was also set up to test whether face-to-face advice was more effective than that given online.

It takes a little while to find out if a business grows or not, so it is too early at the time of writing to know whether the vouchers did indeed lead to faster business growth. But what we do know is that there wasn't great controversy either in the media or business about the randomised element of the scheme. We also know that when the results do come in, they will tell us something very useful: whether or not the scheme should be scaled up from tens to hundreds of millions, or scrapped. The trial has also helped give the business department the confidence to look around the rest of its spending and think about where else a controlled trial might help them pinpoint more effective spending.

The basic argument is not totally new. Some people in and around government have been making the case for more experimental and empirical approaches for many years. Indeed, even an occasional Minister had been trying to push the idea. In the UK, the Minister for Welfare Reform, Lord Freud, who, unusually, had served both Labour and Conservative–Liberal Democrat Coalition Governments, commented that within the complexity of the welfare reforms he had had to make several hundred decisions where he felt he could not be sure which was the right one to make. His radical conclusion was to embed into the Coalition's welfare reform legislation an explicit clause giving government the power to vary the reforms, and even levels of benefit paid, in order to test what was more effective.

What the BIT work with many departments showed, in tangible and practical ways that brought experimental methods alive, was that such trials could be done fast, relatively easily – and that the sky would not fall as a result. BIT helped show policymakers that they didn't have to know the answer. Instead they could build experimentation into routine policy and practice, and gradually find out what *actually* worked.

What works? Industrialising the experimental approach

From 2011 to 2015, a series of institutions were set up to strengthen the use of evidence by policymakers and practitioners in the UK. They had a simple common objective: to collate and build the evidence on what works and to put this evidence directly into the hands of practitioners and commissioners of services. We called them the 'What Works' institutes.

The new institutes were loosely based on the existing National Institute for Health and Care Excellence (NICE), set up during the early days of the Blair government. NICE's job was similar to that of the Food and Drug Administration (FDA) in the USA – not to do primary research, but to trawl through the published evidence on drugs and treatments and to decide whether to:

▲ Recommend the treatment ('NICE approved');

▲ Not recommend the treatment; or

▲ Allow the drug to be used but recommend that further studies be done.

Ultimately its recommendations had to factor in cost. If a treatment had only a very small effect, but was extremely expensive, NICE might not recommend it for general use in the health service. But its primary focus was effectiveness.

If this approach worked for medicine, why wouldn't it work for other areas of policy and practice? Faced with a shrinking budget, it was a particularly pressing question for the Coalition Government: how could we make sure that money was spent on things that worked, rather than things that didn't. With the backing of the Conservative Minister for Government Policy, Oliver Letwin, the Liberal Democrat Chief Secretary to the Treasury, Danny Alexander, and the Cabinet Secretary, Jeremy Heywood, we set about creating institutions that could answer the question.

The original idea was to create one giant 'social policy' NICE, like a big version of the USA's Washington State Institute for Public Policy. The Washington State Institute, led by the economist Steve Aos, was set up to advise the state's legislators about what might be more or less effective, collating empirical evidence that could be trusted across party lines. Steve Aos, in typically understated style, describes its work as being modelled on the Consumer Reports that people turn to when deciding which refrigerator, TV or car to buy.[6]

Yet there was a key difference between Washington State and a medium- to large-size country such as the UK. Operating with a population of around seven million, Washington State legislators made many of the detailed spending decisions directly themselves. But in the UK, with a population nearly ten times larger, most of the comparable decisions were made within the major departments of state or local government. The UK Treasury also has much less line-by-line control of budget spending than many countries. Indeed, many of the key day-to-day decisions are actually made by professionals and practitioners, such as head teachers, senior police figures and the heads of local government. We also felt that many of these discretionary decisions made at this local level were amenable to empirical testing, and were less likely to be so politically contentious. There are a lot more data to compare across 150 local authority areas than at a single national level.

For these reasons we decided to create a series of What Works institutes, each dedicated to a more focused set of questions. From 2011 to 2013, What Works? institutes were established to identify how best to boost attainment in schools (the Education Endowment Foundation); reduce crime (in the College of Policing); intervene early (Early Intervention Foundation); and boost local growth (Centre for Local Economic Growth). More recently, What Works institutes were added to identify how best to promote a healthy and satisfying later life (Centre for Ageing Better); subjective well-being (a particular interest of the Prime Minister, see Chapter 10); and centres covering Wales (with a special focus on poverty) and Scotland (with a special focus on system reform). All of the centres have been set up with independent governance, and with a range of funding including from the (independent) Economic and Social Research Council; the BIG lottery; and from government departments. Each of the centres is dedicated to the generation, transmission and adoption of better evidence.

The example of What Works in education

Founded in 2011, with an initial endowment of £120 million from the Department of Education, the Educational Endowment Foundation (EEF) illustrates the kind of impact that a What Works institute can have. As Kevan Collins, its head, has noted, the EEF has 'laid to rest the idea that you cannot do randomised control trials (RCTs) in education'. It has already funded more than 90 large-scale trials – all but five of which are RCTs – across more than 4,000 UK schools and involving more than 600,000 children. In short, and in less than four years, the EEF has conducted more large-scale trials than have been conducted across the entire education sector *ever*.

Yet the principal output of the EEF is not a set of academic or research papers. Rather, it is a toolkit designed for school heads, teachers and parents that summarises the results of more than 11,000 studies in education, as well as the EEF's own world-leading studies (see Figure 44). The toolkit enables a head teacher, or anyone else, to get a rapid sense of the overall effectiveness of each type of intervention in terms of impact, expressed as the number of months of educational advance (see the last column, marked 'impact'). It also shows how much the intervention tends to cost, as applied to a class size of 25 (£ 'cost'), and the strength of the evidence that underpins these conclusions (number of padlocks for how secure the evidence is).

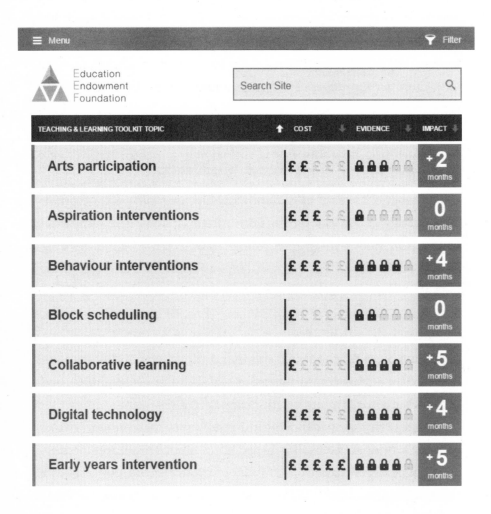

Figure 44. The Educational Endowment Foundation toolkit (truncated), which summarises more than 11,000 educational research studies, including its own large-scale trials. It is designed to enable head teachers and others to get a rapid overview of What Works to boost educational attainment, and particularly that of children from disadvantaged backgrounds. (See http://educationendowmentfoundation.org.uk/toolkit/ for more details.)

For some academic researchers, the toolkit will be seen as an oversimplification of a large and complex literature. But for behavioural scientists, and many practitioners, the trade-off is well worth making (see Chapter 3). Around half of the UK's 24,000 schools say they now use the toolkit to help decide how to spend the money they receive. In particular, British schools now receive around £2 billion per annum as a 'pupil premium' for more disadvantaged students, currently worth around £1,400 extra per year for each student they take from a disadvantaged background. Schools have total discretion how they spend this money. The EEF toolkit helps them make these decisions, but it doesn't force their hand.

The toolkit makes it easy to see at a glance which interventions are effective and cheap. For example, peer tutoring tends to boost progress by half a year, is relatively inexpensive and the evidence behind it is strong. Teaching 'meta-cognition' – essentially teaching kids about how to learn – is even more effective, and similarly cheap and well documented.

The findings of the EEF have not always been popular. For example, their work suggests that extra teaching assistants – at one time a major focus of government spending – are a relatively expensive and generally not very effective way of boosting performance. Further examples of relatively ineffective interventions include having school uniforms, performance pay and setting or streaming. There are even some fashionable educational ideas, the EEF have concluded, that are both expensive and actually set disadvantaged children back, such as making children repeat a year.

Kevan Collins is always careful when speaking to schools not to overclaim or be too dogmatic. A head teacher who has spent hundreds of thousands on teaching assistants may find it hard to accept that they have a relatively modest effect, at least relative to their cost. Kevan notes that in their particular school or circumstances, and with those teaching assistants, it is possible that the effect may be

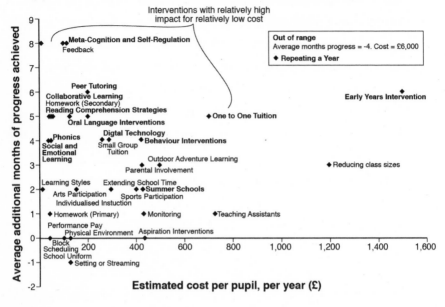

Approximate cost and effect size for 34 education interventions

Figure 45. Approximate cost and effect size for 34 education interventions. Text highlighted in bold signifies interventions for which the evidence on effectiveness is extensive or very extensive according to the toolkit definitions. Cabinet Office analysis based on the Sutton Trust/EEF Teaching and Learning Toolkit technical appendices.[7]

more substantial. Indeed, the EEF is actively studying when and how such assistants can be used to maximum effect.[8] But he'll point out that in other, comparable schools, their effect is small, and will urge the head teacher to look at the other options that generally have bigger impacts.

Sometimes a negative result can stimulate new thinking. For example, while performance-related pay as widely applied appears to have little impact, this result has stimulated some to think about it from new angles. The economist John List, a leading figure in the growing field of experimental approaches in education and now a collaborator with the EEF, has recently shown that while conventional performance-related pay does not work, a behaviourally inspired approach based on people's aversion to loss can boost performance. He found that telling teachers at the beginning of the year what their bonus would be but that it would be cut if their pupils failed to reach a certain standard did lead to a boost in performance. If this result is confirmed, then the toolkit will evolve to show this, distinguishing between the null result of conventional performance-related pay, and the positive impact of loss-based performance pay.

It is a credit to the then Secretary of State Michael Gove that the EEF came into being, albeit perhaps encouraged by the deeply rooted dislike of departments to return end of year underspend to the Treasury. Gove himself, like many of us, was prone to take strong views on what he felt should happen in schools, but he was also often driven to distraction by the weak evidence base and fashion that gripped many of the areas of policy his department funded. When he stood down as Education Secretary in 2014, the controversies of his tenure attracted much press attention, but, oddly, his funding of the EEF went almost without comment. History will lend a very different view, I suspect. The EEF shows every sign of transforming what happens in classrooms not only in the UK, but across the world, with a number of other countries now using its toolkit. It is rebuilding the foundations of teaching into an evidence-based profession, just as NICE, Cochrane and his colleagues helped to move medicine from an art into the science that we recognise today.

Applying the What Works approach to everything we do

Most of the What Works centres do not have the size of endowment given to the EEF, but the core of their approach remains the same. Each of them is dedicated to creating similar toolkits, all designed for the equivalent of head teachers and parents in every field.

The Early Intervention Foundation (EIF), created in around 2012, is working through the cost-effectiveness of early interventions to address a range of social problems. At the same time as they are collating the evidence, they are working with a range of local authorities across the UK to systematically try out new and old approaches, and seeking to plug the gaps in what we still don't know. Though still young, the EIF reviews have already caused a stir. For example, their systematic review of domestic violence interventions offended some when it showed that one of the most popular interventions, focusing on gender relations, did not work. Similarly, an early finding of their work that many local authorities were using interventions in populations and in ways that were known to be ineffective risked causing offence, but also has helped to encourage shifts in spending to more effective interventions.

The What Works Centre for Local Economic Growth (LEG), led by its forthright head, Henry Overman, has also ruffled a few feathers with its early findings. It concluded that local authorities that spent large sums of money building shiny new business parks and industrial estates did little to boost economic growth overall, but simply stole a few jobs from the area next door. Overman didn't win many friends in the arts community either when his centre concluded that most local sports and arts expenditures did little or nothing to boost growth (though they might, of course, be beneficial in other ways, such as boosting health or well-being). In contrast, LEG concluded that, though much less exciting politically, local skills training could boost growth and jobs, and especially relatively short, employer-led forms of training. LEG is likely to put a few dodgy consultants out of business – the ones who will generate whatever answer the local vested interests were hoping for to back their pet project. On the other hand, it should help at least some local politicians and communities to use their spending power to greater effect. In the case of the UK, this particularly concerns the many billions of pounds that are distributed to Local Enterprise Partnerships (LEPs) which, for the most part, have had to spend their money blind until now.

In early 2015, the What Works Centre for Crime Reduction, based within the College of Policing, released its toolkit, along with a £10 million knowledge fund to encourage work to plug the evidence gaps. Its primary audience are the newly elected Police and Crime Commissioners who decide how to spend crime and policing budgets across the UK, and also the wider community who are interested in how best to reduce crime. No doubt it will cause ripples just like the other What Works centres. Just as in education and local growth, large sums of money have often been spent on criminal justice interventions with little or no evidence to back up what it was spent on, and the underlying literature itself has often been weak and gappy. Yet as we saw at the start of the chapter with the example of 'scared straight', where good studies have been carried out the results have often shown that what we thought worked did not. At the same time, other studies have shown that other interventions have sometimes been highly and unexpectedly effective, such as the dramatic reduction in motorbike thefts when the requirement to wear helmets was introduced (see Chapter 3), or evidence that video games, and other forms of diversion, can reduce crime (and may even help to explain the cross-national falls in crime over the last 15 years!).

'Radical incrementalism': keep getting better

It should now be clear that I am a big advocate of the What Works approach. Indeed, one of my roles in British government over the last few years – alongside my day job as head of the Behavioural Insights Team – has been to serve as the newly created UK's National Adviser on What Works. This means that I champion the use of better evidence in government, and push the shift to more widespread, robust, and faster evaluations of government policy and day-to-day professional practice.

There is a slight danger that policymakers and practitioners get half the idea of what works: that there needs to be a review of the evidence, perhaps by one of the What Works centres, and that's it. But the What Works centres are just one part of a bigger story. The centres' collation of the evidence into toolkits is reliant on an ongoing supply of evidence.

In the area of medicine, NICE and the FDA are able to draw on a large number of studies, or medical trials, conducted by private drugs companies seeking approval. But this is atypical. Most of the What Works centres find that in many areas the evidence is distinctly thin, despite the trillions spent by governments on policy interventions and research across the world every year. Even in health, the evidence base is often patchy. The financial returns and regulatory framework around pharmaceuticals drive a large evidence-building industry, even if it is far from perfect.[9] But turn to public health, or even service innovations within healthcare, and the number of robust studies drops dramatically.

To plug this gap we need policymakers and practitioners to do their jobs differently. As discussed earlier, we need policymakers and practitioners to deliberately try out alternatives, and to admit that we often do not know what works best. If we can bring these two elements together – policymakers and practitioners that actively experiment, and What Works centres that independently collate and spread the results – we will have created a powerful dynamic to improve everything that we do. I call this approach 'radical incrementalism' (see box).

Most people, and governments, forget important things they've learnt. That's one of the reasons why we need institutions: to pass on learning from one generation to another. I am by no means the first or only person to argue for the greater use of evidence or RCTs

Radical incrementalism

'Radical incrementalism' is the idea that dramatic improvements can be achieved, and are more likely to be achieved, by systematically testing small variations in everything we do, rather than through dramatic leaps in the dark. For example, the dramatic wins of the British cycling team at the 2012 London Olympics are widely attributed to the systematic testing by the team of many variations of the bike design and training schedules. Many of these led to small improvements, such as getting the cyclists to bring their own pillows when away to reduce the likelihood of getting sick and missing training, but when combined created a winning team. Similarly, many of the dramatic advances in survival rates for cancer over the last 30 years are more due to constant refinements in treatment dosage and combination than to new 'breakthrough' drugs.

Applying similar 'radical incrementalism' to public sector policy and practice, from how we design our websites, to business support schemes, we can be pretty confident that each of these incremental improvements can lead to an overall performance that is transformative in its cost-effectiveness and impact.

in government, but I hope I will be one of the last who has to keep making the case.

As National Adviser, I recently gave a talk to the Department for Environment, Food and Rural Affairs about how they might use more empirical approaches in their work, including the use of RCTs. There was genuine interest in the room, but also some scepticism about whether such approaches could really work in their area. So I asked them if they knew who Ronald Fisher was. There were blank looks. 'The Fisher Test, or the F-test?' I suppose I was feeling mischievous. One or two with more analytical backgrounds started to nod. 'He was one of the most famous and important statisticians of the last century,' I explained, 'and your predecessors in this department funded him.' They looked puzzled. So I explained how Fisher's work, and many of the key foundations of contemporary statistics, was based on literal 'field studies' to establish what variables and treatments affected crop yields. Much of this work was done at the Rothamsted Experimental Station in Harpenden, Hertfordshire.

It feels like an important lesson. Even in a government department that once sponsored and led the development of experimental approaches, and the foundations of modern statistics itself, they had fallen out of the habit. To geeks like me, and perhaps to you, it seems obvious that we often don't know the answer and therefore that we need to experiment, evaluate and iterate. But clearly it isn't obvious, judging from widespread practice. It may not even persist in institutions that once used or funded the 'radical incrementalism' approach themselves.

Going international

Most governments, and professionals, across the world are ultimately wrestling with similar questions. How to boost (sustainable) growth? How best to educate our children? How to boost employment; to reduce crime and conflict; and to boost health and well-being? We can't answer these questions in our armchairs. It is a hard slog to build an evidence base, and to continually 'test, learn and adapt' to do better.[10] What is found to work in one context won't always work in another, but often it will.

To do their jobs properly, What Works institutes and evidence clearing houses need to review studies from across the world, not least to get more variability in the range of interventions considered. Their toolkits, and the intervention studies on which they are built, are a classic public good: they impose costs on those who produce them, but are of benefit to all. As such, we should support them as international public goods, too.

It would be so much more sensible and cost-effective if countries, cities and professional bodies clubbed together to commission systematic reviews, and to build a common evidence-building and disseminating structure together. To some extent we have already started down this road. Bodies such as the OECD and the World Bank might be considered cross-national What Works institutes, building and collating evidence. Some governments have also sought to support collaboration in evidence-building and collation in other ways, such as Norway's support for the Campbell Collaboration (which conducts non-medical systematic reviews). But these institutions are still far being from the linchpins of 'radical incrementalism' that they could be. Much of what counts as evidence are still cut-and-paste comparisons of what different countries are doing, with little purchase on causality or cost-effectiveness. At the same time, most of the outputs remain more akin to rarely read academic papers than the user-friendly, practitioner-focused 'consumer report'-style outputs that might actually change practice on the ground.

I hope that one of the things we'll see emerging in the next couple of years is a more effective cross-national clearing house or platform that enables policymakers and practitioners from across the world to be better able to access and build the evidence on What Works. There is no shortage of opinions and even research, but patching together evidence is not a democratic process in the sense that evidence varies greatly in its quality, and that based on better and more robust methods should be accorded much more weight.

Central to this platform will be a set of toolkits like that of the EEF we saw above (see Figure 44), but with an important extra column that shows the range of countries and places where the intervention was found to be effective (or not). A policymaker – or public service provider – can be much more confident about importing an intervention that has been replicated in five or six countries than one that has only been shown to work in one place alone.

Another key element of this clearing house or platform should be that it will capture and highlight gaps. In this respect, it should work more like a 'kick-starter' for systematic reviews and intervention studies. After five or six countries, states or professional bodies have searched for an answer or review and not been able to find what they are looking for, this needs to be picked up so that a What Works centre or some other body can step forward to plug the gap. The commissioners will get a better review or study, and at a much lower cost since the charge for the work can be spread between them.

The What Works movement should not be something for wealthy nations only. In 2015, the Millenium Development Goals were updated. Generating a list of targets is the easy bit; the difficult question is not what the targets should be, but how they can be delivered. Aid is only a small part of this answer. As a colleague in the Department for International Development pointed out, even in some of the poorest nations of the world aid budgets are increasingly dwarfed by developing nations' own resources. As such, an increasingly valuable gift is knowledge – how to spend precious resources well. If we can figure out a better way of teaching maths in Birmingham, this should definitely be of interest in Berlin, but will almost certainly be of equal interest anywhere else in the world where maths is taught.

BIT, and some of the more innovative trials of organisations such as J-PAL, have shown that rapid, low-cost trial methods can be utilised across the world. We should also introduce in their wake the toolkits and institutional frameworks to translate and adopt these methods and results.

This is not a trivial, 'nice to have' matter. Serious world leaders have concluded that it is the lack of basic competence and effectiveness in the delivery of government and public services that often brings instability, frustration and the fall of governments. Of course, other factors such as honesty and corruption matter, too, but a solid and utilised evidence base is a good foundation stone for a world where governments are trusted and respected by the citizens they serve.

Conclusion: the rise of experimental government

In a postscript to his *Effectiveness and Efficiency*, Archie Cochrane – who did so much to push medicine towards being an evidence-based profession – wondered if he'd been too harsh on his medical colleagues:

> ... I may have been too critical of my colleagues for whom I actually have the greatest admiration and affection ... If one adopts a comparative approach I would like to stress how very far ahead the medical profession (particularly in the UK) is of other professions. What other profession encourages publications about its error, and experimental investigations into the effect of their actions? Which magistrate, judge, or headmaster has encouraged RCTs into their 'therapeutic' and 'deterrent' actions?

It has taken more than 40 years, but other professions and policy areas are finally catching up. The What Works centres meet on a quarterly basis and together are driving, study by study, a quiet revolution in the quality and character of public services and policy. These What Works institutes are engaging in a seemingly simple set of tasks: systematic testing; collating the evidence; and putting this evidence in the hands of commissioners and professionals in an easy and accessible form. As the UK's Minister for Government Policy, Oliver Letwin put it: 'We will surely look back in 10 or 20 years and think it very strange that we ever did it in any different way.'

In business, too, the idea of systematic trials and testing is starting to break out of a few historical footholds, such as marketing and retail, and becoming increasingly widespread.[11]

Once, over lunch at the Treasury, I compared notes with James Manzi, a leading expert on the use of controlled trials in the commercial world, on the relative 'hit rate' that BIT was achieving in our trials compared with those commonly seen in the commercial world. He reckoned that most commercial players, such as retailers, would be lucky to get a hit rate much better than 51:49 – they would be doing well if one or two out of a hundred trials came back with a significant improvement in sales relative to baseline. Since some of them were running thousands of trials a year, this could still lead to valuable improvements. In contrast, in BIT we were getting a hit rate closer to 80:20.

It would be nice to think that this was because we were terribly clever, but a big element of our high success rate has simply been that most of the public sector is virgin territory for the use of systematic trialling, as well as behavioural approaches. The habit runs deep to jump to a single solution, often at national level, and to presume that the way things have always been done must be effective. Unlike in the private sector, there is often little or no competition, and where there is, 'exits' of underperforming institutions and practices are slow or absent. No wonder, then, that BIT was able to have such dramatic success.

Most fundamentally, the experimental methods pursued by BIT, and spread by the What Works movement, bring with them something new and deeply important to policy and practice: humility. As Richard Feyman, the celebrated physicist, quipped, 'science is the belief in the ignorance of experts'. His point was not that scientists were 'ignorant' in the usual sense, but that science was about embracing 'doubt' – being open to the possibility, even likelihood, that your theory was wrong. In his wider writing and lectures, he rightly urged others to embrace this disruptive essence of science.[12]

As experimental studies have shown, and this chapter has argued, we are all prone to overconfidence. Ask a colleague a set of ten factual questions, such as how many people died on the roads last year, but ask him to give the answer as a range within which he is 90 per cent confident such as 'I'm pretty sure the number who died on US roads last year was between 30 and 40 thousand.' Do the same for a group, and you'll often find the average answers are quite accurate. But look at the range for each individual and you will find it is much too narrow. Most individuals will be lucky if they get five out of ten answers to fall in their 90 per cent confidence intervals, let alone nine out of ten. But the good news is that, shown this exercise, most people can learn from the experience to widen their estimates and to adjust for their overconfidence.[13]

We all need to learn this lesson, and we need to build institutions and practices to help us. There is still so much we don't know – but could easily find out. We need to recognise our dangerous tendency to overconfidence and our presumption that what we do know is 'right'. We need to follow in the footsteps of Archie Cochrane and Richard Feyman. We need to embrace doubt. We need to test, learn and adapt.

While writing this chapter I was at a meeting in the House of Commons with three senior Ministers and some officials to resolve a policy issue. Such meetings happen most days. In this case there was a disagreement between two major departments about which of a range of psychological therapies might be utilised to reduce depression and also get people back to work faster (depression now accounts for more years of productive life lost than any other single condition). The Department for Work and Pensions wanted to try a wider range of approaches, but the Department of Health were uneasy about supporting approaches that had not been signed off by NICE, the What Works centre for medical treatments. Much to my delight, one of the Ministers made a suggestion: 'Could we try out these approaches as an RCT …?' There were nods around the table. 'Yes,' agreed the senior official from the Department of Health, 'that would do it.' The more senior of the Ministers grinned at me, then scanned the table. 'We have an agreement, then?' he declared. We did indeed – and something much more. We had moved into a world where Ministers begin to know the merits of a controlled trial, and demand it of their officials.

It is a very different worldview from the brash self-confidence of conventional politics, and falsely confident professional practice, that we have become used to. But it is a worldview that brings results, and will probably be the most important legacy of the quirky empiricism that BIT brought to the heart of British government in 2010, and is now spreading through the world.

SECTION 4

▲

WHERE NEXT?

We have seen how behavioural insights can be used to improve the practical workings of a vast range of processes and practices, and also used to reshape how we think about policy, society and the economy more fundamentally.

In this final section we shall think about the political and practical limits of behavioural and experimental approaches. Just because an approach is effective doesn't mean that it's right. Do nudges, and other behavioural approaches, wear off? If behavioural approaches are so powerful, should there be tighter limits and controls on those who use them, both in government and business?

We shall also have a glance at the next generation of challenges and frontiers that behavioural scientists are looking at – and whether you, as a citizen or consumer, should be worried or delighted. Probably the answer is both. You decide.

CHAPTER 11

▲

RISKS AND LIMITATIONS

It was a warm sunny morning in 2003. My colleagues and I in the Prime Minister's Strategy Unit were looking forward to the day ahead. It was the morning we were publishing a 'think piece' entitled *Personal responsibility and behaviour change*. It was the first serious attempt by a national government to think through the implications of behavioural science for mainstream policy. We'd had to make a few compromises, but it was still a good piece of work, and it was nice to publish it, unlike much of our policy work for the PM which was regarded as too hot to print. Just in case, the words 'this is not a statement of government policy' was printed on the bottom of each of its 70 pages, just as we had done for previous think pieces.

Walking into Admiralty Arch it was obvious immediately from the panic on people's faces that there was a problem. A report of the paper was already on the front page of *The Times* proclaiming: 'PM's Strategy Unit proposes fat tax' together with a picture of big pork pie.

The No. 10 Press Office was on one line, wanting to know what the hell was going on. The Department of Health was on another. Health officials weren't pleased with the lack of consultation, but said they were pretty interested in the idea and asked for No. 10 to please keep the option open. Geoff, then Head of Unit, was none too pleased either, and worried about the damage to our political capital.

The *Times* article was based on a brief reference in our paper to whether price differences between healthy and unhealthy foods might encourage healthier consumption, as had recently been argued for by the British Medical Association.[1] We'd noted that differential duty on leaded versus unleaded fuels had led to a rapid switch to unleaded fuels, and though our paper avoided a firm conclusion on whether or not this would work for food, the implication had made a good headline.

There was pressure to put out a statement that differential taxes on food were impractical and would be ineffective. The No. 10 Press Office wasn't in much of a mood to be told that this was probably wrong on both counts. In the end we haggled over a statement, and put out a line to remind people that this was not government policy and that the government had no plans for a 'fat tax'.

With turmoil in the office, I thought I'd get a breath of fresh air at lunch and stay away from the canteen. But as I walked up to the Whitehall café, outside I noticed that someone had scribbled on the board above the daily special: 'Get your sandwich with butter before the fat tax!' We really were in trouble.

The statement was already too late to stop the tabloids going with the story as well. By the next day they were running front pages with pictures of the leading members of Cabinet with an estimate of their weight under each picture. The relatively large weight of Deputy Prime Minister John Prescott was of particular interest, twinned with the irresistible headline: 'How much fat tax will Prezza pay?'

Shortly afterwards, the Prime Minister, Tony Blair, made a major speech distancing himself from the use of behavioural approaches by government.

Handle with caution?

It would take nearly a decade and a change of government to resuscitate the overt use of psychology and behavioural insights in British policy. The easy account is that a poorly placed briefing and politically awkward headline simply delayed the inevitable. But an alternative view is that the reaction reflected deep-seated public concerns about the use of behavioural insights by government. It makes a lot of people uneasy. And maybe it should.

Making unhealthy foods more expensive, or healthier foods cheaper, wouldn't even be counted as a nudge by Thaler and Sunstein. It is a deliberate attempt to sway the behaviour of citizens – although so is most policy. So why the big fuss?

This chapter discusses the risks and potential downsides of governments using behavioural insights in the design of policy. The potential benefits are clear. But if behavioural insights are powerful, they can be misused, too – not just by business, but also by unscrupulous governments and bureaucrats. Can we have the good, without the bad? Will governments use behavioural insights to do things that they want to do, not what you or the public might want them to? For example, over the last couple of years, governments have been relatively quick to see the power of using behavioural insights to get taxes and fines paid, while politicians have already used BI on their electoral campaigns, and especially in the USA. But have they been as quick to use BI to ensure consumers get a better deal, or to develop more effective methods of citizen scrutiny over what they do?

At the heart of the issue is the question of what constitutes a better choice, and who should decide. A basic implication of many nudges, especially around defaults, is that someone other than you is making a judgement about your best interest and that of society. In other words, the implication is that government, or an expert choice architect, knows best. Yet this is a claim that at least some would dispute, both politically and empirically. Who are the 'nudgers' to say they know better than individual citizens going about their everyday lives?

This chapter will look at these issues and concerns head on. It will move on to discuss what measures might be put in place alongside the use of behavioural insights in policy. The discussion is organised around three broad areas of concern:

▲ Lack of **transparency** – that behavioural approaches are too close to the dark arts of propaganda and subconscious manipulation (a concern of the right).

▲ Lack of **efficacy** – that behavioural approaches are an excuse for not acting more decisively and effectively (a concern of the left).

▲ Lack of **accountability** – that the behavioural scientists and decision-makers behind these approaches need to be more answerable to those they affect (a concern of liberals and democrats).

Nonetheless, with suitable measures and safeguards in place, including enhanced democratic oversight and accountability of the nudgers, I will argue that behavioural insights can bring many benefits, and even enhance the character of democracy itself.

A dark art? The transparency challenge

A deep-seated concern, especially on the right, is that there is something devious or underhand about nudge approaches. As one senior policymaker privately put it in the late 2000s, 'It's not how government should act.'

This is a concern that should be taken seriously. 'Nudge-style' approaches at their core are based on the idea that many decisions and behaviours are rooted in very rapid, often unconscious patterns of thought. If people tend to avoid the highest and lowest priced of a set of choices, be it a beer or a financial product, once sellers have this information they can 'trick' consumers into paying more by adding extra high-price items at the top and trimming out the lower price options. Similarly, armed with the knowledge that people strongly anchor to the default option, couldn't governments and businesses get away with all kinds of mischief? The very automatic nature of such decision-making suggests that the skilled nudger can influence our behaviour without us even noticing.

In a strong form, one could argue that such approaches bring a lack of transparency and constrain freedom, and are even inherently anti-democratic since they are not consciously chosen by the citizens who are affected. Isn't it, to use a word that would send shudders down the spine of any libertarian, *manipulation*?

It is this manipulation concern about nudging that strikes a particularly raw nerve in the USA, and one that Cass Sunstein especially had to wrestle with in the White House. It is an argument that he continues to wrestle with now that he has the freedom to write again back in academia. Similarly for Richard Thaler, always a Chicago economist at heart, this critique of nudging as 'manipulation' is one that he has always been extremely sensitive to.

For Sunstein and Thaler, the originators of the term 'nudging', their first response has always been that nudges should be both 'choice-enhancing' – or at least not choice-restricting – and transparent. In this sense, the nudge is to be seen as an alternative mandating or banning. For example, changing the default on a pension scheme from one that is an opt-in scheme for employees to an opt-out does not eliminate the choice. Employees are still free to opt out if they wish to do so. It is transparent what the choice is, and employees are informed by law about it. In contrast, in some western countries you are obliged to save – though you may have some choice about your pension provider.

There's no neutral choice

Nudgers often talk about 'choice architecture' – the way that options are presented. The everyday example that is often discussed is the order in which food is presented in a cafeteria. Which do you see first: the salad or the chips? It turns out that the order matters. When you walk in hungry, whichever option you see first is very likely to end up on your tray. As Brian Wansink has shown, conference-goers fill up 68 per cent of their plates with the first three items they come across, regardless of whether the items are healthy fruit or a rich cooked breakfast.[2] In fact, we now know that almost every aspect of the cafeteria affects what and how much you eat, from the menu, to the plate size, to the size of the serving implements, to whether or not there are trays.

Few of these effects are mediated by conscious choice. The Thaler and Sunstein argument, and one that is increasingly used by nudgers in governments across the world, is that there is no neutral choice. The cafeteria has to be arranged in one way or another. So policymakers – and restaurant owners, school heads, hospital administrators and so on – should choose options on the basis of what would be best for most people.

If you think about the alternative, this seems irresistibly sensible. Once you know that food order or plate size affects what we eat and how much waste the restaurant produces, isn't it obvious – even incumbent – on the decision-maker to choose the healthier, more environmentally friendly option?

This argument gets a lot more complicated when we move beyond a simple example like the school canteen, to a less clear-cut example like a pension plan. But even in the case of the canteen, it gets more complicated once we acknowledge that there could be more than one way of deciding which option is best. How do we decide the criteria for the default where a different criterion might lead to a different result? For example, let's suppose that salad is a lower profit margin item than the chips – it's then quite a big ask of the cafeteria owner to put the salad first (though the smaller plate sizes might still be attractive). And what if the chips result in the kids in the school staying better focused in the afternoon classes – then how would we decide?

Another issue is that the best default for one person is not necessarily the best for another. In schools where many kids are obese, putting the salads first might be the best choice for most kids, but for a minority with eating disorders like anorexia, this might be very bad. Turning to pensions, where people's circumstances and preferences might differ greatly, having a single default for everyone looks especially problematic.

For many leading behaviourists, including Sunstein, Laibson and Loewenstein, the answer is to have 'tailored defaults'. This means having not one default, but a series of defaults that have been crafted for particular population segments. This is hard to do in a cafeteria, unless you could have more than one line, perhaps directing people one way or another according to their BMI measured as they walk across a sensor on the way in. But for pensions and many other products it is very possible. For example, rather than having a single default for everyone, 'smart defaults' might instead seek to differentiate according to workers' age, marital status and recent or forthcoming pay increases to set a more personalised saving rate and product.

I think this is a good start as an answer, but it isn't enough. Even with personalised defaults, there remain tricky questions about who sets these defaults, and we'll return to this question presently.

Effective communication versus propaganda

A lot of what BIT does, along with other similar units emerging across the world, concerns communication, at least in a broader sense.

A lot of the issues we are asked to work on are about informing, encouraging and persuading. In this sense, the choice architecture is left unchanged, but the focus is on making one action feel more, or less, attractive than another. Indeed, occasionally overseas visitors look at what we do and say, 'Isn't this just comms?'

Some of it is clearly about 'comms', though we'd like to think that we're a bit more scientific and rigorous about it than your average ad agency. To recall the phrase from that master of persuasion Robert Cialdini, from the session he did in the State Dining Room at No. 10 in 2006: 'It's about *effective* communication.'

Governments, and businesses, communicate with people all the time. We are bombarded by signs, texts, emails and letters. Many of these messages are intended for our own benefit, such as to warn us of a hazard ahead on the road; to let us know that a product may be harmful, especially if used in a certain way; or to remind us of our obligations, such as to pay taxes that we owe. If we think it's appropriate and acceptable for such communications to occur, it seems sensible to expect those designing or writing them to make them effective and easy to understand – and not to be misunderstood.

If we're going to introduce a tax break to encourage businesses to invest more in R&D, I think that very few people would consider it wrong to ensure that the communications about this tax break should be as clear and simple as possible. Similarly, I doubt many would object to the use of personalised messages segmented to businesses that the tax break might be most relevant to, or designing prompts that come up on search engines highlighting the tax break when people entered the search term 'reducing your corporate tax bill'. Better to have the business decide to invest more in R&D than to take its profits offshore.

Yet where should we draw the line between effective communication, and unacceptable 'PsyOps' or propaganda? Long before there were 'nudge units' appearing across the world, many governments have had Psychological Operations Units (at least to influence the citizens of other nations, if not their own), and many have had Ministries of Information, some with distinctly Orwellian overtones.

Within BIT there were a number of lines in the sand that we did not cross. First, we were careful to ensure that any claim we made was actually true. If we tried using social norms to encourage a given behaviour, such as by adding the line that 'nine out of ten people paid their tax on time', we took care to make sure this was true. When working with the World Bank to conduct similar work to boost the tax take in Guatemala, the same line would not have been true so we didn't use it. Instead we identified the actual percentage of people who did declare and pay the particular tax in question. In this case, it was around 65 per cent, but we reasoned that many people would still be surprised to discover that a majority of their fellow citizens complied and paid any tax. So we tested including the actual proportion of people who paid the tax in reminder letters to those who had not declared for tax purposes. (Fortunately, it was still very effective, boosting tax paid by 5.6 percentage points, or by 43 per cent more than a control letter without the social norm message.)

A second principle was to be transparent and monitor public concerns. The unit has been open about its work, publishing research protocols and regular public documents on a range of issues that we were working on. We also sought to be attentive to public concerns about whether a particular approach caused offence or confusion. In the UK tax trials using social norms, for example, we tracked levels of complaints, and found that they fell substantially relative to those of the previous year. In contrast, in one trial that we ran, which involved giving small businesses feedback about their credit ratings (which affect their ability to borrow and the rate they may have to pay), we got much more negative feedback. The background to the trial was that small businesses were struggling to get adequate access to finance from banks or others in the ongoing fallout from the

2008–12 financial crisis, and one contributory reason was that small businesses had relatively poor credit ratings yet were unaware of what actions they could take to improve these. Some of these actions were not necessarily obvious, such as how credit ratings companies score a small business better if the owner is on the electoral register (which is optional in the UK). However, in an initial mail-out of 1,000 letters, we received several complaints from people who received them, partly because they didn't really understand why they were sent the letter or felt that it wasn't the government's business. Though the number of complaints were small in absolute terms, at less than a dozen, the concerns seemed genuine and heartfelt so we abandoned the trial.

A third principle was to ensure that we had some form of independent checks and balances outside the team itself to give a view on the ethics of our trials and work. Avoiding lying and being sensitive to public concerns are necessary but not sufficient conditions for ethical behaviour. A key check and balance came from setting up an independent academic advisory panel, which included Richard Thaler and around half a dozen other leading academics with behavioural expertise. The panel was later chaired by Lord O'Donnell, the former Cabinet Secretary, who combined both a deep interest in behavioural approaches and a deep knowledge of the workings of government (and remains chair of the advisory panel today).

On some occasions the panel did indeed push back, and there were BIT interventions that were revised as a result. The health behaviour expert on our panel, Professor Theresa Marteau also felt that we needed to strengthen the transparency and independence of the ethical clearance process for some of our trials, to bring it into line with those found in medical trials. This led to a robust debate across the panel about the right balance between the sophistication of the ethics clearance process and the pressure to act fast. What level of ethical clearance process was appropriate for changing the wording

Figure 46. London's Senate House that helped inspire Orwell's idea of the 'Ministry of Truth', as part of his dystopian vision 1984 of a society based on state-based mind control. The building housed the British wartime Ministry of Information, where his wife worked. Nudge units need to ensure that they are embedded in an institutional framework that ensures they stay well away from Orwell's vision. As it happens, Senate House is now part of University College London, whose master's programme in behavioural science has supplied BIT with several students, and one of whose professors sits on our advisory board.

on a tax reminder letter, versus a new drug trial, noting that millions of such letters were sent out every year without any clearance process at all? Some panel and team members also thought that there was an important difference between trials run in autonomous and independent academic institutions versus those run within a government context answering to democratically elected Ministers. This debate led us to clarify our clearance processes, and to set up a more formal and independent ethics and trial protocol clearance process drawing on independent academics outside Whitehall.[3]

Behavioural predators

Governments are not the only, or even the main, users of behavioural science or nudging. Back in 2003–4, when writing the original PMSU report on behaviour change, we coined the term 'behavioural predators' to refer to the commercial, and sometimes criminal, influencers whose intent was far from benign.[4] Unfortunately, there are a lot of people and businesses who are busy persuading others to do things which are very much not in their interests and that they will probably regret.

Tobacco companies developed extremely sophisticated marketing campaigns to make smoking seem glamorous and attractive, particularly to young people and segments that had yet to take up the habit. Door-to-door salesmen developed a highly commercially successful trade in getting people to switch to alternative energy suppliers in Britain, that were often much more expensive than the best alternatives in the market. Banks and other financial services have learnt how to sell more expensive finance to less sophisticated borrowers, and how to ensure that they don't switch to better deals. And many online businesses have become adept at adding extra charges, terms and conditions that people don't notice.

Robert Cialdini's original book *Influence: The Psychology of Persuasion* is full of examples of clever 'tricks of the trade' that range from how skilful waiters and salesman can boost their earnings, through to overt scams. Of course, Cialdini's point is to understand how they work, and to arm the reader against them. Similarly, there are some excellent books and courses emerging explaining how marketers and businesses can use behavioural science to get an edge on the competition.[5] But there's nothing to stop an unscrupulous individual or trader studying the same approaches to use on unsuspecting consumers.

Actually, that's not quite true. There *should* be something to stop the unscrupulous trader using and abusing clever behavioural approaches to take advantage of others. Most countries have laws against deceitful practices; regulations to enforce fair trade and consumer rights; and regulators to intervene and back them. More fundamentally, well-designed and functioning markets can also offer some protection against large-scale abuses, though also opportunities for innovative malpractice, too.

This need, and demand, to intervene on behalf of citizens by governments and regulators means that they are drawn into the world of behavioural insights whether they like it or not, and even if they themselves do not wish to use the approaches. In a world of poachers and predators, you need a few gamekeepers, too.

The line between abusive practice, improper influence and effective marketing can be a subtle one. It is not enough for regulators to say 'it is a competitive market, so everything is fine'. Unregulated markets, and particularly those dealing with complex products and busy consumers, can often find stable equilibriums with a high level of 'consumer detriment' or, in everyday language, people getting ripped off. For example, the widespread use of click-box acceptances of complex terms and conditions buried in long documents is a recipe for abusive practice, and draws directly on our tendency to go for the easy option (click the box, versus actually read the document). Regulators are right to probe the limits of what firms can get away with burying in such terms and conditions. Regulators are right, for example, to insist that anything that bears on the price of the product or service should not be buried in these terms and conditions.

Whether we like it or not, the world has many behavioural predators. A government or legitimate business that fails to engage in this reality is putting their head in the sand. More importantly, a government that fails to respond is, in my view, failing in its duty to protect the people it works for and represents. Failing to engage is not neutral – it means leaving the field open to the bad guys.

Choosing not to choose

There is a paradox that follows from the US-style approach to nudging that roots the approach in the requirement to be choice-enhancing. People use mental shortcuts to prevent the slow, deliberative part of our brains from being overwhelmed by choices and decisions. A sensible choice, therefore, will often be to 'choose not to choose'.

We've all had experiences when a keen salesman, or family member, has ground us down with endless choices. Which of these colours do you prefer? Which of these options? Eventually we reach a point where we say in exasperation, 'Look, I just don't care – you decide.'

Governments, businesses and communities face endless decisions that they are often making on behalf of other people. Indeed, one good reason for having elected politicians, love them or hate them, is that we're asking them to make many of these decisions on our behalf so the rest of us can get on with our lives. Relative to most people, I'm a policy nerd and interested in some of these choices, but even I don't want to be asked about every safety feature that might be added on the route I take into work, or the way in which my tax bill is presented.

Cass Sunstein in particular has rehearsed this puzzle in recent years, not least to needle some of the cruder critics of his work from when he was in government.[6] Online defaults and software installations often have the logical structure of offering the option of choosing not to choose. Early on in the installation procedure, the programme asks the user if they wish to go for the default installation, or if they wish to go through a longer, more personalised installation process. It is clearly defensible, and often rather sensible, to choose not to choose, and to trust someone else's expertise on what is probably the best thing to do.

Of course, like all such puzzles one question begets another. At what level, and at what time, should we be offered the choice not to choose? And once we have done so, how binding should it be? There is clearly no general answer to this question, but there are some rules of thumb that policymakers might use. For example, where most people offered the choice end up selecting the same option – even with expert and impartial advice on hand – it would seem sensible to move that option into a second-order choice or menu that most people could skip. Similarly, where there are many options but they rest heavily on expert judgement, such as how to diagnose and treat a given medical symptom, it would seem reasonable that people might wish to choose not to choose. There are also many situations in which people might wish to bind in their future selves by deliberately restricting their own choice. People on a diet may choose not to go down the dessert aisle, and would prefer their partner not to keep offering them seconds at dinner. Gamblers may choose not to be allowed into casinos, and not to be given the option to bet.

Yet we can also see the risks attached to a blanket judgement that people often choose not to choose. Bureaucrats and businesses might justify their lack of consultation on the basis that most people were not interested in the detail – that the public had, in effect, chosen not to choose. Messy though it is, this is an area that needs checks and balances. What form these should take we shall return to later in the chapter.

An excuse for not acting? The efficacy challenge

A very different argument against nudging is that it is an excuse for not acting more decisively – a fig leaf for inaction. Unlike the arguments that we have seen so far, which tend to have their roots in libertarian concerns from the right or centre, this is a critique that comes more commonly from the left – or, perhaps more accurately, from the paternalists.

From this viewpoint, if something is right or wrong it should be outlawed, mandated or taxed directly. Nudges, it is argued, are a not-so-subtle right-wing conspiracy to avoid taking proper action. Particularly in Europe, state paternalism has a much more respectable and popular pedigree than in the USA, and indeed than in most Anglo-Saxon countries. In European discussions, the words 'there's nothing wrong with paternalism' will often be heard. Proponents point out that we have long believed in educating kids, not just to make sure we have productive economies, but 'for their own good'. We don't ask our children if they'd like to read and write, we just get on and teach them. Similarly, well-organised states across the world, from efficient city-states such as Singapore to the high-trust Nordic nations of northern Europe, just get on and do stuff, from building housing to organising elaborate welfare safety nets. Viewed through such a lens, the nudge approach can look strangely anaemic and hesitant, leaving citizens exposed to risks that could easily be addressed more directly.

One area where we ran into this critique on more than one occasion was in relation to public health. In crude terms, if a behaviour or activity is known to be unhealthy, and especially if it might be harmful to others, why mess around with a nudge? Why not just ban it? Public health is also home to a rival ethical principle to choice: the precautionary principle. This states that if a product or behaviour is not known to be safe, or if considerable uncertainty exists over its safety, then access to it should be limited or banned.

You can see the logic of the approach. If a pharmaceutical company develops a new drug, it should have to show that it is safe to use on humans before it is widely available for sale. Similarly, when your teenage son says he's got a great idea for a new stunt on his motorbike involving a home-made ramp and your new garden shed, you might err on the side of saying 'no'. You don't know that it won't work out, but do you really want to take the chance? It was this line of reasoning that set much of the public health community so strongly against e-cigarettes (see Chapter 8).

Some on the political left also worry that nudge-style approaches might be used as an excuse to avoid more decisive action on poverty and disadvantage. For example, some might feel that what the unemployed really need is a massive job creation scheme, perhaps driven by a major investment programme in housing or infrastructure. From this point of view, designing a nudge to improve the job search activity of the unemployed, or one to encourage businesses to take on a few extra workers, looks like sideshow – or, even worse, a deliberate distraction from what really needs to happen.

Being a pragmatist, my own view is that we should do whatever works, particularly if it has minimal costs (see Chapter 10). As a head of a government department once said to me during a strategic review of government priorities, 'a large department doesn't have to have just one or two objectives – we have more than 2,000 people and a budget of more than £10 billion – we ought to be able to manage to do several things at once'.[7] That said, I think there are real dangers in getting too carried away with thinking that nudges are the answer to everything.

An example of a policy area where this applies is climate change. Don't get me wrong: I think there are some very neat behaviourally based interventions that can help chip away at the challenge, such as how giving people feedback on their energy use relative to their more efficient neighbours can trim a couple of per cent off consumption, with an effect size comparable to a 10–20 per cent price shift. It's fast, cheap and worth doing. But we shouldn't kid ourselves that this will make much of a dent on carbon emissions. If anything, behavioural insights tell us that human beings are ill suited to addressing climate change without decisive government action. The problem is diffuse, with short-term costs dominating over long-term gains. We should be very wary of convincing ourselves that nudges, without major regulatory changes and increases in the price of carbon, are likely to save the planet for our children.

Relative efficacy – nudging versus other tools

There is an academic version of the nudge versus other policy tools argument. It goes something like this. A nudge is a policy intervention that is intended to influence behaviour, but does not involve any incentive or sanction, mandate or regulation, and is more than just giving people information. Having defined nudging, and the use of behavioural insights, in the narrowest possible terms, the proponent can then argue that 'nudging is not enough'.

I confess that I don't think this is a very interesting argument, and it's also misleading. As a recovering academic myself, I recognise the style of the argument well enough, which is to create a narrowly defined 'straw man' proposition that can then be taken apart. The argument may have some purchase in the US context where some commentators have sought to define behavioural approaches specifically as choice-enhancing nudges. But it doesn't really recognise what BIT, and other leading practitioners, actually do.

The way we use behavioural insight approaches is as a tool or lens through which to view all policy interventions. We are certainly interested in, and often consider, tax and incentive design. We spend a lot of time on the design of regulations (just as Sunstein did in the USA), and we're also interested in the form and detail of communications, information and transparency, and how information can be presented to be easy to understand and influential. In essence, we seek to introduce a more realistic, empirically grounded model of what influences human behaviour and decision-making.[8]

Just as an engineer with a better understanding of air flows and wind resistance can use this knowledge to design a more economical car, a better turbine, or a faster plane, so we try to use behavioural insights to improve the design of lots of different policy levers. This sometimes identifies new policy options along the way, such as the power of nudges like feedback on social norms or changing defaults. But equally important is how behavioural insights can be used to subtly refashion conventional policy tools, such as redesigning a tax incentive to make it more effective. For example, behavioural insights might lead us to conclude that we should apply tax at the point of purchase of a gas-guzzling car rather than relying on the more classical approach of putting the extra tax on petrol. Applied in this way, behavioural insights are more incremental rather than revolutionary in their impact, just as the engineers' use of a wind tunnel does not fundamentally change the design of a car, but subtly reshapes it to be more efficient, and better suited to the task it is made for.

Will impact fade as people become familiar with the approach?

At public events and discussions, very often someone will ask, 'I can see that when you first get a personalised text reminder, or a letter that tells you that most people pay their tax on time, it would be effective. But what happens after lots of agencies start using the same approach, or after you get the tax letter for several years in a row? Won't the effect fade out?'

This is a really important empirical question. We have to acknowledge that because these approaches haven't been used for very long, at least by governments, our answer has to be a tentative one. I do worry that certain approaches will get overused, or even inappropriately and insensitively used as familiarity with them spreads, and that their positive effects may wash out. For example, social norm messages are increasingly used on official letters, road signs and elsewhere. We're not far off being able to make the joke that 'nine out of ten government agencies now use social norm messages' (not a very funny joke, I admit).

We know that certain types of behavioural intervention do seem to fade out over time. The most notorious and familiar of these is dieting. Millions of people across the world work very hard to shed a few pounds, and many succeed. But the evidence is that most of them put the weight back on again in the six months following. Behavioural scientists, such as Kevin Volpp, have experimented with different types of incentive that can help slimmers be more successful. For example, Volpe has shown that organising slimmers into groups of five people, and offering them a collective reward for their overall performance, is more effective than incentives offered to each separately (social pressure kicks in). But even so, when the incentive scheme ends, such slimmers are still likely to pile those pounds back on.

Nonetheless, looking at the 'fade-out' issue more broadly, there are good reasons to think that behavioural approaches can have great longevity. This applies both in terms of the longevity of the effects and the continued efficacy of particular approaches.

The first point to make is that some behavioural interventions only need to work once. If the objective is to encourage someone to insulate their attic, then the nudge only has to work once. It is not like dieting that requires an effortful behaviour every time the person is confronted with food. Other changes that require upfront one-off effort or costs have a similar profile. Setting up a pension plan can be unravelled relatively easily if the person wants to do so, and payments into it stopped, but for most people the real barrier is getting the plan set up in the first place and once it is in place they tend to stick with it (and are happy they did so).

Second, many behavioural changes when made – unlike diets – are 'sticky'. This can either be because a new 'habit' is established by the person themselves or, very importantly from a public policy perspective, because a new 'behavioural equilibrium' is established that is reinforced by other people. A well-documented example of this phenomenon comes from interventions to encourage higher voter turnouts in the USA. Such interventions, such as prompting people to think about how, and at what time, they will go to the polling station, have been found not only to boost turnout in a coming election, but also in subsequent elections even without further intervention. Todd Rogers, at the Harvard Kennedy School of Government, has likened the persistence of the voting effect to moving the person into a 'behavioural rip-tide'.[9] The intervention not only changes the person's behaviour directly, it also moves it into the flow of other influences. In this example, once you become an active voter in the US, you come on to the 'radar' of local party activists who are then likely to reach out to you in subsequent elections. But it is also that you start to think of yourself as a voter; that you now know where the polling station is and how to get there; and perhaps that you start to become slightly more interested in politics and elections.

The behavioural effect is particularly likely to persist, or even amplify, if the nudge is applied to many people at once. An increasingly familiar illustration of this effect in many countries is the remarkable impact of restrictions on smoking in public places. These have often worked much better than governments expected. The reason is that they become self-reinforcing. The change prompts lots of smokers to give up at the same time, as smoking becomes more inconvenient, creating social reinforcement or 'social proof'. Individual smokers who might have wavered suddenly no longer see fellow smokers lighting up, and if they were to do so the disapproval of others would soon remind them of the change.

Yet there is still the question of whether the efficacy of specific types of nudges will wear off as people become more familiar with them. This may well be true for novel approaches, and especially where they involve being persuaded to do something that in retrospect the person might regret. Given that this is exactly the territory of abusive nudges, or swindles, this habituation is no bad thing: 'once bitten, twice shy' as the expression goes. Indeed, let me share a personal story.

Some years ago, as I paused to check the departure board as I hurried for my train from London, I was confronted by two women and a small child giving me a tiny sprig of lavender with the stem wrapped in a piece of foil. As I looked in puzzlement, one of the women put out her other hand and said 'for the little children'. This turns out to be a pretty standard 'play', and one you might recognise from Chapter 5 or the wider literature: it's reciprocity coupled with a direct ask. Before I'd had a chance to think about it, I'd given them a pound. Afterwards, of course, I thought about it and felt slightly irritated at having been played. But I also thought I'd learnt something, and if it happened again I'd either shake my head, or look a little closer to see if they really needed the money. The point is, as a scam, you wouldn't keep falling for it every day. But it does also critically depend on both a novelty and whether, on reflection, you wanted to give the money. Recall the experiment we ran with the merchant bankers where they were given a tiny tub of sweets with the request that they give a day of their salaries to the bank's designated charity for that year. When this was run again the next year, while it worked just as well on people who hadn't experienced it before, the effect roughly halved on those who had got the sweets the year before. In contrast, most people in Britain buy a poppy every year to support injured servicemen. We know the script, and know it's a sort of nudge, but we're ultimately happy to go along with it so it keeps working.

This, it seems to me, is at the heart of many behavioural approaches and their acceptability. The power of many nudges and other behavioural influences is that, in the moment, they work on an 'automatic', 'system 1', basis. This brings great advantages. It is less effortful for the person concerned, and also means that they tend to work across socio-economic groups much more evenly (unlike, say, traditional informational or educational campaigns). But if they are used inappropriately, such as when companies start sneaking extra charges on the basis that you have to unclick them if you don't want them, people do start to notice and to actively, or wilfully, habituate. On the other hand, when nudges are used appropriately to go with the grain of things that people, on reflection, want to do, the effects persist – perhaps we might even say that people purposefully allow the effects to persist. For example, Katherine Milkman and colleagues found that they could boost gym attendances by 50 per cent by giving people an iPod with a novel on it to listen to while exercising. It's known as 'temptation bundling' – people are tempted back to the gym to hear what happens next in the story, at the same time as getting a workout. Since the extra nudge is helping them to do something they wanted to do anyway, its effects last over weeks and months.[10]

Let me give one last, everyday example that illustrates this wilful lack of habituation. When, at discussions or seminars, people ask about the issue of the effects of nudges wearing off, I sometimes ask for a show of hands of those who set their watches a few minutes fast. Of course, quite a few people don't use watches any more, but I generally find that about a third or more of those who do keep their watch a few minutes fast. Isn't that fascinating? They have a pretty good idea why they do it. When pressed, most say something like 'so I'm not late'. Yet at the same time, they all know their watch is fast, and generally know exactly how fast it is. So what is this nonsense? Why does it work?

It works because it takes a tiny mental effort to look at your watch and correct it for the few minutes that it is fast. If you are not in a hurry, you will readily do this. But if you are under pressure – you are late and running for your train (which is why you are glancing at your watch) – you won't bother to make the calculation.

I have to confess that I am one of those people. My watch is generally about three minutes fast. Occasionally I have thought this rather odd, and decided on a 'rational' basis to set my watch for the right time. I've then spent the next week missing my train and being late for lots of meetings, until eventually giving in and setting my watch fast again.

But now, years of nudging have taught me to be more respectful of the human condition. Given the brains we actually have, and not the ones that economists presumed we had, it's not so dumb – and certainly not irrational – to set our watches fast. People will generally adapt to abusive or inappropriate nudges, but ones that go with the grain of what we want to do anyway, or that help to form a new behavioural habit or equilibrium, will persist and sometimes even amplify in effect.

Who nudges the nudgers? The accountability challenge

The original title of Thaler and Sunstein's book *Nudge* was, as we discovered earlier in this book, *Libertarian Paternalism*. In the years since publication, and especially for US audiences, practitioners have tended to emphasise the 'libertarian' bit of the story, but there is a 'paternalist' aspect to the approach, too. Behavioural approaches very often involve adjusting the 'choice architecture' to encourage one behaviour over another for some intended benefit, such as healthier eating, getting back to work faster and so on. The nudger becomes the architect. But why should we trust the nudger to know better?

Maintaining choice, tailoring defaults and ensuring transparency ease the problem but they do not eliminate it. This is powerfully illustrated by George Loewenstein et al.'s recent work showing that even when people are told that a default has been set for them on a random basis, they still show extremely strong anchoring to the arbitrary default they were given even when they have an opportunity to change it. The researchers weren't asking about some trivial matter: it was about end-of-life treatment, and the circumstances under which a doctor could switch off your life support system.[11]

This example illustrates the potentially great power that sits in the hands of the nudger, or choice architect, be they in government, business, or a professional – whether they are aware of it or not. Given this, my own view is that it is not enough to point to the libertarian aspects of the approach and say there's no further issue. The nudgers need to answer to someone – and it can't just be themselves.

Of all people, those who study behavioural biases should be especially attuned as to why nudgers need to answer to someone else. As Max Bazerman, Dan Ariely, Susan Fiske and others have shown, we all have self-serving attributional biases, and these can get us into real trouble when we start to drift into conflicts of interest. It is just too easy for us to tell ourselves a story that the 'best' option for another person just happens to be the one that is in our own best interest, too. Financial advisers persuade themselves, as well as their clients, that the best deal on the table happens to be the one that has a juicy commission. Doctors persuade themselves, as well as their patients, that the best treatment happens to be quite expensive. Why should we think that policymakers are any different?

The ethics of experimentation

A major part of the BIT approach, and that of the What Works movement (Chapter 9), is the use of experimentation. Sometimes people ask whether it is unethical to do trials, or experiments on people, and especially in the context of public services. By their nature, people taking part are generally unaware that they are involved in an experiment, or at least what exactly the nature of the experiment is. Methodologically, it is generally regarded as better that 'subjects' be unaware – or what social scientists call 'blind'. Ideally, all those in direct contact with the subjects should also be unaware at least of which 'arm' of the experiment each subject is in – or what social scientists call 'double blind'. This is considered better because it avoids the risk that otherwise, when people are aware that they are in a 'special' experimental group, they might act differently just because of this knowledge.

From an ethical point of view, many people instinctively feel it would be better if all those involved knew they were participating in a trial. This is what would commonly happen in a medical trial. After a long ethical clearance process, during which there would be an assessment of the possible risks of giving patients the new treatment, a target sample of people would be identified for the trial, typically patients being treated for a given condition. The patients would be asked if they wanted to participate in a medical trial and, provided they agreed, would be assigned to one of a number of conditions. In the simplest form, half would get the new drug and half would get a placebo that looked exactly the same. This control, or placebo group, are very important, because we know that a certain proportion of people given a pill that contains no active drug will show a recovery of their own accord (a fascinating phenomenon in its own right). In this situation, the subjects are still blind to which pill they have been given, but they know they are part of an experiment.

In contrast, imagine we want to find out if adding an extra line to a letter reminding people that they have yet to pay their tax, or want to find out if particular motorway gantry messages reduce dangerous driving. We could, in principle, try to find a way of telling people in advance that they are about to become participants in a trial. We could write to the tax debtors in advance to let them know that they are about to receive one of several variations of a tax letter to test their reactions, or on motorways by putting up a sign saying that motorists are about to be subjected to one of several messages, and if they do not wish to participate in this trial they should leave the motorway at the next exit. But you can immediately see that the disclosure is both intrusive and distorting of the actual experiment.

This is not unusual in the social sciences or in business. Many experiments are run which depend on the subject not knowing that they are part of an experiment. For this reason, the academic community has developed extensive ethical clearance processes so that someone other than the experimenter themselves is involved in making the judgment as to whether the experiment is acceptable to perform. These rules and conventions have tightened over the years. Indeed, many of the most famous experiments in psychology from the 1950s and 1960s would probably no longer be given ethical clearance, such as Milgram's compliance experiments at Stanford (see Chapter 1).

Governments have different checks and balances from those in a university. Ministers sign off most key decisions. They in turn are subject to the test of regular elections and can be thrown out by the voting public. In this sense, they are much more accountable than your average academic; when did you last hear of the vice chancellor of a university being thrown out on the back of a student vote, let alone a wider public vote of all of those who might have been subject to the university's research?

As mentioned in Chapter 8, there were occasions when Ministers did block a trial, such as when we proposed to test whether tax payers would be more likely to file on time if we entered early returners into a lottery to say 'thank you'.[12] We also sought to add an additional check and balance through sharing trial protocols with the academic advisory panel and asking them whether the trials we were running might be harmful or cause offence. We later scaled this up to run potentially sensitive trials through a fully external ethics panel.

Yet for some people this still might not seem enough. Some might argue that governments should never conduct such experiments, especially where subjects are blind to the fact that one is happening. Indeed, in the case of the some governments, such as in Germany, it is arguable that their constitution explicitly forbids them from doing so, at least without the clearance of Parliament.[13]

For me, this is going too far. In fact, let me put it more strongly: I think it is unethical for governments *not* to do trials.[14]

Governments, public bodies and businesses regularly make changes to what they do. Sometimes these changes are very extensive, such as when welfare systems are reformed, school curricula are overhauled, or professional guidelines are changed. No doubt those behind the changes think they are for the best. But without systematic testing, this is often little more than an educated guess. To me, this preparedness to make a change affecting millions of people without testing it is potentially far more unacceptable than the alternative of running trials that affect only a small number of people before imposing the change on everyone.

Public voice

The more we are persuaded that behavioural interventions and experimentation works, the more we need to couple checks and balances to make sure that these approaches are appropriately used. Ultimately it is the public, not the nudgers, who should decide.

This may seem a paradox. One of the characteristics of many nudges is that they operate on the automatic, unconscious level, and a key benefit for the public is precisely because they do not tax our busy and valuable 'system 2', or conscious thinking. But now I'm saying that the more effectively they work on this unconscious level, the more important it is that the public be aware of what is going on and participate in making the choice.

Of course, the answer is that we don't all have to be thinking about everything all of the time. There is a good reason why people invented representative democracy. Most people have better things to do than ruminate over every choice and decision that governments and societies need to make. The same applies to nudging, where many of the decisions to be made can be rather detailed, and frankly rather

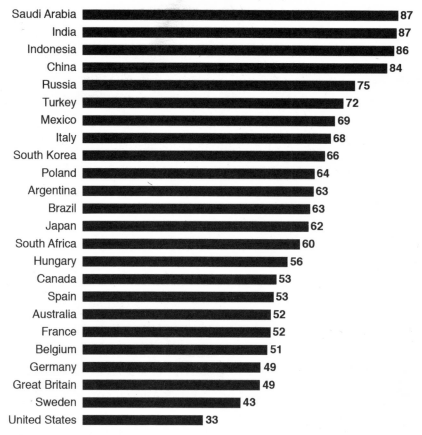

Government should ban...

% Strongly support/ tend to support
Average over all four policy areas

Saudi Arabia	87
India	87
Indonesia	86
China	84
Russia	75
Turkey	72
Mexico	69
Italy	68
South Korea	66
Poland	64
Argentina	63
Brazil	63
Japan	62
South Africa	60
Hungary	56
Canada	53
Spain	53
Australia	52
France	52
Belgium	51
Germany	49
Great Britain	49
Sweden	43
United States	33

Base: c.500–1,000 residents aged 16–64 (18–64 in the US and Canada) in each country, November 2010.
Source: Ipsos Global @dvisor

Figure 47. Cross-national differences in public support for tougher government action. The measure averages attitudes to banning unhealthy foods; banning smoking; banning environmentally unsustainable products (such as things that can't be recycled); and requiring people to save for their pensions. Note that while only around a third of Americans support such actions, in many parts of the world a large majority support tougher action. In South Africa, India, Indonesia and China, more than 80 per cent support such actions. (Data from Ipsos MORI.)[15]

dull to most people – even if their impact may be quite large.

BIT was staffed by civil servants. We took – and still take – our instructions from elected representatives, and an elected government. Yet when it comes to big issues, and particularly those that affect the day-to-day lifestyle choices of our citizens, is this enough? Minsters are themselves subject to many other demands. Similarly, when the public come to vote, the detailed changes made by one of many small parts of government do not loom large in their decision, let alone subtle changes that they may not even have noticed. Of course, for most people elections are really about choosing people that you trust (or least distrust) with principles and positions that are broadly aligned with your own, rather than working down a checklist of specific policy options.

It is also really important to note, given the strong North American roots of much of the behavioural literature, that public attitudes differ greatly across countries. The emphasis placed on 'choice-enhancing' principles in US academic and political debate, alongside a deeply rooted distrust of government action, is not seen in many countries (see Figure 47). In many rapidly developing nations, there is far more appetite for aggressive and direct government action. In India and China, for example, around 85 per cent of the public support outright bans on smoking and unhealthy foods, and more than 95 per cent support tough action against companies in these sectors.

Governments also consult the public between elections, though often the main people who respond to these consultations are businesses, lobby groups and other special interest groups rather than the public at large. But there are mechanisms designed to deliberately reach out to the 'normal' public. These include surveys 'town hall' meetings open to all, citizens' juries, and deliberative forums. The latter option involves bringing together a statistically representative sample of the public for a day or more, briefing them in detail about the issue from different viewpoints, and asking the sample – this microcosm of the wider public – what they think is the right thing to do now that they have seen the arguments.[16]

A public consultation of this type accompanied the UK's Pensions Commission, headed by Adair Turner, that led to the decision to change the defaults for saving into workplace pensions in the UK. During this process, hundreds of members of the public were shown the facts and figures on pensions, and the early evidence on how changing from an opt-in to an opt-out scheme might change savings rates. In a very real sense one can argue that it was the public that then gave government permission to make the change. Without this sense of public permission, Ministers might never have made the change in the original legislation, and it certainly would have been much harder to persuade the new Prime Minister, government and business to stick with the change as the deadline drew near.

In my view, this is true of many of the changes that nudgers might want to make, and especially when the change concerns lifestyle. Want to reduce the amount of chocolate and sweets at checkouts? Want to encourage more rainy-day saving by defaulting a few per cent of people's wages into high-interest accounts? Want to encourage more people to walk or cycle to work by making it more inconvenient or expensive to use their cars? Be you the government or business, better ask the public, your workers or customers first before you make such changes. It's not just that you may get a lot of angry letters if you don't, but also because it is *their* behaviour and their lives you are messing with. If they're not persuaded by the case, it will probably not work anyway. Moreover, a good consultation can itself be a key part of the process behaviour change. We care about what other people think, and particularly those who seem like us. The fact is, people may be much more likely to adopt or accept a change if they feel that people like them recommended it.

I actually think this is so important that we should have a new kind of parliament – not to replace the ones we've got now, but as a supplement to them. Once a month or so, when our Houses of Parliament are otherwise empty, we should ask 100 to 300 randomly chosen members of the public to come and help us decide on some new aspect or detail of lifestyle policy, just like the questions listed above. They should have the argument presented, hear from those against, and be asked to give a view. At the same time, government departments wrestling with behavioural and lifestyle issues would ask to have their issue presented at one of the 'people's parliaments'. The conclusion would be advisory, not binding, but governments would be expected to publicly explain how they followed or ignored the results.

Some legislators, officials and Ministers will be appalled at this idea. Some will particularly dislike the idea that they will be ceding power and authority to this new mechanism. But this is a misreading of both behaviour and power. There are many areas of behaviour where governments (and businesses) have only fragile legitimacy to act, and some of the stronger methods of nudging themselves rest on shallow public acceptance. Showing the public the power of the forces that shape their behaviour, and the options for how it might be affected, can give permission for governments to act in new ways on behalf of the public. It's not about taking power from one group and giving it to another. It is about increasing the total pot of power, enabling the public to shape their own destiny – and enabling them to direct, and to nudge, the nudgers.

Conclusion

Behavioural-based approaches are increasingly being applied by governments, and businesses, across the world. Citizens themselves are using them, too, such as through mobile apps, or actively choosing products and services that enable them to shape their own behaviours.

The two most frequent critiques that we in BIT heard in the early years of our work were seemingly contradictory. Some worried that the Nudge Unit might be bringing powerful new forms of 'mind control' or PsyOps into the hands of governments. This has been a particular concern in the USA, and has led its leading advocates there to focus on 'choice-enhancing nudges'. In contrast, other critics have worried that governments were turning to an ineffective new fashion as an excuse for not pursuing 'proper' policies. This has been more of a concern in north European countries with a strong tradition of more assertive government action, and generally a higher level of trust in government itself.

Of course, neither concern really captures the reality. Behavioural insights have proven to be an effective tool to help refine and improve the cost-effectiveness of policies; to make services easier for citizens to use; and in some cases have opened up thinking to create new kinds of policies altogether. Yet there is an element of truth, or appropriate concern, in both critiques.

Behavioural insights, like any other form of knowledge, can be used for good or bad. But there is a particular concern that, by their very nature, behaviourally based interventions can operate below the conscious radar of busy citizens. This suggests that the more governments and businesses draw on these types of insights, so they need to match this with appropriate transparency and, in my view, strengthened forms of public consultation and 'permission'. More sophisticated forms of public consultation don't come cheap – a single deliberative forum can cost hundreds of thousands of pounds. But I think enhanced public deliberation is the way to go, at least for policy changes that directly relate to lifestyle choices and that ultimately rest on public permission to be both acceptable and effective.

One thing governments can't do is to put their heads in the sand. Behavioural effects and influences play a major role in consumer markets, and far beyond. Even the most sceptical libertarians look to government and the courts to deliver the rule of law and justice. But we know that courtrooms and legal processes are riven with behavioural biases, from witnesses' ability to recognise a suspect or recall what happened, to the likelihood of judges awarding parole according to the time of day and the period since lunch. Whether we like it or not, the way a form is written, the way a call is answered, the way a tax or incentive scheme is constructed – all influence behaviour.

At the same time, businesses have moved from occasionally stumbling on behavioural effects, such as in a more effective marketing campaign, to overt and systematic testing of how behavioural biases can be exploited. This includes finding better ways to hold on to 'sticky customers'; how best to squeeze an extra sale or margin; and developing new products and sales that can be used to help master our biases, as well as others designed to exploit them. For this reason alone, governments and regulators across the world are being pulled into the world of behavioural insights. Digital and online trading is accelerating this trend still further.

Governments shouldn't be afraid to respond to this changing environment. Indeed, governments and regulators are failing in their duty if they do not. Our citizens also expect us to use this knowledge to improve public services, as well as to respect the fact that people's cognitive capacity and time is a valuable asset that the public do not want wasted. We have all got better things to do with our lives than to wade through complex forms and confusing bureaucracy.

At one level, introducing a more realistic model of human decision-making is just like an engineer using a wind tunnel to make a better car, and as such we should expect and demand it. Yet at the same time, understanding human behaviour is not the same as understanding air flows and wind resistance. Nudgers, or behavioural scientists, must be very wary about setting themselves up as unconstrained engineers and architects of the human condition. If we are to be architects – remembering that no option is neutral or without some effect – then we must at least be clear who we work for. Nudgers, like architects and engineers, should work for the client, and the client should be the public. The client is you.

CHAPTER 12

CONCLUSION

Where Next?

The use of behavioural insights and the systematic empirical study of What Works is here to stay. These approaches have been used in some form or other for decades by marketers, albeit often driven by success and failure in consumer markets rather than by systematic study. The use of big data and large-scale commercial experimentation, augmented by digital and web-based live testing, has taken it to another level. Companies are increasingly testing every aspect of what they do to find out what is most effective: the colour, shape and gaze of characters on packaging; the 'choice architecture' on webpages; and the finest detail of pricing.

Governments are being pulled into this world of consumer psychology, if only to figure out how to protect citizens from abusive use of such practices by business, or sometimes to protect consumers and businesses from ourselves when the shortcuts in our heads get multiplied into systemic failure. The 2008 near-financial meltdown showed that this wasn't a marginal issue: economic models based on unrealistic assumptions about perfect information and all-knowing, hyper-rational economic agents can get us into real trouble.

From strategy to 'the last mile'

When I joined No. 10's newly formed Prime Minister's Strategy Unit in 2001, 'strategy' seemed an obvious gap to plug. Of course governments, and businesses, should have a sense of the big picture: a strong analysis of the key challenges being faced and a coherent plan for what should be done. Without it, there was a high likelihood that different parts of government or business would go off in different directions, with nothing much being achieved.

More than a decade later, it now seems equally obvious that governments and businesses need more than high-level strategy. Many of the grand plans of government and business end in failure, or at least disappointment. Sensible-seeming incentives are left unclaimed, the intended behaviour largely unchanged. The majority of new products released by business fail to sell. Very often, these plans and products fail because we in turn failed to attend to the 'small details' that are of little interest to our grand strategists. These failures arise because we neglect what the behavioural economist and business school professor Dilip Soman calls 'the last mile'.[1]

Heads of government and business were traditionally not much interested in the details of forms and procedures that their citizens and customers had to deal with. Turns out that's a big mistake. However good your strategy or product, if the person the product or intervention is aimed at has to wade through a poorly designed form or process, they will probably give up and do something else. Your strategists will be left back at HQ saying, 'What went wrong?'

Getting these design details right has proved fertile ground for behavioural scientists. Much of what such scientists do is familiar to the design professions and ethnographers who study how real people interact with products and services. By understanding how people actually use services and products – what they like and what they get frustrated with – designers can reshape the products and services until they feel easier and more intuitive to use. But behavioural scientists have added two extra elements into the mix. First, they bring in the systematic study of how people think about the world and how they decide, including the mental shortcuts that we all rely on to get through everyday life. This gives the behavioural scientist a more informed idea about what might work better, including sometimes identifying seemingly counter-intuitive alternatives to the current set-up. Second, behavioural science brings in the practice of systematic testing and trialling. The combination, mixed with a little design flair, can prove highly effective (as we saw in Chapters 3 to 6).

Addressing these design challenges is about more than 'nudges'. It is about applying behavioural insights to everything that we do, from how information is presented to how an incentive or regulation is structured. In this sense, we can use behavioural insights on any challenge, from gently encouraging people to pay their tax on time, to encouraging the adoption of healthier lifestyles. Building on what has already been shown and achieved, we can be confident that the application of behavioural science to the nuts and bolts of government and business can bring forward hundreds of millions of pounds' worth of unpaid tax, lengthen the lives of millions, help save the planet, boost educational attainment, prevent crime and fear, and improve the efficiency and quality of services. No wonder behavioural insight specialists have gone from curiosity to 'must have' in many organisations and governments over the last few years.

Refashioning policy

Yet as Section 3 of this book showed, behavioural science is about more than patching up the last mile of the customer or citizen experience, critical though that is. It is a thread that, once you pull it, leads you back to the very foundations of what governments and businesses do.

Behavioural insights are forcing policymakers to question some of their basic assumptions. Regulators are prompted to think about markets, and market failures, in new ways, and to consider new and innovative ways to shape and sanction market players. Senior civil servants and Ministers are prompted to think about the challenges they face in new ways; to think about using new tools, and to look at old tools, like legislation and incentives, in a new light. Would laws work better if people could understand them directly? Would spending go further and have more of an impact if it were shaped by the new principles of behavioural science?

Behavioural science poses fundamental questions about the objectives of governments and businesses, too. The systematic study of subjective well-being – of happiness and life satisfaction – raises profound questions about what we're all trying to do. The same mental shortcuts that make us prone to eat more than we should, and leave us saving too little today for our pensions tomorrow, also guide many of the bigger choices we make in life. Many of these key drivers of life satisfaction are largely neglected by governments and business, such as the role played by social relationships. Bosses focus too much on extrinsic rewards, such as cash bonuses, and not enough on intrinsic rewards, such as feedback and the pleasures of the job. Similarly, policymakers focus so hard on the direct outcomes of their policies that they often miss the fundamental importance to citizens of other factors such as being kept informed, or being treated with respect and dignity.

The experimental methods that behaviourists have helped popularise may prove their greatest legacy of all. The use of rapid randomised controlled trials has helped catalyse a more empirical approach to policy and delivery. This in turn has stimulated a shift from a policy model of 'smart people know best' to one of humility and 'radical incrementalism' – acknowledging that policies and practices should be designed to allow the testing of multiple variations, just like a gardener always plants two seeds in a pot, then clips the weaker of the two. Within BIT, the approach was called 'test, learn, adapt',[2] but as it has gone mainstream it has become part of the wider What Works movement. By mid-2014, the UK had created a network of independent What Works centres covering medical practice, education, early intervention, crime, local economic growth, well-being and better ageing, together with specialist centres emerging in Scotland and Wales. Together they cover more than £250 billion of spending. The What Works movement shows every sign of going international. In the USA, it is joining up with the Coalition for Better Evidence and empiricism of the US more generally.[3] The World Bank and OECD are looking to how they can embed and extend it across countries. And there is serious discussion about how UN development goals can be systematically supplemented by a foundation of not just what we are trying to do, but how it can be done.

The Anglo-Saxon countries have been the fastest to adopt behavioural and what works approaches, but these approaches are also spreading across northern Europe and into Asia. After the UK and USA, Singapore and New South Wales in Australia have been early adopters, with the state of Victoria not far behind. Germany, the Netherlands and Israel have moved to create their own BITs, while Denmark has absorbed the approach through its MINDLAB and behavioural exchange network. France, Italy, Finland, Canada, Portugal and the UAE are all actively looking to create such capacities, generally linked to their Prime Minister's offices. The No. 10 Behavioural Insights Team has itself been commissioned by more than half a dozen other national governments.

A repeated public and media reaction has been initial wariness and scepticism, but where governments have been open about how they are using the approaches, the public has warmed to the 'common sense' nature of the changes to policy that have followed. After all, shouldn't forms and processes be designed to be easier to follow, letters to be easier to understand, and markets made to work better for the consumers who use them?

New challenges

For me and the team it has been an exciting few years. The application of behavioural insights to policy and practice has gone from a crazy idea to mainstream thinking, or at least close to it. BIT grew from seven people in 2010, to 15 by late 2013 and to 50 by early 2015 as the team became able to help other public services and countries. As I write, we have around a hundred trials under way, and advise on a wide range of policy in the UK and beyond.

Yet I'm still left with a profound sense of how we are still just scratching the surface. There have been some great successes, but then I think about how many letters and communications remain difficult to understand and untouched by a behavioural insight lens. I think about how most years of healthy life are lost as the result of behavioural factors, yet this is not where our health ministries spend more than a fraction of their money or professional focus. I think about the extent to which economies are driven by 'animal spirits' of confidence and sentiment, yet this is something about which our business departments, treasuries and central banks have almost nothing to say. And I think about the billions we spend across all our departments to make the world a better place, and yet how weak our direct focus is on the fundamental drivers of human well-being and flourishing.

We need to turn public policy from an art to a science, and with it the professions that underpin it. We should be restless about expanding the scale and ambition of behavioural science to every corner of public service, albeit twinned with strong democratic safeguards and consultations to make sure that it is the public that set and approve the nudgers' agenda. But, ultimately, our ambition should be about more than scale: it's about impact. It's time for us to move beyond getting taxes paid on time and get people to the gym, important though these are. It is time to challenge the behavioural science community to take on some of the biggest, and seemingly intractable, challenges of our time. Let me take three examples.

Social mobility and entrenched disadvantage

Work stretching back decades has shown that many of the mediators of disadvantage are subtle, pervasive and not just rooted in the external environment. Disadvantage and poverty seep into how we think about the world, how the world thinks about us, and is often passed from one generation to another.[4]

Successive generations of policymakers have tried many approaches to break such cycles of disadvantage. There have been successes but, in general, it is an area where great efforts have led to only modest results. In many countries, massive investments in state education have dragged up overall results, but the gap between social groups has often remained stubbornly unchanged.[5] Massive programmes to enable the poor to escape low-income neighbourhoods have, when systematically tested, led to only small effects on subsequent social mobility.[6] And well-intentioned welfare and income support programmes have alleviated poverty in the short-term but have often failed to be the springboard out of long-term poverty that its designers had hoped.[7]

This history of disappointment has led many to characterise entrenched poverty and disadvantage as a 'wicked problem'. It has complex and self-reinforcing causes that make it extremely hard to unravel, reinforced still further by deep-seated drivers towards greater inequality within modern economies. Yet against this bleak background, behavioural scientists have come up with a few results that suggest that more focused, potentially relatively cheap, interventions could make a big difference.

Carol Dweck's extraordinary work has shown how seemingly tiny differences in how children are given feedback can set them on a trajectory of success or failure. In essence, children who are steered towards believing that a test result is a measure of their inherent ability ('good result: you're a smart kid') show less persistence and lower subsequent performance on a difficult task than children who are steered towards believing that a test result is a measure of their effort (good result: good effort). In Dweck's words, the latter type of feedback creates a 'growth mindset', or a theory of mind that personal achievements come from effort,[8] leading the child to try harder and not give up in the face of personal challenge. As she demonstrates, these effects are very large. More positively, they suggest very practical and specific actions that parents and teachers can take to set a child on the road to personal discovery, resilience, and seizing the opportunities when they come along.

In a different body of work on adults, Sendhil Mullainathan and Eldar Shafir have shown how poverty has far more powerful cognitive effects than we were previously aware.[9] Having money worries seems to preoccupy a chunk of our minds, even if we are not aware of it. The effect size on IQ is roughly equivalent to having had no sleep the night before, but on an ongoing basis. This gives useful clues to how welfare systems might be adapted, not just by throwing more money at them, but by avoiding systems and processes that factor in this unseen cognitive load.

We have seen similar glimpses in our own work. The reworking of the interaction between jobseekers and advisers in UK jobcentres, by Rory Gallagher, Alex Gyani, Sam Hanes and others in BIT (with Department of Work and Pensions colleagues) showed that we could get the unemployed back to work significantly faster (see Chapter 8). Importantly, it showed that these changes could have the biggest impact on the motivation and outcomes of some of the most disadvantaged and 'at risk'. The fact that we've been able to replicate, and even improve on, these results with colleagues in Singapore and Australia makes us think that we could do even better yet.

Perhaps even more strikingly, with an effect size that even shocked us, was the results of our recent intervention to try to narrow the gap between white and ethnic minority recruits into the police (Chapter 6). Simon Ruda and Elizabeth Linos, who led the intervention, found that the addition of a motivational message – encouraging applicants to reflect on why they wanted to join the police and why it mattered to their community – boosted the pass rate of minority group applicants by 50 per cent, while leaving white applicants unaffected. It had previously been thought that the difference might be the result of differences in proficiency in English or even, some had suggested, cognitive ability. Instead, this seemingly simple prompt, provided just before the applicants clicked through to do the online test, was enough to eliminate entirely the pass rate between groups.

It's worth reflecting how extraordinary these results are. We don't know how much of an impact they might have on entrenched disadvantage, but they suggest that such effect sizes might be much more than experts have previously thought. At the very least, these results should be grounds for revisiting the great challenge of social mobility and disadvantage with a more behaviourally sophisticated lens, and seeing where it leads.

Conflict

People have been fighting and falling out with each other for as long as there have been people. Indeed, at least in respect of homicide, the evidence is pretty compelling that we used to do even more of it – at least in Europe – in previous centuries than in modern times.[10] Nonetheless, the world remains scarred by intergroup conflict, with around two new wars starting every year, half of which are the reigniting of a previous conflict.[11]

Humility is needed here. Doubtless some of these wars are sparked by shortages of natural resources or other factors well outside the purview of a behavioural scientist. And many great minds and efforts have gone into both the specific and general causes of such conflicts. The challenge to behavioural scientists is, do we have anything to add? Is there some clue, mental process, or intervention that we might humbly suggest that could make a difference?

At least some behavioural scientists are thinking that, just maybe, we do have something to add. George Loewenstein, one of the most productive and thoughtful behavioural scientists in the world today, certainly thinks so. It is early days, but his most recent work is edging into this space. Building on his previous work about how negotiations often reach an 'irrational' impasse and how we mispredict our own behaviour from an emotionally cold to hot state, Loewenstein is trying to unravel the behavioural roots of conflict. There is much that he can draw on. The long body of work on 'social cognition', that leads from the early work of Fritz Heider to the contemporary work of Susan Fiske and others (see Chapter 1), maps in some detail how our near-instant judgements and classification of others forms the building blocks of conflict and prejudice. Figures like Eldar Sharif are also musing on similar issues, wondering what practical interventions, if any, might ease the deep-seated tensions in some of the world's most troubled hotspots. There's also interesting and important neuroscience work by Tania Singer and others on the subtle differences between the pathways behind empathy and sympathy, and the development of specific approaches to develop such skills and capacities in young people and adults.

Again, we can't know if these routes will lead anywhere. But behavioural science has shown a remarkable capacity to bring new insights and creative new solutions to many other areas, so it may surprise us again.

The evidence on evidence: spreading better government and practice

This might not seem as grand as the previous challenges, but evidence on evidence goes to one of the greatest puzzles of our time: why don't people do 'what works'? My father used to say, 'if you're sat on a nail, you should move'. In technical parlance, this puzzle combines the study of 'fixation' – why people get stuck on a given practice or solution, even if it doesn't work – with the study of diffusion and innovation – why better ideas and practices fail to spread more rapidly.

We started to poke around this issue in Chapter 10. But there's a question that sits above the generation of evidence for specific questions in education, crime and so on, which is what some have called 'the evidence on evidence'. For example, if a medical team somewhere figures out a better way of treating cancer, why does it take so long to diffuse – and, more importantly, what can be done to accelerate this spreading of best practice? Smart policymakers and professionals are quietly obsessed by this question, and many reforms are aimed at trying to do something about it. Introducing market mechanisms, controversial though they sometimes are, is generally driven largely by a belief that a market can spread effective practice rapidly through a system, through the expansion of the best providers and the exit of those who aren't doing a good job. Professional training, journals, even books like this, are all about the spreading of new – and hopefully better – ideas and practices, though they may also bring more 'noise' and error too.

Yet the science on science, or evidence on evidence, is amazingly thin. What we do know is that the spread of ideas, or lack of it, has deeply psychological and behavioural roots. The biases in our heads make us much more inclined to absorb ideas that fit with our prior beliefs. Similarly, we know that ideas and practices spread through social networks, and yet that these networks often work to keep out new ideas, too. Even in science it's often remarked that 'science progresses one coffin at a time', as people so rarely change their views within their lifetimes.[12]

So what are the best ways of spreading new ideas and better practices? Is it peer-to-peer learning, or new forms of online education? Can we reshape incentives and market designs to catalyse the spread of better practice? These might seem less grand questions than how to address disadvantage or conflict, but they are fundamental to economic and social progress.

A linked issue is to focus behavioural science on to organisations and governments themselves. It's a common question at seminars, to which we have only a partial answer, as to how behavioural science can make organisations work better. Progress towards answering these questions is being pushed forward by a clutch of outstanding young behavioural scientists such as Mike Norton, Francesca Gino, Adam Grant and Nina Mazar, who are offering new insights around motivation and honesty in commercial organisations. I hope that these and other behavioural scientists will explore interventions to improve the performance and probity of governments too. Across the world, one can make a strong case that much conflict and extremism is rooted in the failure of governments to do their job properly.

Corruption and incompetence offer rich soil for restlessness and violence to grow. I'm tired of being told that while we might be able to use behavioural science and more empirical methods to help identify a better way of increasing uptake of vaccination rates or saving, the business of improving the efficacy and probity of governments is too complicated. Fostering and supporting effective governance is the number one priority of aid agencies across the world today. In other domains, behavioural science has had a lot to say about how to: make transparency and information more impactful; prompt honesty; improve recruitment; reduce errors in decision-making;

and improve the spread and adoption of best practice. It will be more complicated than your average lab study, but we've every reason to think that behavioural science could make governments, and other large organisations, work better too.

Knowing yourself

Evolution has shaped our minds, and the mental shortcuts that spin within them, but that does not mean we are prisoners to these processes. Just as physicists push the frontiers of our understanding of the universe, with the remarkable forces and particles that compose it, and biologists push our understanding of the wonderful complexity of life itself, psychologists are pushing the frontiers of understanding our minds.

We can all use this knowledge to help us understand our own minds, and, to some extent, to reshape them for the world we now live in. We can try to factor in how we discount the future, and misremember the past. We can use knowledge of how our habits form to reshape those habits we wish to cultivate and weaken those we wish to disrupt. We can seek to understand how our beliefs and behaviours are influenced by the people and environments around us, and reshape these interpretations and environments to influence ourselves and others for the better. In short, we can use behavioural insights to become engineers of our own minds and lives.

Minds that evolved through the struggle for survival among our ancient ancestors have bestowed on us remarkable talents that we take for granted, from razor-sharp reactions to interpret fleeting patterns of light and sound, to ways of interpreting the multifaceted intentions of others. But the world and challenges we face have changed. We need to attune and refine our minds for the one we live in now.

One of the nicer, human twists of BIT's work was for me the rediscovery of that deep curiosity about how our minds work. When

Rory and Alex were busy leading the retraining of 25,000 jobcentre staff, many of the questions that came up were not about the new process per se, but about the science that lay behind it. The jobcentre advisers wanted to understand more about the anchoring effects that meant that looking for at 'least three jobs' was problematic. They wanted to understand why prompting a young unemployed person to think about when and how they would search for a job would make a difference, or why it mattered that the jobseeker themselves wrote down the actions to be taken. The advisers wanted to understand how these effects occurred in their own minds and lives, too.

If you've got this far into this book, and the literature on which it is built, you are also well on the road to achieving that understanding. Perhaps that's one of the most human and adaptive aspects of our minds – our curiosity. We want to know how things work. We want to know what others think, and to share our own thoughts and feelings. We even want to know *why* we want to know. Enjoy it. It's quite cool being human.

A final word

Governments, organisations and individuals across the world are starting to use behavioural insights to reshape what they do and how they do it. This varies from the simple rewording of letters so that people can understand them more easily, to the fundamental redesign of policies to promote healthier living, energy conservation or getting people back to work.

This book has introduced a simple framework that can be used not only by policymakers, but by anyone: EAST. If you want to encourage a behaviour – in yourself or in others – make it easy, attractive, harness social influence, and choose a time when most receptive. My sister-in-law recently told me how she had used the EAST framework to change part of her work – chasing unpaid bills – and how it had saved her hundreds of hours of wasted phone calls and effort, and saved her clients time and hassle as well. Hopefully you will find it just as useful.

Behind the shroud of our consciousness, a myriad of processes race to interpret the world and to act upon it. We need to think of cognitive capacities as a wonderful, but precious resource. When we design services and products, we should be respectful of this resource, and remember that people have generally got better things to do than wade through bureaucracy or the puzzling 'rationality' of the state or big business. We have to design what we do around people, not expect people to have to redesign their thinking and lives around us.

If there is one great risk to the application of behavioural insights to policy, it is that the thread of public permission wears too thin. If governments, or indeed communities or companies, wish to use behavioural insights, they must seek the permission of the public to do so. When behavioural science moves from the lab to the world around us, its experiments are not just about efficacy, but about acceptability, too.

This book is intended to be part of that openness. Ultimately, you – the public, the so-called 'ordinary citizen' – need to decide what the objectives, and limits, of nudging and empirical testing are.

In 2014, as a result of demand for its services from public services and other countries, the Behavioural Insights Team became a social purpose company co-owned by the British government, the innovation charity Nesta, and its employees. The team is still small by the scale of governments or business, but its influence has already been remarkable. Policy changes driven by BIT and its sister units have led, and are leading, to millions of healthy life years saved, hundreds of thousands getting into work faster, and millions in revenue brought forward.

There is still much that we do not know. Will some of the effects we see today diminish as they become overused and familiar? Will better-informed governments, pushed by better-informed consumers, clamp down on the use of nudging by big business? Who knows? But one thing is sure: nudging – the use of behavioural insights and the experimental methods it has brought in its wake – are here to stay.

NOTES

Preface

1 The use of images for speeding offences was based on an account from a French official. I do not know if they ran it as a systematic trial. The last bit, about 'threatening' to send it, was shameless embellishment.

Chapter 1: Early Steps

1 One of the most basic psychological effects is how familiarity breeds liking, from random sequences of notes to how much we like and trust institutions.

2 I'm grateful to Rory Sutherland for first drawing my attention to the fascinating example of how Frederick the Great encouraged Prussians to adopt the potato.

3 Quoted in *Quarterly Journal of Military History*, August 2009.

4 UCLA Department of Epidemiology, School of Public Health; http://www. ph.ucla.edu/epi/snow/victoria.html.

5 The Rotherhithe Tunnel was opened around 1908, and today carries the A101 road from Limehouse to Rotherhithe. As its sharp turns are now considered dangerous, it has a speed limit of just 20 mph.

6 Heide, Robert, and Gilman, John, *Home Front America: Popular Culture of the World War II Era*. p.36 ISBN 0-8118-0927-7 OCLC 31207708.

7 Festinger, L. (1957). *A Theory of Cognitive Dissonance*. Stanford, CA: Stanford University Press. A classic illustration of the effect, was a study in which students had to do a boring, repetitive task, but were then paid either $1 or $20 to persuade someone in the waiting room that it was fun. When subsequently asked to rate the experiment, those paid just $1 were much more likely to rate it as interesting than those paid $20. Festinger argued that those paid the smaller sum restructured their beliefs in line with their behaviour: it must have been interesting, since I did it and told someone else it was interesting, just for a measly $1. Festinger, L., & Carlsmith, J. M. (1959), *Cognitive consequences of forced compliance. Journal of Abnormal and Social Psychology*, 58(2), 203.

8 Often referred to as the 'Cocktail Party Effect'; Moray, N. (1959). 'Attention in dichotic listening: Affective cues and the influence of instructions'. *Quarterly Journal of Experimental Psychology*,11(1), 56–60.

9 Ratliff, F. (1965). Mach bands: quantitative studies on neural networks in the retina.

10 Milgram, S. (1963). 'Behavioural Study of Obedience', *The Journal of Abnormal and Socal Psychology*, 67(4), 371.

11 Asch, S. E. (1956). 'Studies of independence and conformity: 1. A minority of one against a unanimous majority'. *Psychological Monographs: General and Applied*, 70(9), 1. ; Haney, C., Banks, W. C., & Zimbardo, P. G. (1973). 'Study of prisoners and guards in a simulated prison'. *Naval Research Reviews*, 9(1–17).; Latane, B., & Darley, J. M. (1968). 'Group inhibition of bystander intervention in emergencies'. *Journal of Personality and Social Psychology*, 10(3), 215.

12 Tversky, A., & Kahneman, D. (1973). 'Availability: A heuristic for judging frequency and probability'. *Cognitive Psychology*, 5(2), 207–232.

13 For clarity, it's the thickness of the paper $x2^{100.}$ For further illustrations see Kahneman, D. (2011), *Thinking Fast and Slow*, Farrar, Straus and Giroux; though this example with the paper is my own. For a laboratory-based illustration of how we struggle with exponential-type calculations, see an early experiment by Tversky and Kahneman (1974). Subjects were asked to estimate, after seeing the question for five seconds:
   $1 \times 2 \times 3 \times 4 \times 5 \times 6 \times 7 \times 8 = ? \dots$ or $\dots 8 \times 7 \times 6 \times 5 \times 4 \times 3 \times 2 \times 1 = ?$
   Subjects who saw the first sequence estimated 512 on average, but those who saw the second sequence estimated 2,250. People use a mental shortcut of starting to multiply the first few numbers, then roughly extrapolate. They then anchor to their early estimate, failing to intuitively grasp an exponential-type function. The correct answer is 40,320.

14 See, for example, Susan Fiske's long-standing work on emotion; the MINDSPACE report for a quick overview of many of the more robust effects; or Daniel Kahneman's own excellent summary of the field in *Thinking Fast and Slow*.

15 A recent estimate for the UK, which alone spends billions of pounds a year on health-related research, is that less than 1/200th of this money is spent on behavioural factors, and, of this, the majority is spent on medical compliance.

16 For a sense of these lectures, see 'Social Psychology and Policy', Chapter 18, in Fraser and Burchell (eds), *Introducing Social Psychology* (2001). Oxford: Polity

17 The 'Forward Strategy Unit', created in 2001, formed a sister unit to the existing Performance and Innovation Unit created in the wake of the 1997 election. Both were later merged to form the PM's Strategy Unit, which lasted until it was shut down by the 2010 Coalition Government of Cameron and Clegg in early 2011.

18 Cialdini, R. B. (2003). 'Crafting normative messages to protect the environment'. *Current Directions in Psychological Science*, 12(4), 105–109.

19 Interestingly, the Welsh Government did continue to pursue the idea of presumed consent. Organ donation was also on the list of early topics for BIT in 2010, though with a subtly different solution in mind.

Chapter 2: Nudging Goes Mainstream

1 In my view Richard Thaler's work is sufficiently outstanding and impactful in its own right to merit the Nobel Prize in economics, a view I know to be shared by many others. For a recent and accessible overview of his work, see Thaler, R. (2015), *Misbehaving: the Making of Behavioural Economics*. Norton & Co.

2 *Options for a New Britain* (2010) and its predecessor, *Options for Britain* (1996); three 'Strategic Audits' conducted by the PMSU (2002, 2005, 2008); and various other works.

3 For example, I'd seen Paul present a year or two earlier on the strengths and limitations of Quality Life Adjusted Years, including the systematic biases that were inadvertently built into their method; and we'd also brought him in to participate in seminars linked to a big Department of Health review at which he impressed, including on his interest in framing and priming effects. He is now better known for his recent book on happiness.

4 Dolan, P., Hallsworth, M., Halpern, D., King, D. and Vlaev, I. (2010) MINDSPACE Institute for Government, London. http://www. instituteforgovernment.org.uk/sites/default/files/publications/MINDSPACE. pdf

5 In the British system, the Prime Minister and politicians make very few appointments – not much more than 50 across the whole of government, and virtually all of which are constitutionally constrained 'Special Advisers' ('SpAds') who are specifically prohibited from instructing civil servants. Instead, permanent civil servants are assigned to take on the roles and tasks set by the new government. Ministers are allowed to refashion the system itself, if not choose the people. In contrast, the US President gets to make nearly 10,000 appointments.

6 This was arguably driven rather more by political optics than realistic assessment. The UK centre of government, that is No. 10 and the Cabinet Office, is unusually small in international comparison, as are the number of political appointees. Furthermore, there was an early naivety around the needs of Coalition, as opposed to the 'normal' majority government arrangements. Coalition Government needs more people in the centre when every policy has to be negotiated between two parties.

7 It turned out that there was a good alternative candidate: an extremely talented deputy director in the Strategy Unit who had drafted an outline note for the new team. I thought the outline was excellent, and tried to get her on to the team. Alas, the then director of the Strategy Unit had no intention of letting her go.

8 The original seven full-time members of the team were: Kate Marshal, the original deputy director seconded from the BRE; Rory Gallagher; Maren Ashford, a marketing expert recruited (slightly controversially) from a previous role in the Conservative party; Sam Nguyen; Henry Ashford, recruited externally with a social enterprise background; Rosie Donarchie, an all-round policy analyst from the PMSU; and Ben Monks, from the PMSU on a temporary basis.

Chapter 3: Easy

1 *Automatic Enrolment Opt-out Rates: findings from research with large employers*, DWP, 2013. https://www.gov.uk/government/uploads/system/uploads/attachment_data/file/227039/opt-out-research-large-employers-ad_hoc.pdf. See also Benartzi, S. (2012) *Save More Tomorrow*, Portfolio Publishers. For an early advocacy of the idea, see Thaler, R. (2002), 'Save More Tomorrow: a simple plan to increase retirement saving', *Capital Ideas*, vol. 4, no.1, Chicago Booth.

2 In contrast, some policymakers in Asia worried that people saved too much, and really needed to be encouraged to spend and consume more.

3 In the US pension system, not only does the employer match employee contributions to the pension, they can also withdraw that money once the person reaches 59 years old – in effect, the employee can get the equivalent of 1.6% of their annual salary, or on average more than $500, by using the manoeuvre. More than a third of people nonetheless leave this money 'on the table'. James J. Choi, David Laibson, and Brigitte C. Madrian (2011) $100 Bills on the Sidewalk: Suboptimal Investment in 401(k) Plans . Rev Econ Stat. 2011 Aug; 93(3): 748–763.

4 Presentation at BX 2014, Sydney.

5 Mayhew, Pat, Clarke, Ronald V., and Elliott, David (1989), 'Motorcycle Theft, Helmet Legislation and Displacement', *Howard Journal of Criminal Justice*, vol. 28, issue 1: 1–8.

6 The 44 per cent was found in a study of 19 Texas cities (http://www.smarter-usa.org/documents/IIHS-Helmet-Q&A.pdf). A fall of 36 per cent in motorcycle thefts was seen in the Netherlands in 1975 following the introduction of laws to require helmets (Mayhew et al., 1989).

7 See Kreitman (1976). 'The coal gas story: UK suicide rates, 1960–1971'. *British Journal of Preventative and Social Medicine*, 30, 86–93 and more recently, Hawton, 'Restricting access to methods of suicide: rationale and evaluation of this approach to suicide prevention'. *Crisis*, 28, 4–9(2007).

8 http://www.dol.gov/regulations/20120622OIRAReducingReporting PaperworkBurdens.pdf

9 Bettinger, E., Long, B.T., Oreopoulos, P., and Sanbonmatsu, L. (2012) 'The Role of Application Assistance and Information in College Decisions: Results from the H&R Block Fafsa Experiment'. *Quarterly Journal of Economics*, 127, Issue 3; 1205-1242. https://econresearch.uchicago.edu/sites/econresearch.uchicago.edu/files/Bettinger%20Long%20Oreopoulos%20Sanbonmatsu%20-%20FAFSA%20paper%201-22-12.pdf.

10 The rise was from 19.2 to 23.4 per cent of people. See BIT 'EAST'.

11 Hawton, K., Bergen, H., Simkin, S., Dodd, S., Pocock, P., Bernal, W., Gunnell, D. and Kapur, N. (2013) 'Long term effect of reduced pack sizes of paracetamol on poisoning deaths and liver transplant activity in England and Wales: interrupted time series analyses'. *BMJ*; 346 doi: http://dx.doi.org/10.1136/bmj.f403 (published 7 February 2013).

12 Even MINDSPACE had, in retrospect, relatively little to say on 'make it easy' – though it did get covered under 'D' for defaults.

13 See, for example, see Max Bazerman's *The Power of Noticing* (2014), Simon and Schuster.

Chapter 4: Attract!

1 Nakamura, R., Pechey, R., Suhrcke, M., Jebb, S. A., and Marteau, T. M. (2014), 'Sales. Impact of displaying alcoholic and non-alcoholic beverages in end-of-aisle locations: an observational study', *Social Science & Medicine*, vol.108; 68–73. doi: 10.1016/j.socscimed.2014.02.032.

2 Neslin, S. A., and Van Heerde, H. J. (2009), *Promotion dynamics*, 3: 177–268. Chan, T., Narasimhan, C., and Zhang, Q. (2008), 'Decomposing promotional effects with a dynamic structural model of flexible consumption', *J Mark Res*, 45: 487–498. Ni Mhurchu, C., Blakely, T., Jiang, Y., et al. (2010), 'Effects of price discounts and tailored nutrition education on supermarket purchases: a randomized controlled trial', *Am J Clin Nutr*, 91: 736–747.

3 See EAST for a summary of these results in more detail. We also tested adding both the name and the amount. This was slightly more effective than the amount alone, but slightly less effective than the name alone.

4 *What's Psychology Worth? A Field Experiment in the Consumer Credit Market.* Bertrand, Karlan, Mullainathan, Shafir and Zinman. 7 June 2005. http://cep.lse.ac.uk/seminarpapers/10-06-05-BER.pdf

5 Slovic, P. (2007). '"If I look at the mass I will never act": Psychic numbing and genocide'. *Judgment and Decision Making*, 2, 79–95. Available at www.decisionresearch.org.

6 Santiago-Chaparro, Kelvin R., Chitturi, Madhav, Bill, Andrea, and Noyce, David A. (2012), 'Spatial Effectiveness of Speed Feedback Signs', *Transportation Research Record: Journal of the Transportation Research Board*, vol. 2281: 8–15.

7 Van Houten, Ron and Nau, Paul A. (1981), 'A comparison of the effects of posted feedback and increased police surveillance on highway speeding', *Journal of Applied Behavior Analysis*, vol. 14, issue 3: 261–71.

8 Sandberg, W., Schoenecker, T., Sebastian, K. and Soler, D. (2009) *Long-Term Effectiveness of Dynamic Speed Monitoring Displays (DSMD) for Speed Management at Speed Limit Transitions*, Washington, Dakota and Ramsey Counties. http://www.informationdisplay.com/httpdocs/docs/MinnesotaStudy.pdf.

9 http://wheels.blogs.nytimes.com/2010/11/30/speed-camera-lottery-wins-vw-fun-theory-contest/?_php=true&_type=blogs&_php=true&_type=blogs&_r=1

10 This 10-fold return wasn't a randomised control trial (RCT), and one could argue that the result was not robust – in other words, it's possible, though unlikely, that the extra switching to direct debit might have arisen from some other change over the period in these areas.

11 Frey, B. (2001), *Inspiring Economics: Human Motivation in Political Economy.* Frey, B., and Osterloh, M. (eds) (2002), *Successful Management by Motivation: Balancing Intrinsic and Extrinsic Incentives.*

12 Roberto, C. A., and Kawachi, I. (2014), 'Use of psychology and behavioral economics to promote healthy eating', *Am J Prev Med.*, 47(6): 832–7. doi: 10.1016/j.amepre.2014.08.002.

13 Van Kleef, E. et al., (2014) 'Nudging children towards whole wheat bread: a field experiment on the influence of fun bread roll shape on breakfast consumption'. *BMC Public Health,* 14:906 http://www.biomedcentral.com/content/pdf/1471-2458-14-906.pdf. Belot, M., James, J and Nolen, P. (2014) *Incentives and Children's Dietary Choices: A Field Experiment in Primary Schools.* University of Bath. http://www.bath.ac.uk/economics/research/working-papers/2014-papers/25-14.pdf.

14 Dolan, P., Hallsworth, M., Halpern, D., King, D. and Vlaev, I. (2010) MINDSPACE Institute for Government, London. http://www.instituteforgovernment.org.uk/sites/default/files/publications/MINDSPACE.pdf.

Chapter 5: Social

1 See the wonderful MIT student study of revolving and swing doors by Cullen et al., (2006). In their survey of students, 61 per cent said they would take the revolving doors if the person ahead did so. http://web.mit.edu/~slanou/www/shared_documents/366_06_REVOLVING_DOOR.pdf

2 Cialdini, Robert B., Reno, Raymond R., and Kallgren, Carl A. (1990), 'A Focus Theory of Normative Conduct: Recycling the Concept of Norms to Reduce Littering in Public Places', *Journal of Personality and Social Psychology*, vol. 58, no. 6: 1015–26.

3 Salganik, Matthew J., Dodds, Peter Sheridan, and Watts, Duncan J. (2006), 'Experimental Study of Inequality and Unpredictability in an Artificial Cultural Market'. https://www.princeton.edu/~mjs3/salganik_dodds_watts06_full.pdf

4 Darley, J., and Latene, B. (1968), 'Bystander intervention in emergencies: diffusion of responsibility', *Journal of Personality and Social Psychology*, vol. 8, no. 4: 377–83

5 Burger, J., and C. Shelton (2011), 'Changing everyday health behaviors through descriptive norm manipulations'. http://www.scu.edu/cas/psychology/faculty/upload/Burger-Shelton-2011.pdf

6 Alice Isen found that giving sweets to clinicians led to them considering a wider variety of options and a more accurate diagnosis. Erez, A. & Isen, A.M. (2002). 'The Influence of Positive Affect on Components of Expectancy Motivation.' *Journal of Applied Psychology*, 87(6): 1055-1067.

7 For a closely related argument from my ex-colleague from the political side at No. 10, see: Steve Hilton, Jason Bade, and Scott Bade (2015), *More Human: Designing a World Where People Come First.*

8 We also know from Amy Cuddy's work at Harvard that this itself matters for getting a job: candidates who walk into an interview having previously stood in a 'power-pose' for a two-minute period are rated more highly at interview, and therefore more likely to get the job.

9 For an accessible route into this literature, drawing heavily on the USA long-running Framingham study, see: Nicholas A. Christakis and James H. Fowler (2009), *Connected: The Surprising Power of Our Social Networks and How They Shape Our Lives.*

Chapter 6: Timely

1 Charles Duhigg (2012), *The Power of Habit: Why We Do What We Do in Life and Business*, Random House.

2 The documented numbers leaving the UK without further prompt rose from around 18 to 22 per cent. This figure is a substantial underestimate of the total leaving due to incompleteness in the data tracking exits at the time the study was conducted, but the proportionate size of the effect should still hold true.

3 Shu, L. L., Mazar, N., Gino, F., Ariely, D., and Bazerman, M. H. (2012), 'Signing at the beginning makes ethics salient and decreases dishonest self-reports in comparison to signing at the end', *Proceedings of the National Academy of Sciences*. 109(38), 15197–15200

4 We ran a version of this intervention to encourage people to be more honest in declaring if their residential status had changed such that they were no longer entitled to a single-person discount on their local council tax. It did boost declarations, but we found that a simplified letter was able to do at least as well in this trial. At the time of writing, a trial is being run with 40,000 tax forms to see if moving the signature earlier can prompt more honest declarations.

5 https://www.gov.uk/government/uploads/system/uploads/attachment_data/file/350282/John_Lewis_trial_report_010914FINAL.pdf

6 Marcel, A. J. (1983), 'Conscious and Unconscious Perception: Experiments on Visual Masking and Word Recognition', *Cognitive Psychology*, 15: 197–237.

7 Vohs, K. D., Mead, N. L., and Goode, M. R. (2006), 'The psychological consequences of money', *Science*, 314(5802): 1154–6.

8 Barrera-Osorio, Felipe, Bertrand, Marianne, Linden, Leigh L., and Perez-Calle, Francisco (2011), 'Improving the Design of Conditional Transfer Programs: Evidence from a Randomized Education Experiment in Colombia', *American Economic Journal: Applied Economics*, 3(2): 167–95.

9 Read and van Leeuwen (1998): 74 per cent chose fruit a week in advance, but when the delivery turned up and offered the choice, 70 per cent chose chocolate.

10 Read, D., Loewenstein, G., and Kalyanaraman, S. (1999) 'Mixing virtue and vice: combining the immediacy effect and the diversification heuristic', *Journal of Behavioral Decision Making*, Dec 1999, 12, 4. http://online.wsj.com/public/resources/documents/ReadLoewenstein_VirtueVice_JBDM99.pdf

11 Soman, Dilip (2015), *The Last Mile: Creating Social and Economic Value from Behavioural Insights*, Rotman–UTP Publishing.

12 Muraven, M., and Baumeister, R. F. (2000), 'Self-regulation and depletion of limited resources: does self-control resemble a muscle?', *Psychol Bull.*, 126(2): 247–59.

13 Danziger, S., Levavb, J., and Avnaim-Pessoa, L. (2011), 'Extraneous factors in judicial decisions', *Proceedings of the National Academy of Sciences*, vol. 108, no. 17: 6889–6892, doi: 10.1073/pnas.1018033108

14 Dai, H., Milkman, K. L., Hofmann D. A., and Staats, B. R. (2014), 'The Impact of Time at Work and Time Off From Work on Rule Compliance: The Case of

Hand Hygiene in Health Care', *Journal of Applied Psychology*, http://dx.doi.org/10.1037/a0038067

15 Linder, J. A., Doctor, J. N., Friedberg, M. W., Nieva, H. R., Birks, C., Meeker D., and Fox C. R. (2014), 'Time of Day and the Decision to Prescribe Antibiotics', *JAMA Internal Medicine*, vol. 174, no. 12: 2029–31.

16 Duflo, Esther, Michael Kremer, and Jonathan Robinson (2011), 'Nudging Farmers to Use Fertilizer: Theory and Experimental Evidence from Kenya.' *American Economic Review*, 101 (6): 2350–90.

17 The drop-out rate fell from 25 to 16 per cent. It is worth noting that these FE colleges are only paid for students who show up, and complete the course, so this is a very important result for them!

Chapter 7: Data and Transparency

1 An added reason for dropping the term RECAP is that no one could remember what it stood for, even Richard Thaler, who coined the term.

2 As is often the case, we were going to call it 'mydata' or something similar in the Green Paper, but someone else was already using the phrase.

3 A great deal of the business of government, and certainly in No. 10, occurs in the corridors and lobby of the building. It's also worth noting how much legislation occurs by attaching extra ideas on to Bills passing through. It's often referred to negatively as 'Christmas tree' legislation – people add clauses like decorations on a tree. But it is sometimes quite effective. The Bill can serve as a rallying call for ideas in an area. Hence a government or PM can say, 'We need a Bill on X.' Officials have a rattle around their cupboards and drawers for some policy ideas that might work, new or old. By the time the Bill has worked its way around Whitehall and through Parliament, what started out as a skeleton has flesh and muscle. Of course, the Bill can also end up as a rather overweight Frankenstein ...

4 As an aside, I still have the same GP in Cambridge that I signed up with as an undergraduate 30 years ago even though I've moved house, and even city, many times in between. My practice scores well, but it's not one of the best. I'm sure I would have been influenced by these ratings if they'd been around back then.

5 British Crime Survey, July 2014.

6 Leslie K. John, Alessandro Acquisti and George Loewenstein, (2011) 'Strangers on a Plane: Context-Dependent Willingness to Divulge Sensitive Information'. *Journal of Consumer Research*, Vol. 37, No. 5 (February 2011), pp. 858–873.

7 http://www.hsph.harvard.edu/obesity-prevention-source/obesity-trends/ For very recent estimates, see the latest reports of the World Health Organisation, now projecting virtually the entire populations of some countries to be obese or overweight by 2030.

8 The Behavioural Insights Team (2014), *Reducing Mobile Phone Theft and Improving Security*. Home Office. https://www.gov.uk/government/uploads/system/uploads/attachment_data/file/390901/HO_Mobile_theft_paper_Dec_14_WEB.PDF

9 *Which?*, 3 November 2014.

10 Both George Loewenstein and Christine Roberto have independently found that visual heuristics have a bigger impact on marginal food choices, and that the inclusion of a human figure increases impact. The Australians have recently gone with a within-category overall star rating, with early indications that it is already driving reformulation.

11 Hoffrage U., and Gigerenzer, G. (1998), 'Using natural frequencies to improve diagnostic inferences', *Acad. Med.*, 73: 538–40.

12 http://www.surveyandtest.com/do-epc-ratings-affect-house-prices.

Chapter 8: A Different Approach to Big Policy Challenges

1 The 'red boxes' are the distinctive briefcases that Ministers are given in British government to carry their official papers in. Much of the rhythm of Whitehall, and governments across the world, beats with the filling and unfilling of these boxes.

2 See, for example, how the majority of the public in many countries say that politicians put their 'personal interest' above that of the public interest, and the extensive coverage of how Parliaments have overly long summer recesses and Prime Ministers being on holiday during crises.

3 Tetlock, Philip E. (2005), *Expert Political Judgment: How Good Is It?*, Princeton University Press.

4 See the work of Robert West et al. for the latest UK statistics on smoking quit rates. http://www.smokinginengland.info/

5 If we attributed say 50,000 a year, or around a quarter, of the increase of the number of extra smokers now quitting to e-cigs – noting that this is the primary change in the pattern of quitting, and taking the conservative assumption supposing that it just brought forward the date of quitting enough to save a two years of life on average, this would suggest that e-cigs are currently saving around 100,000 years of life per annum.

6 WHO Framework Convention on Tobacco Control, 21 July 2014, p.2. http://apps.who.int/gb/fctc/PDF/cop6/FCTC_COP6_10-en.pdf?ua=1

7 This built on evidence suggesting that people are more likely to complete a sequence of tasks if they feel they have already made a good start. Hence customers at a coffee shop given a loyalty card that gives them a free coffee after they have bought ten, with a stamp each time they buy a cup, will buy their ten coffees significantly faster if given a card with 12 slots but with the first two already stamped, than if given a blank card with just ten slots.

8 Ioannidis, J. P. A. (2005), 'Why Most Published Research Findings Are False', http://buster.zibmt.uni-ulm.de/dpv/dateien/DPV-Wiss-False-Research-Findings.pdf

9 The sample size for this much larger trial was around 110,000. See forthcoming detailed analysis and econometric modelling by Gallagher, Gyani, Sanders et al.

10 There are around 2.4 million accepted claims for Jobseeker's Allowance in a typical year, paid at £57 for under 25s and about £72 for over 25s. Historically the most common duration on benefits is in the range 13 to 26 weeks, with around 800,000 people on the allowance at any one time. A rough estimate is

therefore 2.4 million x 2–4 (days saved) x £60–70 (average benefit level per week) ÷7= £48–96 million.

11 The term 'animal spirits' is generally attributed to John Maynard Keynes, from his 1936 book, *The General Theory of Employment, Interest and Money*.

12 At least one of these ideas did later come to fruition, in the form of the mobile phone theft index – one of a number of ideas to de-shroud the relative vulnerability of consumer and online products, to in turn nudge manufactures to build products that were safer and more secure for consumers (see Chapter 7).

Chapter 9: Well-being – Nudging Ourselves, and Each Other, to Happier Lives

1 See Halpern, D., (2009) *The Hidden Wealth of Nations*, for a plot of commuting time versus life satisfaction. This exact size of the effect remains a contested issue: it's hard to fully separate individual differences and selection effects. See also Stutzer and Frey (2008), 'Stress that doesn't pay: the commuting paradox', *Scandinavian Journal of Economics*, 110 (2): 339–66

2 Aristotle, *The Nicomachean Ethics*, 1098a.

3 *An Inquiry into the Original of Our Ideas of Beauty and Virtue* (1725).

4 *The Principles of Moral and Political Philosophy* (1785).

5 *An Introduction to the Principles of Morals and Legislation* (1789).

6 Inglehart, R. F. (1989), *Culture Shift in Advanced Industrial Society*, Princeton University Press.

7 Donovan, N., and Halpern, D. (2002), 'Life satisfaction: the state of knowledge and implications for government', Prime Minister's Strategy Unit, discussion paper.

8 This method of measuring well-being is known as the Experience Sampling Method (ESM).

9 Lewis, J., 'Income, Expenditure and Personal Well-being, 2011/12' (2014), Office for National Statistics.

10 In a recent and bound to be controversial paper, Oswald has noted that the gene linked to depression appears to be lower in the high life-satisfaction country of Denmark. Furthermore, he has noted that there is a correlation between the level of this gene across a number of countries and their average level of subjective well-being. This sets up the argument, albeit tenuous at this point, that genetic differences might after all explain at least some of the national differences in SWB, and, therefore, that these in turn might affect growth rates. It will be an extraordinary development if others are able to confirm or extend the result.

11 MacKerron, G., and Mourato, S. (2013), 'Happiness is greater in natural environments', *Global Environmental Change*, 23(5): 992–1000.

12 Dunn, E. W., Gilbert, D. T., and Wilson, T. D. (2011), 'If money doesn't make you happy, then you probably aren't spending it right', *Journal of Consumer Psychology*, 21(2): 115–25. Subsequently expanded into the book *Happy Money*.

13 See Halpern, D., (2005), *Social Capital*, Polity Press, for a summary of the literature. For a more recent meta-analysis see Holt-Lunstad et al., including 148 independent studies which used data from over 300,000 individuals followed for an average of 7.5 years. This shows that individuals with adequate social support experience a 50 per cent increase in the odds of survival than their counterparts with poorer social connections. Holt-Lunstad, J., Smith, T. B., and Layton, J. B. (2010), 'Social relationships and mortality risk: a meta-analytic review', *PLoS medicine*, 7(7), e1000316.

14 Pennebaker, J. W., Kiecolt-Glaser, J. K., and Glaser, R. (1988). 'Disclosure of traumas and immune function: Health implications for psychotherapy'. *Journal of Consulting and Clinical Psychology*, Vol. 56, pp. 239-245.

15 Oswald, A. (1997), 'Happiness and economic performance', *Economic Journal*, 107: 1815–31.

16 Helliwell, J.F. and Huang, H., (2010) 'How's the Job? Well-Being and Social Capital in the Workplace'. *ILRREVIEW*, Vol. 63 (2) http://digitalcommons.ilr. cornell.edu/ilrreview/vol63/iss2/2/.

17 Gallup data summarised in John Helliwell's blog: https://socialcapital. wordpress.com/tag/john-helliwell/. He also noted from the same data that *employees who report having a best friend at work were:*

- *43% more likely to report having received praise or recognition for their work in the last seven days.*
- *37% more likely to report that someone at work encourages their development.*
- *35% more likely to report coworker commitment to quality.*
- *28% more likely to report that in the last six months, someone at work has talked to them about their progress.*
- *27% more likely to report that the mission of their company makes them feel their job is important.*
- *27% more likely to report that their opinions seem to count at work.*
- *21% more likely to report that at work, they have the opportunity to do what they do best every day.*

18 Layard, R. (2011) *Happiness: Lessons from a New Science.*

19 These are from 2011 data, though published in 2014. http://www.ons.gov.uk/ ons/dcp171766_363811.pdf

20 Gilbert, D. (2007) *Stumbling on Happiness*, Knopf.

21 See Carol Dweck's personal site for an overview of her work: https://web. stanford.edu/dept/psychology/cgi-bin/drupalm/cdweck , or for an overview: Dweck, C. S. (2006), *Mindset: The New Psychology of Success*. For Angela Duckworth's closely related work on 'Grit' see https://sites.sas.upenn.edu/ duckworth/pages/research .

22 Richard and I have often been on panels together, such as a session with Angela Merkel in 2013, and he has used this phrase a few times, and it always strikes a chord.

23 Fujiwara, D., & Dolan, P. (2014). Valuing mental health. *Policy*, 4, 2-1.

24 Spence, R., Roberts, A., Ariti, C. and Bardsley, M. (2014). 'Focus on: Antidepressant prescribing. Trends in the prescribing of antidepressants in

primary care', *Quality Watch*. http://www.health.org.uk/publications/focus-on-antidepressant-prescribing/. The rise is not accounted for by shorter prescription periods, nor by changes in the strength of tablets prescribed.

25 Personal communication, David Clark (Oxford, and head of the UK's Improving Access to Psychological Therapies Programme). A commitment to expand e-CBT was made in the March 2015 budget and championed by the Deputy Prime Minister, Nick Clegg

26 Dunn, E. W., Aknin, L. B., and Norton, M. I. (2008), 'Spending money on others promotes happiness', *Science*, 319(5870): 1687–8.

27 https://www.ipsos-mori.com/Assets/Docs/Publications/SRI-National-Citizen-Service-2013-evaluation-main-report-August2014.PDF

28 http://www.behaviouralinsights.co.uk/publications/evaluating-youth-social-action

29 Halpern, D., (1995), *Mental health and the built environment*. Taylor and Francis. Also, Halpern, D. (2008) 'An evidence-based approach to building happiness building for happiness, in RIBA-edited volume, Jane Wernick, J (ed) *Building happiness: architecture to make you smile*. RIBA Building Futures, Black Dog Publishers.

30 This is an idea suggested by Paul Resnick in the USA, that is still oddly rare.

31 Alice Isen, ibid. – ref. 6 in 'Social' (Ch. 5).

32 Revision of the 'magenta book', which sets out how evaluations are done, has also been undertaken – the impacts of policies on well-being should also be measured, and where possible using the newly developed ONS measures.

33 Brickman, P., Coates, D., and Janoff-Bulman, R. (1978), 'Lottery winners and accident victims: Is happiness relative?', *Journal of Personality and Social Psychology*, 36(8): 917. In fact, these results are often incorrectly reported as showing that winning the lottery or becoming paralysed has no long-term impact on well-being. This is not the case, but the effects are still much smaller than most people think they would be.

34 Fujiwara, D., and Campbell, R. (2011), *Valuation Techniques for Social Cost-Benefit Analysis: Stated Preference, Revealed Preference and Subjective Well-Being Approaches. A Discussion of the Current Issues*. HM Treasury.

35 Inglehart, Ronald F., Foa, R., Peterson, C., and Welzel, C. (2008), 'Development, Freedom, and Rising Happiness A Global Perspective (1981–2007)', *Perspectives on Psychological Science*, 3(4): 264–85. DOI. Abstract. Public Access. Local Access.

36 Halpern, D. and Reid, J. (1992); 'Effect of unexpected demolition announcement on health of residents'. *BMJ* 304:1229; Halpern, D (1995), *Mental health and the built environment*. Taylor and Francis.

37 Buell, Ryan W., and Michael I. Norton. The Labor Illusion: How Operational Transparency Increases Perceived Value.' *Management Science* 57, no. 9 (September 2011): 1564–1579. Buell, Ryan W., and Michael I. Norton. 'Think Customers Hate Waiting? Not So Fast...' *Harvard Business Review* 89, no. 5 (May 2011).

38 The event was run in March 2007, with Ipsos MORI selecting a random stratified sample of the public.

39 See Halpern, D., (2009), *Hidden Wealth of Nations*, Polity Press, for more detail on background, including of the Canadian work. For more on the introduction of the Friends and Family Test into NHS England, see http://www.england. nhs.uk/ourwork/pe/fft/

40 Epley, N., and Schroeder, J. 'Mistakenly seeking solitude', *Journal of Experimental Psychology: General*, vol. 143(5), Oct 2014, 1980–1999.

41 In this case of the UK's controversial HS2, you might decide you've got to build a new railway for other reasons anyway, such as lack of capacity. But changing the valuations of the time saved may still open up other cheaper possibilities, such as increasing the capacity of your existing lines, or building a slower but more comfortable service.

42 For example, the UAE have set increasing well-being as their top priority in their 2015 strategy.

43 Putnam, R. D., Campbell, D. E., & Garrett, S. R. (2012). *American Grace: How Religion Divides and Unites Us*. Simon and Schuster.

Chapter 10: What Works? The Rise of Experimental Government

1 Petrosino, Anthony, Buehler, John, and Turpin-Petrosino, Carolyn (2013), 'Scared Straight and Other Juvenile Awareness Programs for Preventing Juvenile Delinquency: A Systematic Review', http://www. campbellcollaboration.org/lib/project/3/

2 https://www.gov.uk/government/publications/test-learn-adapt-developing-public-policy-with-randomised-controlled-trials

3 Cochrane, A. (1972) *Effectiveness and Efficiency: Random Reflections on Health services*, Cochrane, p.6.

4 Shepherd, J. P. (2007) 'The production and management of evidence for public service reform'. *Evidence and Policy*; 3: 231–51. Jonathan more recently revisited this issue in: Shepherd, J. P. (2014), *How To Achieve More Effective Services: The Evidence Ecosystem*, Project Report [Online],Cardiff: Cardiff University; available at: http://www.scie-socialcareonline.org.uk/ how-to-achieve-more-effective-services-the-evidence-ecosystem/r/ a11G0000006z7vXIAQ.

5 There are some other methodological alternatives. For example, a 'discontinuity design' can use a comparison between what happens to firms, or people, just above and just below a threshold at which the grants are given. In effect one can argue that those either side of the line are virtually the same, and then compare their subsequent performance. But it gives you a smaller sample, and is potentially problematic where you have a particularly varied population, as is true for businesses.

6 Consumer Reports is the US equivalent of 'Which?' http//:www. consumerreports.org/cro/index.htm. I was always very taken by the idea that an independent institution might provide such advice to Parliament, and proposed this in a piece written with Stewart Wood (later an adviser to Gordon Brown and then Ed Miliband) that we should create just such an institution linked to our own Parliament. The idea was set out in the introduction to *Options for Britain* (1996), co-edited with Stewart Wood, Stuart White and Gavin Cameron.

7 http://educationendowmentfoundation.org.uk/toolkit/about-the-toolkit/ (see Cabinet Office, November 2014).

8 http://educationendowmentfoundation.org.uk/news/teaching-assistants-should-not-be-substitute-teachers-but-can-make-a-real-d/

9 Goldacre, B (2012) *Bad Pharma: How Drug Companies Mislead Doctors and Harm Patients,* 4th Estate.

10 See 'Test, Learn and Adapt', BIT, for a summary of this approach.

11 Manzi, James (2012) *Uncontrolled: The Surprising Payoff of Trial-and-Error for Business, Politics, and Society,* Basic Books.

12 Feyman, Richard, *The Meaning of It All: Thoughts of a Citizen-Scientist.* Lectures originally given in 1963.

13 Max Bazerman, a central figure in the world of applying behavioural science to practical problems, uses this exercise in his classes at the Harvard Business School.

Chapter 11: Risks and Limitations

1 Marshall, T. (2000), 'Exploring a fiscal food policy: the case of diet and ischaemic heart disease', *BMJ,* 320: 301–5.

2 Wansink, Brian (2014), *Slim by Design: Mindless Eating Solutions for Everyday Life,* New York: William Morrow.

3 The rapid trial ethics and protocol process set up by the team's Head of Research, Michael Sanders, in effect piggy-backed on systems built for UK universities, and Bristol in particular.

4 http://webarchive.nationalarchives.gov.uk/+/http:/www.cabinetoffice.gov.uk/media/cabinetoffice/strategy/assets/pr2.pdf. It was actually my co-author Clive Bates who came up with the phrase. In his previous role working for the anti-smoking campaign group ASH, he got to see some pretty strong examples of such predatory behaviour.

5 Thaler, R., (2015) *Misbehaving: the Making of Behavioral Economics.* Norton &Co; Soman, D., (2015) *The Last Mile: Creating Social and Economic Value from Behavioural Insights.* Rotman–UTP Publishing.

6 Sunstein, C. (2014), *Why Nudge?: The Politics of Libertarian Paternalism.* Yale

7 Sir Robin Young, then Head of the UK's Department for Business and Industry, as part of the PMSU's Strategic Audit exercise, 2002–3.

8 George Loewenstein uses a very similar formulation to talk about the role played by behavioural insights.

9 Todd Rogers has examined this in some detail, including the mechanisms that lie behind persistence of effects; http://www.behaviouralinsights.co.uk/blogpost/ideas-and-results-harvard-part-iii.

10 Milkman, K. L., Minson, J. A., and Volpp, K.G.M. (2014), 'Holding the Hunger Games Hostage at the Gym: An Evaluation of Temptation Bundling', *Management Science,* vol. 60(2): 283–99.

11 Loewenstein, G., Bryce, C., Hagmann, D., and Rajpal, S. (2014), 'Warning: You Are About to Be Nudged'. http://papers.ssrn.com/sol3/papers.cfm?abstract_id=2417383.

12 As mentioned earlier, Ministers were concerned that the lottery would be seen as unfair, not least since tax returns are disproportionately filled in by the more affluent.

13 Personal communication with senior figures in the German Chancellery.

14 Ben Goldacre, among others, has also expressed a similar view.

15 https://www.ipsos-mori.com/DownloadPublication/1454_sri-ipsos-mori-acceptable-behaviour-january-2012.pdf

16 See Halpern, D. (2009), *The Hidden Wealth of Nations*, chapter 5, for a more detailed description of these types of democratic innovation.

Conclusion

1 Soman, Dilip (2015), *The Last Mile: Creating Social and Economic Value from Behavioural Insights*. Rotman–UTP Publishing.

2 https://www.gov.uk/government/publications/test-learn-adapt-developing-public-policy-with-randomised-controlled-trials.

3 http://coalition4evidence.org/ See also the activities of the Arnold, Bloomberg and Sloan Foundations.

4 For a recent and powerful account, see Putnam, R. (2015), *Our Kids: The American Dream in Crisis*, Simon and Schuster.

5 This has been a clear pattern in the UK for several decades, particularly affecting white working-class kids. A previous chief economist at the Department of Education described the attainment gap as trying to squeeze a balloon: if you gripped it in one place, the bulge seemed to move somewhere else, i.e. to the next level of qualifications or market differentiator.

6 Note the large-scale evaluations of the US Department of Housing (HUD) Moving to Opportunity Programs. Extremely modest, and sometimes negative (in the case of young males) effects were found for both adults and their kids – a bitter disappointment for such an ambitious, expensive and well-intentioned programme (see for example, http://www.nber.org/mtopublic/MTO%20 Overview%20Summary.pdf.) Though not as systematically analysed, similar disappointment followed many of the large-scale urban relocation programmes in the UK, France and elsewhere in the 1950s to the 1970s.

7 See, for example, the persistent, and sometimes cross-generationally expanding, levels on Incapacity Benefit (IB) in many UK regions in the 1970s to 2000s.

8 Dweck, C., (2006), *Mindset: The New Psychology of Success*. Random House.

9 Mullainathan, Sendhil, and Shafir, Eldar (2013), *Scarcity: Why Having Too Little Means So Much*.

10 Eisner, M. (2003), 'Long term historical trends in violent crime', *Crime and Justice*, 30: 83–142. http://www.vrc.crim.cam.ac.uk/vrcresearch/ paperdownload/manuel-eisner-historical-trends-in-violence.pdf

11 Collier, Paul (2010), *Wars, Guns and Votes: Democracy in Dangerous Places*, Bodley Head.

12 This phrase is generally attributed to Max Planck, not least as picked up through Kuhn's work on paradigm shifts in scientific thinking. Planck's actual

phrasing was: 'A new scientific truth does not triumph by convincing its opponents and making them see the light, but rather because its opponents eventually die, and a new generation grows up that is familiar with it.' *Wissenschaftliche Selbstbiographie. Mit einem Bildnis und der von Max von Laue gehaltenen Traueransprache*, Johann Ambrosius Barth Verlag (Leipzig 1948), p. 22, as translated in *Scientific Autobiography and Other Papers*, F. Gaynor (trans), pp. 33–34 (as cited in T. S. Kuhn, *The Structure of Scientific Revolutions*).

ACKNOWLEDGEMENTS

There are many people who deserve thanks and credit for the work and results of the Behavioural Insights Team that this book describes, and a rather shorter list for the writing and editing of the book itself.

There are a number of people who deserve explicit credit for the creation and early support of the team, many of whom I hope I remembered to mention in section 1. These include the two Cabinet Secretaries, Lord Gus O'Donnell and Sir Jeremy Heywood, without whose steadfast support – and that of their fantastic private offices – the team would not have had anything like the impact that it has, and without whose personal support I would certainly not have returned to No. 10 to do another 'tour of duty'. Very special thanks also must go to Richard Thaler for the unique and supportive role he has always played in the team, and his personal support to me: he has always managed to get the balance exactly right between deeply thoughtful and good-humoured advice, and a light and unobtrusive touch (and I am sorry about the No. 10 food). On the political side, particular thanks go to Prime Minister David Cameron, and to Rohan Silva, Steve Hilton, Oliver Letwin and Polly Mackenzie. Others who deserve recognition for their support over the years from within the No. 10, Cabinet Office and Treasury community include: Susan Acland-Hood, Paul Bate, Mike Bracken, Tim Chatwin, Will Cavendish, Nick Clegg, Ivan Collister, Melanie Dawes, John Fingleton, Iain Forbes, John Gibson, Miles Gibson, Ameet Gill, Hugh Harris, Rupert

Harrison, Richard Heaton, Guy Horsington, Nick Hurd, Gus Jaspert, Jo Johnson, Emma Kenny, John Kingman, Paul Kirby, Dan Korski, Rob Kramer, Kieran Kumeria, Ed Llewellyn, Gavin Lockhart, Chris Lockwood, Tim Luke, Michael Lynas, Chris Martin, Francis Maude, Liz McKewen, Emily Miles, Ben Moxham, Kris Murrin, Tom Nixon, Elenor Passmore, Maddy Phipps-Taylor, Richard Reeves, Ivan Rogers, Nick Seddon, Grant Shapps, James O'Shaughnessy, Dave Ramsden, Philip Rycroft, Laura Trott, Antonio Williams, Poppy Wood, and Dan York Smith. I'd also like to add a personal thanks for the tireless good humour, and human touch, of the police, staff and custodians on the door and gate of No. 10 – while the rest of us come and go, you keep the place going. Recognition should also go to Liam Byrne, from the end of the previous administration, who signed off the MINDSPACE report that helped form the foundation of the work that was to follow. There is a harsh abruptness to democratic politics, but also something – behind the headlines – hugely admirable about how people across administrations pass the baton to each other with a genuine goodwill to make the world a better place.

We also owe thanks to a number of Ministers, advisers and civil servants from other departments, including from HMRC: David Gauke, Lin Homer, Edward Troup, Rohan Grove, Nick Down; DWP: Robert Devereux, David Freud, Philippa Stroud, Steve Webb, Trevor Huddleston; from Education: Michael Gove, David Laws, Tim Leunig, Chris Wormald, Tom Jeffory, Paul Kissak; from Health and PHE: Jeremy Hunt, Jane Ellison, Una O'Brian, Sally Davis, Felicity Harvey, Duncan Selbie, Kevin Fenton; from BIS: Matt Hancock, David Willetts, Ed Davey, Jo Swinson, Giles Wilkes, Emily Welsh, Amanda Rowlatt and from elsewhere: Mark Walport, David Davis, Jill Matheson, Stephen Aldridge. Thanks are also due to my Cabinet What Works team, Dani Mason, Laura Bayton, Louise Moore and Ross Neilson, and to the Heads of the What Works centres, with the quiet revolution they are driving.

Thanks also go to those involved in the 'spin-out' of the Behavioural Insight Team from inside No. 10 and Cabinet Office into its weird and wonderful current form, a 'social purpose' company. These include Francis Maude, Stephen Kelly, Janet Baker, Andreas Georgiou, Nicky Kerr, Ed Whiting, Ed Welsh, Jazmin Glassborow, Paul Maltby; and to our new partners in Nesta, especially Phil Colligan, with Geoff Mulgan, John Chisham, and the rest of the Nesta team.

The work of the BIT has always built on the ideas of a work of a wide academic community, colleagues and friends. This includes our Academic Advisory group, chaired by Gus O'Donnell: Richard Thaler, Nick Chater, Dan Goldstein, Peter John, George Loewenstein, Theresa Marteau, and Peter Tufano. The team and I are also indebted to the work and counsel of many others, especially to Daniel Kahneman and Cass Sunstein; and also David Albury, Dan Ariely, Jon Baron, Christian Bason, Maurice Biriotti, John Britton, Iris Bohnet, Max Bazerman, Bob Cialdini, Cary Cooper, Angus Deaton, Paul Dolan, Angela Duckworth, Bobby Duffy, Carol Dweck, Gerd Gigerenzer, Ben Goldacre, Pelle Hanson, Tim Hartford, John Helliwell, Felicia Huppert, Paul Johnson, Mike Kelly, Beau Kilmer, Dom King, Christian Kroll, David Laibson, Richard Layard, Steve Levitt, John List, Donald Low, Mike Luca, Robert McCorquodale, Mike Norton, Beth Novack, Philip Oreopoulos, Ben Page, Bob Putnam, Matt Rabin, Todd Rogers, Marty Seligman, Nigel Shadbolt, Eldar Shafir, Jonathan Shepherd, Dilip Soman, Rory Sutherland, Richard Suzman, Larry Sherman, Andrew Skates and Kevin Volpe.

Most of all, I would like to thank the wonderful and talented people who make up and support the Behavioural Insights Team itself. A particular thanks is due to Owain Service, who has been central to building a cohesive team and navigating the complexities of moving from inside government to the current form, and to Andy Jackson and Olly Nguyen to delivering a functioning organisation. One legacy of our shift from government is a fairly 'full' layer of governance for a small entity, but I am really grateful for the work and support of our excellent Board, chaired by Peter Holmes, who brings a genuine independence of mind, commercial nous, and decisiveness to meetings that is a deeply valuable addition to our work; and to our Board members Philip Colligan and Janet Baker, who represent the majority shareholder interests of Nesta and Cabinet Office, and have given us their time, constructive challenge, and support in just the right measures.

Having grown from around a dozen to more than 60 people, there's now too many to credit everyone in BIT, but let me at least call out thanks to some of the key members of the team, and especially those who have been with the team from the early days and who have helped with this book. Thank you to Owain for reading and checking at least some of this book, and especially for howlers that would have caused unintended offence. I hope we caught them all but I take full responsibility for errors or omissions that remain. Thank you to team leads, and wonderful colleagues, roughly in order of joining the team: the hugely talented, and sun-blushed, Rory Gallagher (Australasia); Sam Nguyen (economy and employment); Simon Ruda (international and home affairs); Felicity Algate (consumers and infrastructure); Michael Hallsworth (health and tax); Elspeth Kirkman (North America); Michael Sanders (evaluation and giving); Zhi Soon (education and skills); and Kate Glazebrook (emerging areas). A former Cabinet Secretary once said to me that 'your ambition in life should be to make sure that those who follow and ultimately replace you are even better at what they do than you are'. I'm hopeful.

A further great development of the last couple of years has been the deepening of relationships with colleagues and friends across the world, as others have learnt from, supported, and extended the work of the BIT. Particular acknowledgements are due in Australia to Chris Eccles, Blair Comley, Jerril Rechter, and Lyn Roberts; in the

USA to Maya Shanker, Danny Goroff, and James Anderson; in the World Bank to Marco Hernandez, and Renos Vakis; in Germany to Andrea Schneider; and in Singapore to our outstanding colleagues in the Singapore Government.

Additional thanks, for comments and help on the book, are due to Michael Hallsworth, Jen Rubin, Ariella Kristal, Lauren Bern, and for the final haul to turn it into an actual book, James Pullen, Ed Faulkner, Yvonne Jacob, Richard Collins, and especially Hugo Harper, Sam Hanes and Kate Glazebrook.

Finally, I owe the deepest thanks to my family – to Jen, Aaron and Isaac – and sincerely apologise for all the weekends and holidays lost to this book (and its predecessors). It has been such an intense couple of years – full-on at work, exams at school, family bereavements – it has felt that at times the 'important stuff' of life has got squeezed to the margins. It might have been mad to try to do the book as well. Aaron and Isaac – you are truly wonderful young men, and Jen, I'm not sure what I've done to deserve being with you, but I'm profoundly glad about it. I'm really looking forward to some time for doing nothing in particular with you guys in the years to come.

DSH, June 2015.

INDEX

(page numbers in italics refer to illustrations)